How The
Brain Works

How The Brain Works

**Understanding Brain Function
Thought and Personality**

General Editor:
Professor Peter Abrahams

amber
BOOKS

© 2015 by Bright Star Publishing Plc

Material previously published in the partwork *Inside the Human Body*

This edition published in 2015

Editorial and design by
Amber Books Ltd
74–77 White Lion Street
London
N1 9PF
United Kingdom
www.amberbooks.co.uk
Appstore: itunes.com/apps/amberbooksltd
Facebook: www.facebook.com/amberbooks
Twitter: @amberbooks

ISBN: 978-1-78274-253-1

Project Editor: Sarah Uttridge
Design: Ummagumma

Printed in China

Contents

Introduction

Without a functioning brain and nervous system we would be unable to walk, talk, breath or communicate. Our emotions, our creativity and our ability to reason are all controlled by the complex network of cells that make up the brain, and which communicate constantly with each other and with other systems and structures within the body. In short, the brain and nervous system are what make us functioning human beings.

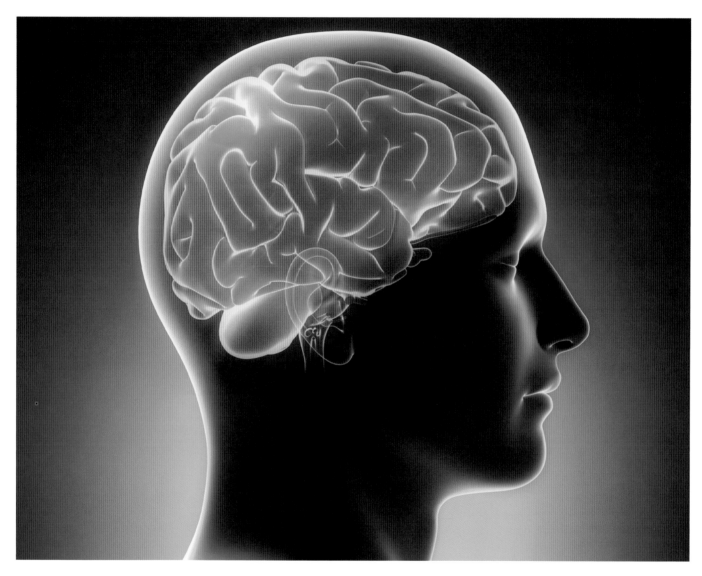

COMPLEX STRUCTURE

The brain is the 'control centre' of the nervous system; it receives messages through the body's peripheral nerves via the spinal cord and processes the information before, for example, telling your eye to blink, your foot to move or your bladder to empty. Each area of the brain has a different function. The cerebrum – the outer part that almost fills the entire skull – deals with language and our consciousness of self whereas the cerebellum, tucked under the cerebellum, ensures that movements are co-ordinated and balanced. Deep within the brain sits the limbic system, an important collection of structures whose functions are not completely understood, but which we know are involved with primitive instincts such as fear, emotions and memory.

WHEN SOMETHING GOES WRONG

Any complex machine is susceptible to malfunction or damage and the brain is no exception. Despite being protected by a bony 'crash helmet' – the skull – the brain is vulnerable to trauma,

The complexities of the brain are still being unravelled today despite rapid advances in technology, and a greater understanding of our psychological make-up.

and head injuries can be devastating, especially in children. Damage to brain tissue, such as that caused by the development of tumours or early degeneration of nerve cells, causes symptoms dependent on the area of the brain that is affected. A stroke, which cuts off the blood supply to brain tissue, is not uncommon in the elderly

Imaging techniques such as CT scanning enable health experts to examine the brain layer by layer to check for any unusual characteristics.

and can lead to weakness in the limbs and even paralysis. Fortunately, earlier recognition of the symptoms has led to more timely life-saving treatment in specialist centres, and the outlook for stroke is improving.

Some disorders are evident at birth and are life-long conditions: for instance, in cerebral palsy, the brain is starved of vital oxygen, affecting movement and speech; and in Down's syndrome children are born with a range of physical and mental symptoms caused by a genetic abnormality. Other conditions are particularly associated with older age – Alzheimer's disease is becoming increasingly common as the world's population ages, and Parkinson's disease primarily affects people over the age of fifty.

COPING WITH MENTAL ILLNESS
One in four of us will experience mental illness in our lifetime – a familiar but unsettling statistic. The experience can range from stress related illness to depression or schizophrenia. Mental illness can affect basic human functions such as eating, for example anorexia nervosa and bulimia, or can affect people at particular times of their lives, such as after having a baby. Medication and 'talking therapies' are the cornerstones of treatment, and these should be tailored to each individual.

LOOKING INSIDE THE BRAIN
Once symptoms develop that may indicate a brain disorder, it is vital that doctors are able to visualize the brain tissue, measure electrical activity within the cells and assess nerve function. Symptoms of neurological disease are often vague and progress slowly or they indicate a number of potential diagnoses. Technological advances over the last 50 years have meant that we can now see brain tissue in minute detail using non-invasive investigations such as computed tomography, magnetic resonance imaging, or PET scanning. These techniques have transformed diagnostic ability. Progress in diagnosing and treating neurological disorders and a better understanding of the brain and how it works means that people have a better chance than ever of a cure or a normal life expectancy.

Close examination of brain structures using on screen brain imaging techniques can reveal abnormalities, such as tumours or bleeding.

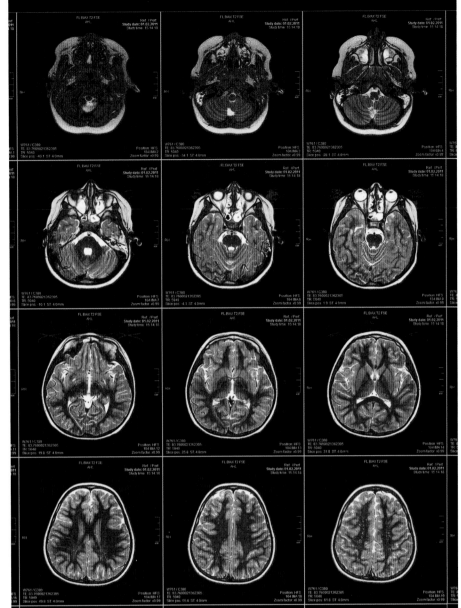

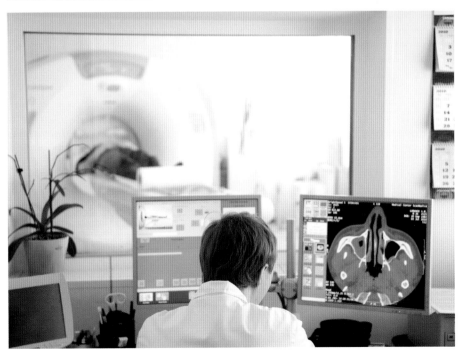

The brain

The brain is the part of the central nervous system that lies inside the skull.
It controls many body functions including our heart rate, the ability to walk
and run, and the creation of our thoughts and emotions.

The brain comprises three major parts: forebrain, midbrain and hindbrain. The forebrain is divided into two halves, forming the left and right cerebral hemispheres.

HEMISPHERES

The cerebral hemispheres form the largest part of the forebrain. Their outer surface is folded into a series of gyri (ridges) and sulci (furrows) that greatly increases its surface area. Most of the surface of each hemisphere is hidden in the depths of the sulci.

Each hemisphere is divided into frontal, parietal, occipital and temporal lobes, named after the closely related bones of the skull. Connecting the two hemispheres is the corpus callosum, a large bundle of fibres deep in the longitudinal fissure.

GREY AND WHITE MATTER

The hemispheres consist of an outer cortex of grey matter and an inner mass of white matter.
■ Grey matter contains nerve cell bodies, and is found in the cortex of the cerebral and cerebellar hemispheres and in groups of sub-cortical nuclei.
■ White matter comprises nerve fibres found below the cortex. They form the communication network of the brain, and can project to other areas of the cortex and spinal cord.

Left cerebral hemisphere

Right cerebral hemisphere

Frontal pole
The most anterior part of the forebrain

Superior frontal gyrus

Precentral gyrus
Contains the motor area of the cortex that controls the skeletal muscles. As well as moving the limbs, this part of the cortex controls movement of the fingers, thumbs and lips

Postcentral gyrus
Contains the sensory area of the cortex

Sulcus
An infolding of the cerebral cortex

Gyrus
A raised ridge of cerebral cortex

Longitudinal fissure
The division between the two cerebral hemispheres

Precentral sulcus

Central sulcus
Separates the frontal and parietal lobes

Parieto-occipital sulcus
Forms a boundary between the parietal and occipital lobes

Calcarine sulcus
Contains the visual part of the cortex

Ridges and furrows

Primary motor cortex

Primary somatosensory cortex

Receptive speech area
(Wernicke's area)

Frontal lobe
Part of the forebrain that deals with emotions

Parietal lobe
An area involved with orientation in space

Motor speech
(Broca's area)

Temporal lobe
The area concerned with sound and spoken language

Occipital lobe
Part of the hindbrain and the main area for visual interpretation

Primary auditory cortex

The four lobes of the cerebral hemispheres are highlighted on this left hemisphere.

The central sulcus runs from the longitudinal fissure to the lateral fissure, and marks the boundary between the frontal and parietal lobes. The precentral gyrus runs parallel to and in front of the central sulcus and contains the primary motor cortex, where voluntary movement is initiated. The postcentral gyrus contains the primary somatosensory cortex that perceives bodily sensations. The parieto-occipital sulcus (on the medial surface of both hemispheres) marks the border between the parietal and occipital lobes.

The calcarine sulcus marks the position of the primary visual cortex, where visual images are perceived. The primary auditory cortex is located towards the posterior (back) end of the lateral fissure.

On the medial surface of the temporal lobe, at the rostral (front) end of the most superior gyrus, lies the primary olfactory cortex, which is involved with smell. Internal to the parahippocampal gyrus lies the hippocampus, which is part of the limbic system and is involved in memory formation. The areas responsible for speech are located in the dominant hemisphere (usually the left) in each individual. The motor speech area (Broca's area) lies in the inferior frontal gyrus and is essential for the production of speech.

Inside the brain

A midline section
between the two cerebral
hemispheres reveals the
main structures that
control a vast number
of activities in the body.
While particular areas
monitor sensory and
motor information, others
control speech and sleep.

SPEECH, THOUGHT
AND MOVEMENT
The receptive speech area
(Wernicke's area) lies behind
the primary auditory cortex and
is essential for understanding
speech. The prefrontal cortex has
high-order cognitive functions,
including abstract thinking,
social behaviour and decision-
making ability.

Within the white matter of
the cerebral hemispheres are
several masses of grey matter,
known as the basal ganglia.
This group of structures is
involved in aspects of motor
function, including movement
programming, planning and
motor programme selection and
motor memory retrieval.

DIENCEPHALON
The medial part of the forebrain
comprises the structures
surrounding the third ventricle.
These form the diencephalon
which includes the thalamus,
hypothalamus, epithalamus
and subthalamus of either side.
The thalamus is the last relay
station for information from the
brainstem and spinal cord before
it reaches the cortex.

The hypothalamus lies below
the thalamus in the floor of the
diencephalon. It is involved in

Corpus callosum
A thick band of nerve fibres, found
in the depths of the longitudinal
fissure that connects the cerebral
hemispheres

Right cerebral hemisphere
One of two
hemispheres
that form the
largest part of
the forebrain

Ventricle
Fluid-filled
cavity

Thalamus
Directs sensory
information from
the sense organs
to the correct part
of the cerebral cortex

Optic nerve
Carries visual information
from the eye to the brain

Pituitary stalk
The pituitary gland is not included when
the brain is removed from the skull

Hypothalamus
Concerned with emotions and
drives, such as hunger and
thirst; it also helps to control
body temperature and the
water-salt balance in the blood

Precentral gyrus

Central sulcus

Postcentral gyrus

Pineal gland
Part of the
epithalamus
that synthesizes
melatonin

Parieto-occipital sulcus
Divides the
occipital and
parietal lobes

Calcarine sulcus
Where most of
the primary visual
cortex lies

Cerebellum
Controls body
movement and
maintains balance;
consists of grey
matter on the outside
and white matter on
the inside

Spinal cord

Midbrain
Important in
vision; links the
forebrain to the
hindbrain

Pons
Part of the
brainstem
that contains
numerous
nerve tracts

Medulla oblongata
Contains vital centres that
control breathing, heart-beat
and blood supply

a variety of homeostatic
mechanisms, and controls
the pituitary gland that
descends from its base. The
anterior (front) lobe of the
pituitary secretes substances
that influence the thyroid
and adrenal glands, and the
gonads and produces growth
factors. The posterior lobe

produces hormones that increase
blood pressure, decrease urine
production and cause uterine
contraction. The hypothalamus
also influences the sympathetic
and parasympathetic nervous
systems and controls body
temperature, appetite and
wakefulness. The epithalamus
is a relatively small part of the

dorso-caudal diencephalon that
includes the pineal gland, which
synthesizes melatonin and is
involved in the control of the
sleep/wake cycle.

The subthalamus lies beneath
the thalamus and next to the
hypothalamus. It contains
the subthalamic nucleus that
controls movement.

Brainstem and cerebellum

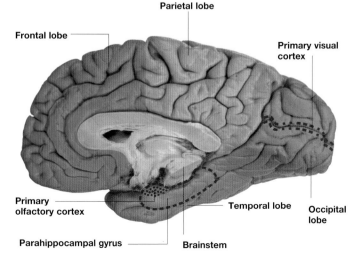

Parietal lobe

Frontal lobe

Primary visual cortex

Primary olfactory cortex

Parahippocampal gyrus

Temporal lobe

Occipital lobe

Brainstem

The posterior part of the
diencephalon is connected to
the midbrain, which is followed
by the pons and medulla
oblongata of the hindbrain.
The midbrain and hindbrain
contain the nerve fibres
connecting the cerebral
hemispheres to the cranial
nerve nuclei, to lower centres
within the brainstem and to the
spinal cord. They also contain
the cranial nerve nuclei.

Most of the reticular
formation, a network of

*A view of the medial surface of
the right hemisphere, with the
brainstem removed, allowing the
lower hemisphere to be seen.*

nerve pathways, lies in the
midbrain and hindbrain. This
system contains the important
respiratory, cardiac and
vasomotor centres.

The cerebellum lies posterior
to the hindbrain and is attached
to it by three pairs of narrow
stalk-like structures that are
called peduncles. Connections
with the rest of the brain and
spinal cord are established via
these peduncles. The cerebellum
functions at an unconscious
level to co-ordinate movements
initiated in other parts of the
brain. The cerebellum also
controls the maintenance of
balance and influences posture
and muscle tone.

Meninges

The meninges are three membranes that protect the brain and spinal cord.

The meninges cover the brain and spinal cord, and serve to protect these important structures. They comprise three layers.

THE DURA MATER
The dura mater is a thick fibrous tissue that lines the inner layer of the skull. It deviates from the contours of the skull by forming a double fold (falx cerebri) that dips down between the cerebral hemispheres, and into the gaps between the cerebral hemispheres and the cerebellum (tentorium cerebelli).

THE ARACHNOID MATER
The arachnoid mater is an impermeable membrane that follows the contours of the dura mater. It is separated from the dura mater by a small gap called the subdural space. The arachnoid mater is connected to the pia mater by bands of web-like tissue (called trabeculae).

THE PIA MATER
The pia mater covers the surface of the brain and spinal cord. The space between the arachnoid and pia (subarachnoid space) is filled with cerebrospinal fluid (CSF). The brain and spinal cord are suspended in this fluid, which provides the most important means of physical protection for the brain.

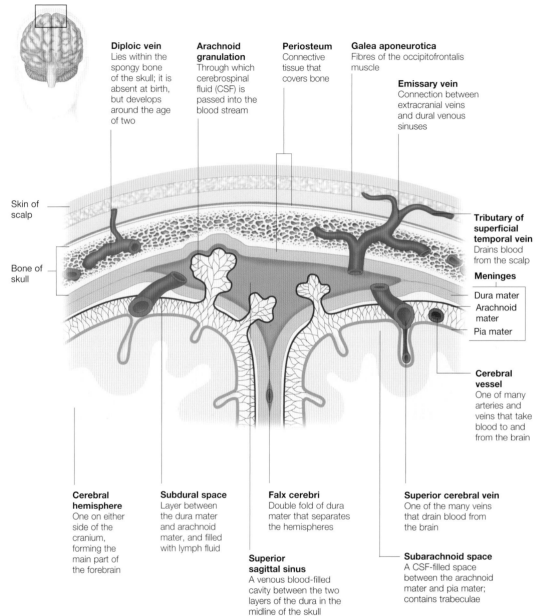

Diploic vein
Lies within the spongy bone of the skull; it is absent at birth, but develops around the age of two

Arachnoid granulation
Through which cerebrospinal fluid (CSF) is passed into the blood stream

Periosteum
Connective tissue that covers bone

Galea aponeurotica
Fibres of the occipitofrontalis muscle

Emissary vein
Connection between extracranial veins and dural venous sinuses

Skin of scalp

Bone of skull

Tributary of superficial temporal vein
Drains blood from the scalp

Meninges
Dura mater
Arachnoid mater
Pia mater

Cerebral vessel
One of many arteries and veins that take blood to and from the brain

Cerebral hemisphere
One on either side of the cranium, forming the main part of the forebrain

Subdural space
Layer between the dura mater and arachnoid mater, and filled with lymph fluid

Falx cerebri
Double fold of dura mater that separates the hemispheres

Superior sagittal sinus
A venous blood-filled cavity between the two layers of the dura in the midline of the skull

Superior cerebral vein
One of the many veins that drain blood from the brain

Subarachnoid space
A CSF-filled space between the arachnoid mater and pia mater; contains trabeculae

---

Potential sites of bleeding

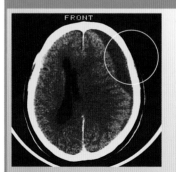

A subdural haemorrhage (circled on this CT scan) can be extensive, compressing a large area of the brain.

Although arteries are found in the arachnoid membrane, the most important of the meningeal arteries is the middle meningeal artery.

This artery is found outside the dura mater (the extradural space), and lies close to the inner layer of the periosteum. It is set in the bone, therefore reducing pressure on the meninges, but if the artery becomes too enlarged, for example through increased blood pressure, the person will suffer from a headache.

The middle meningeal artery runs across the junction of three skull bones. Here, it is susceptible

to injury from fracture. If the artery ruptures, blood will leak into the extradural space, and may result in a quick death if left untreated. Following a head injury, such as violent shaking of the head, bleeding may occur from the intra-cranial venous sinuses – blood-filled cavities between layers of dura (see over). The blood will leak into the subdural space, and may compress brain tissue. If this occurs slowly, gradual loss of brain function or a change in the individual's personality will result. Sometimes, it can occur rapidly, and may cause death.

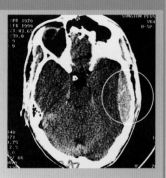

This is the characteristic appearance of an extradural haemorrhage. The leakage of blood into the skull is circled.

Dural venous sinuses

The sinuses play a role in the circulation and drainage of the blood and fluids that protect and bathe the brain.

There are 15 dural venous sinuses – blood-filled cavities between double folds of dura mater. Venous sinuses are lined by endothelium, but unlike other veins, they have no muscular layer. They are therefore very delicate, relying on surrounding tissues for support. The network of sinuses can be seen on the illustrations.

VENOUS CIRCULATION
There are two sets of dural venous sinuses, those in the upper part of the skull and those on the floor of the skull. They receive blood draining from the brain via the cerebral and cerebellar veins, the red bone marrow of the skull via diploic veins and the scalp via the emissary veins. They are crucial to the reabsorption of CSF.

ROUTES OF BRAIN INFECTION
The sinuses are valveless and provide no resistance to the spread of infection. The connections between the veins of the face and the dural venous sinuses allow the possibility of infection on the face spreading to the brain, which can be life-threatening.
   Valveless connections between the veins around the spinal cord and dural venous sinuses allow the spread of infection or cancer cells between the body and the brain.

Falx cerebri
Double layer of dura mater that lies in the midline and separates the left and right cerebral hemispheres

Superior cerebral veins
Can be ruptured following a head injury; this is the most common cause of subdural haemorrhage

Cavernous sinus
Several veins drain into this sinus; cranial nerves and the internal carotid artery also pass close by

Inferior sagittal sinus
Lies in the free margin of the falx cerebri; joins the straight sinus in the midline of the tentorium cerebelli

Inferior petrosal sinus
Joins the internal jugular vein

Transverse sinus
Joined by the inferior cerebral and inferior cerebellar veins to become the sigmoid sinus

Superior sagittal sinus
Receives superficial veins

Sigmoid sinus
Carries blood to the internal jugular vein

Occipital sinus
Passes from the transverse sinus to the sigmoid sinus

Straight sinus
Receives blood from the inferior sagittal sinus and the great cerebral vein

Tentorium cerebelli
Forms roof over the posterior cranial fossa and the cerebellum

Sphenoparietal sinus
Drains into the roof of the cavernous sinus

Superior petrosal sinus
Joins the transverse sinus and cavernous sinus

Great cerebral vein (of Galen)
Drains the deeper parts of the brain

Sinuses in the base of the skull

Ophthalmic vein
Drains blood from eye socket

Diploic bone
Contains red bone marrow

Internal carotid artery
Passes through the cavernous sinus

Cavernous sinuses

Inferior petrosal sinus
Not associated with the dural folds. Leaves the skull separately.

Foramen magnum
Hole in the occipital bone through which the spinal cord passes

The venous sinuses in the base of the skull as seen from above.

Pituitary stalk
Connects the brain to the pituitary gland

Globe (eyeball)

Optic nerve
Essential for normal sight

Middle meningeal artery
Supplies blood to the cranial bones; may rupture following a skull fracture

Sigmoid sinus
Joined on either side by the superior petrosal sinus

Internal jugular vein
Receives the sigmoid sinus and leaves the brain through the jugular foramen

Right transverse sinus
Leads to the sigmoid sinus

There are seven pairs of sinuses on the floor of the skull. These include the transverse, inferior petrosal sinus, superior petrosal sinus, cavernous, sigmoid, sphenoparietal and occipital sinuses.

CAVERNOUS SINUSES
The cavernous sinuses lie on either side of the pituitary gland. The roof of each sinus is continuous with the dural sheet (diaphragma sellae) that covers the pituitary gland, surrounding the pituitary stalk.
   Several important structures lie close to the cavernous sinuses. These include the internal carotid artery, three nerves supplying eye movement, and branches of the trigeminal nerve, which supplies sensation to the skin of the face and enables movement of the muscles of mastication.

Blood vessels of the brain

The arteries provide the brain with a rich supply of oxygenated blood.

The brain weighs about 1.4 kg and accounts for two per cent of our total body weight. However, it requires 15–20 per cent of the cardiac output to be able to function properly. If the blood supply to the the brain is cut for as little as 10 seconds we lose consciousness and, unless blood flow is quickly restored, it takes only a matter of minutes before the damage is irreversible.

THE ARTERIAL NETWORK
Blood reaches the brain via two pairs of arteries. The internal carotid arteries originate from the common carotid arteries in the neck, enter the skull via the carotid canal and then branch to supply the cerebral cortex. The two main branches of the internal carotid are the middle and anterior cerebral arteries.

The vertebral arteries arise from the subclavian arteries, enter the skull via the foramen magnum and supply the brainstem and cerebellum. They join, forming the basilar artery that then divides to produce the two posterior cerebral arteries that supply, among other things, the occipital or visual cortex at the back of the brain.

These two sources of blood to the brain are linked by other arteries to form a circuit at the base of the brain called the 'circle of Willis'.

Inferior (from below) view of the brain

Right hemisphere **Left hemisphere**

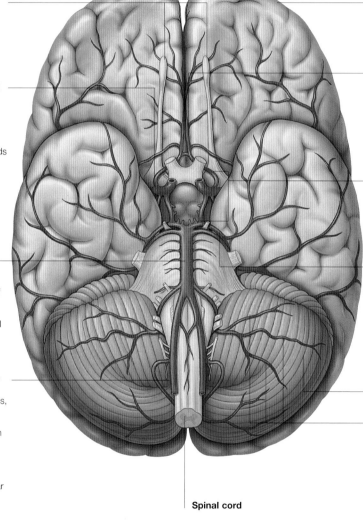

Olfactory bulbs
Organs of smell

Middle cerebral artery
This is the main branch of the internal carotid artery, supplying blood to two-thirds of the cerebral hemisphere and many deep structures of the brain

Basilar artery
A large artery that lies on the inferior surface of the pons; divides to form the two posterior cerebral arteries

Vertebral artery
Arises from the subclavian arteries, enters the skull through the foramen magnum to supply the brainstem, then fuses with its opposite number to form the basilar artery

Spinal cord

Cerebrum

Anterior cerebral artery
Supplies blood to the frontal lobe and to the medial surface of the cerebral hemisphere

Circle of Willis
Circle of communicating arteries at the base of the brain

Posterior cerebral artery
Supplies blood to the inferior part of the temporal lobe and to the occipital lobe at the back of the brain

Cerebellum

Cerebellar arteries
Branches from the vertebral and basilar arteries that provide the blood supply to the cerebellum

What happens if blood supply stops

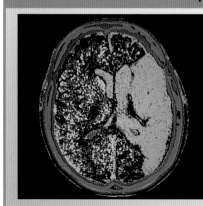

The importance of the blood supply to the brain becomes very clear when that supply is lost, as is seen in a stroke.

Strokes may result from blockage of (ischaemic stroke) or bleeding from (haemorrhagic stroke) an artery. This results in the death

This false-colour CT scan shows an area of dead tissue (blue) caused by a blockage in a cerebral artery. This may be due to a blood clot.

of the brain tissue supplied by that particular vessel.

The effects on the patient depends on which blood vessel is affected. A stroke on one side of the brain can result in weakness or paralysis in the opposite side of the body. This is because the motor cortex, which controls the voluntary movement of muscles on the opposite side of the body, is damaged.

Other symptoms that may be associated with damage to

specific areas of the brain are:
■ Loss of sensation down one side of the body
■ Visual disturbances
■ Language problems (such as slurring, an inability to express oneself or even loss of speech altogether)
■ Confusion. The degree of recovery, depends on the size and location of the damaged area. In some cases, the paralysis or weakness persists, although it often improves.

Veins of the brain

Deep and superficial veins drain blood from the brain into a complex system of sinuses. These sinuses rely on gravity to return blood to the heart as, unlike other veins, they do not possess valves.

The veins of the brain can be divided into deep and superficial groups. These veins, none of which have valves, drain into the venous sinuses of the skull.

The sinuses are formed between layers of dura mater, the tough outer membrane covering the brain, and are unlike the veins in the rest of the body in that they have no muscular tissue in their walls.

The superficial veins have a variable arrangement on the surface of the brain and many of them are highly interconnected. Most superficial veins drain into the superior sagittal sinus. By contrast, most of the deep veins, associated with structures within the body of the brain, drain into the straight sinus via the great cerebral vein (vein of Galen).

FUNCTIONS OF THE SINUSES

The straight sinus and the superior sagittal sinus converge. Blood flows through the transverse and sigmoid sinuses and exits the skull through the internal jugular vein before flowing back towards the heart.

Beneath the brain, on either side of the sphenoid bone, are the cavernous sinuses. These drain blood from the orbit (eye socket) and deep parts of the face. This provides a potential route of infection into the skull.

Superior sagittal sinus
The largest of the venous sinuses; receives blood from many of the superficial cerebral veins and is also the site for reabsorption of cerebrospinal fluid into the circulation

Inferior sagittal sinus
Found at the lower margin of the falx cerebri (a large fold in the dura mater separating the two cerebral hemispheres); receives blood from superficial veins

Straight sinus
Drains blood from the inferior sagittal sinus and the deep cerebral veins via the great vein of Galen

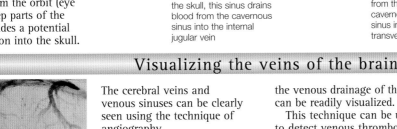

Cavernous sinus
Drains blood from the orbit, deep parts of the face and the pituitary gland

Transverse sinus
Connects the confluence of the sinuses and the sigmoid sinus

Inferior petrosal sinus
Associated with the petrous temporal bone of the skull, this sinus drains blood from the cavernous sinus into the internal jugular vein

Superior petrosal sinus
Drains blood from the cavernous sinus into the transverse sinus

Sigmoid sinus
Drains blood from the transverse sinus to the internal jugular vein; so called because of its 'S' shape

Visualizing the veins of the brain

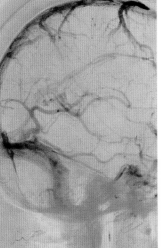

The cerebral veins and venous sinuses can be clearly seen using the technique of angiography.

The procedure involves injecting a radio-opaque contrast medium into the internal carotid artery. After about seven seconds the medium has had an opportunity to reach the venous circulation. A rapid series of X-rays is then taken, and the details of abnormalities or problems with the venous drainage of the brain can be readily visualized.

This technique can be used to detect venous thrombosis (blood clots) and congenital abnormalities in the connections between arteries and veins (arteriovenous malformations, or AVMs).

However, problems with the cerebral venous system are far less common than those associated with the cerebral arteries.

The veins of the cerebrum are visible on this carotid arteriogram (venous phase). The radio-opaque medium shows up as black.

This cast shows the venous sinuses of the brain, which drain deoxygenated (no longer containing oxygen) blood back to the heart.

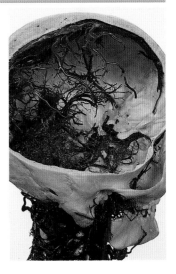

Ventricles of the brain

The brain 'floats' in a protective layer of cerebrospinal fluid – the watery liquid produced in a system of cavities within the brain and brainstem.

The brain contains a system of communicating (connected) cavities known as the ventricles. There are four ventricles within the brain and brainstem, each secreting cerebrospinal fluid (CSF), the fluid that surrounds and permeates the brain and spinal cord, protecting them from injury and infection.

Three of the ventricles – namely the two (paired) lateral ventricles and the third ventricle – lie within the forebrain. The lateral ventricles are the largest, and lie within each cerebral hemisphere. Each consists of a 'body' and three 'horns' – anterior (situated in the frontal lobe), posterior (occipital lobe) and inferior (temporal lobe). The third ventricle is a narrow cavity between the thalamus and hypothalamus.

HINDBRAIN VENTRICLE

The fourth ventricle is situated in the hindbrain, beneath the cerebellum. When viewed from above, it is diamond-shaped, but in sagittal section (see right) it is triangular. It is continuous with the third ventricle via a narrow channel called the cerebral aqueduct of the midbrain. The roof of the fourth ventricle is incomplete, allowing it to communicate with the subarachnoid space (see over).

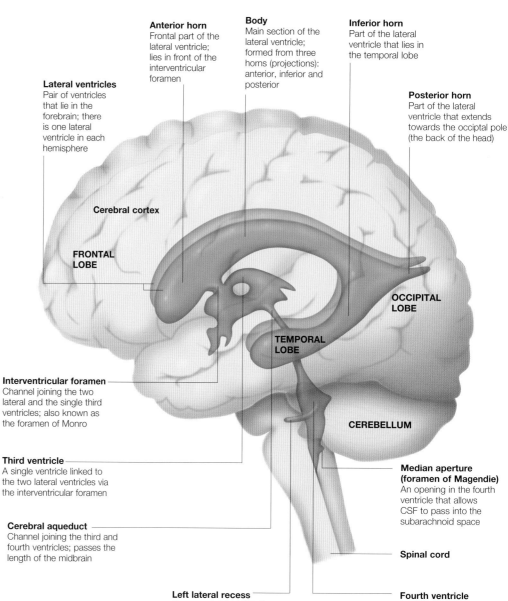

Anterior horn
Frontal part of the lateral ventricle; lies in front of the interventricular foramen

Body
Main section of the lateral ventricle; formed from three horns (projections): anterior, inferior and posterior

Inferior horn
Part of the lateral ventricle that lies in the temporal lobe

Posterior horn
Part of the lateral ventricle that extends towards the occipital pole (the back of the head)

Lateral ventricles
Pair of ventricles that lie in the forebrain; there is one lateral ventricle in each hemisphere

Cerebral cortex

FRONTAL LOBE

OCCIPITAL LOBE

TEMPORAL LOBE

CEREBELLUM

Interventricular foramen
Channel joining the two lateral and the single third ventricles; also known as the foramen of Monro

Third ventricle
A single ventricle linked to the two lateral ventricles via the interventricular foramen

Cerebral aqueduct
Channel joining the third and fourth ventricles; passes the length of the midbrain

Median aperture (foramen of Magendie)
An opening in the fourth ventricle that allows CSF to pass into the subarachnoid space

Spinal cord

Left lateral recess (foramen of Luschka)
Opening in the fourth ventricle that allows CSF to pass into the subarachnoid space

Fourth ventricle
Cavity within the brainstem that extends to the central canal in the middle of the spinal cord

This sagittal section of the brain and brainstem reveals the four ventricles and the foramina and aqueducts that connect them.

Cerebrospinal fluid in the ventricles

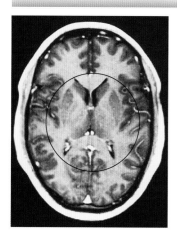

Within each ventricle is a network of blood vessels known as the choroid plexus. This is where the cerebrospinal fluid is produced. CSF fills the ventricles and also the subarachnoid space surrounding the brain and spinal cord, where it acts as a protective buffer. CSF is also believed to remove waste products into the venous system. The appearance of CSF can often provide clues to infection.

The symmetrical arrangement of the ventricles can be seen on this MR scan (circled).

CSF can be taken from various locations, usually along the spinal cord, in a procedure known as a 'tap'. A small hole is made in the dural sac (the outermost layer of meninges surrounding the brain and spinal cord) and into the lumbar subarachnoid space, where fluid can be aspirated (sucked out).

As CSF is normally a clear, colourless fluid, any change from this can indicate disease. A red appearance, for example, might suggest that the CSF contains blood from a recent haemorrhage.

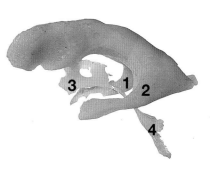

The ventrical system consists of four communicating cavities, as seen on this resin cast.

Circulation of cerebrospinal fluid

Cerebrospinal fluid (CSF) is produced by the choroid plexus within the lateral, third and fourth ventricles.

The choroid plexuses are a rich system of blood vessels originating from the pia mater, the innermost tissue surrounding the brain. The plexuses contain numerous folds (villous processes) projecting into the ventricles, from which cerebrospinal fluid is produced.

From the choroid plexuses in the two lateral ventricles, CSF passes to the third ventricle via the interventricular foramen. Together with additional fluid produced by the choroid plexus in the third ventricle, CSF then passes through the cerebral aqueduct of the midbrain and into the fourth ventricle. Additional fluid is produced by the choroid plexus in the fourth ventricle.

SUBARACHNOID SPACE

From the fourth ventricle, CSF finally passes out into the subarachnoid space surrounding the brain. It does this through openings in the fourth ventricle – a median opening (foramen of Magendie) and two lateral ones (foramina of Luschka). Once in the subarachnoid space, the CSF circulates to surround the central nervous system.

As CSF is produced constantly, it needs to be drained continuously to prevent any build-up of pressure. This is achieved by passage of the CSF into the venous sinuses of the brain through protrusions known as arachnoid granulations. These are particularly evident in the region of the superior sagittal sinus.

Superior sagittal sinus
A space receiving venous blood from the cerebral hemispheres

Arachnoid mater
The middle of the three meninges of the brain

Lateral ventricle

Dura mater
The outermost of the three meninges of the brain

Choroid plexus of the third ventricle
Responsible for the production of cerebrospinal fluid

Arachnoid granulations
Structures through which CSF passes into the venous sinuses

Subarachnoid space
Gap between the arachnoid and pia meninges through which CSF circulates; arrows indicate the direction of flow

Interventricular foramen
The opening through which CSF passes from the lateral ventricle to the third ventricle; blockage of this opening can lead to hydrocephalus

Cerebral aqueduct
Carries CSF to the fourth ventricle

Pituitary gland
Regulates the production of hormones

Lateral aperture of fourth ventricle
Channel through which CSF passes into the subarachnoid space

Central canal of spinal cord
Continuous with the fourth ventricle and extending through the spinal cord

Median aperture
Opening in roof of fourth ventricle, allowing CSF to pass into the subarachnoid space

Third ventricle

Cistern of the great cerebral vein
An area where CSF can be sampled

Choroid plexus of fourth ventricle
Produces CSF

Cerebellomedullary cisterna
One of a number of cisternae (enlarged subarachnoid space) from where CSF can be sampled

The circulation of CSF is plotted on this section of the brain and brainstem. The arrows show the movement of CSF: blue denotes the route of the fluid through the ventricular system; yellow the route through the subarachnoid space.

Hydrocephalus

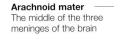

As CSF is continually being secreted, raised intracranial pressure will result if there is interference in the circulation. Such a situation will result from blockage of the interventricular foramen, the cerebral aqueduct or the apertures in the roof of the fourth ventricle,

Hydrocephalus results from an obstruction of the flow of CSF within the ventricular system or through the subarachnoid space. As a result, pressure builds up and the skull becomes enlarged as shown in this picture. In babies, hydrocephalus is usually due to a congenital malformation, or follows meningitis or a brain haemorrhage.

and will produce the condition known as hydrocephalus (water on the brain). A patient with this condition presents with headaches, unsteadiness and mental impairment.

In the newborn, hydrocephalus may produce a tensed and raised anterior fontanelle and an enlarged skull, and will require immediate treatment to relieve the pressure. If a sample of CSF is required for analysis in an adult, a lumbar puncture may be performed. In this procedure, a needle is inserted into the subarachnoid space between the bones of the fourth and fifth lumbar vertebrae. This does not damage nervous tissue, as the spinal cord normally terminates at a higher level (between the first and second lumbar vertebrae).

PET brain imaging

PET is a non-invasive imaging technique that reveals
local changes in brain activity. It is very useful at showing changes
associated with mental processes and nervous system diseases.

PET (positron emission tomography) is a technique for imaging brain function that makes use of small amounts of radiation from positron (sub-atomic particle) emitting isotopes or tracers.

The isotope is injected into the bloodstream and taken up into the brain. Depending on the particular isotope used, the tracer becomes most concentrated in certain areas, such as those with the highest rates of metabolism.

CROSS-SECTIONS OF THE BRAIN

The scanner uses a set of sensors to detect radiation emitted from the head after the injection and uses this data to construct detailed cross-sections of the brain. The level of radiation coming from each area can be colour-coded to produce a map of activity in the different brain regions.

While PET does not show brain structure clearly (as an MRI would), it gives unique information on functional activity. PET scans can now be superimposed onto MRI scans of the same person to combine the strengths of both techniques.

PET scans yield immediate results, as the technician receives images of cross-sections of the brain during the scan (screen on centre left). Metabolic activity shows up as 'hot spots'.

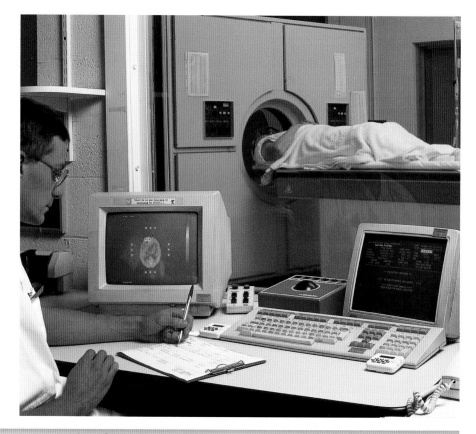

Applications

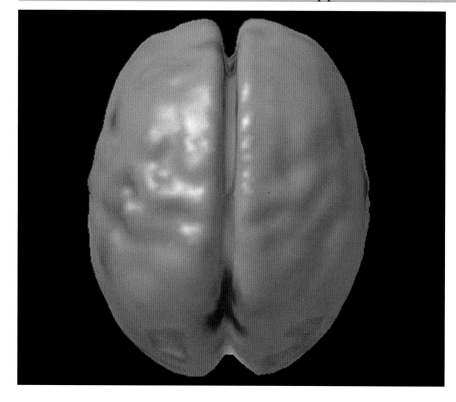

In healthy subjects, the short half-life of the isotopes used in PET scanning means that several scans can be carried out in the same session, monitoring changes in the brain during different activities such as movement, speaking or memorizing. PET scans have shown increases in blood flow in specific regions of the brain during different tasks, providing new information about the organization of brain function.

Other uses of PET scanning include:
■ Helping to discover which area of the brain is active at the beginning of an epileptic seizure. Although highly active during a seizure, the abnormal brain region will also often show reduced glucose metabolism between seizures
■ Estimating the rate of metabolic activity in brain tumours: more malignant tumours show higher levels of metabolism
■ In patients previously treated for brain tumours, helping to decide whether changes seen on MRI following surgery are due to the effects of the treatment or recurrence of the tumour.

PET imaging shows activity within different areas of the brain. This scan of the brain at rest demonstrates that there are still small areas of activity (shown in green) at the front and back of the brain.

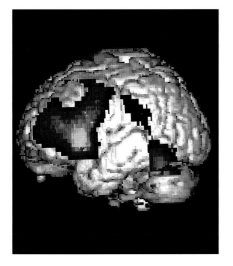

A PET scan showing areas of brain activity associated with turning thoughts into speech. The smaller area is involved in checking for cognition (understanding).

Generating speech

PET scanning can demonstrate the brain areas involved in speech generation. A region known as Broca's area in the frontal cortex is particularly involved. In most people, this is located in the left frontal lobe and so the left hemisphere is said to be dominant for speech.

Other areas are also activated during speaking, including the supplementary motor area in the frontal lobe, part of the motor cortex and the cerebellum.

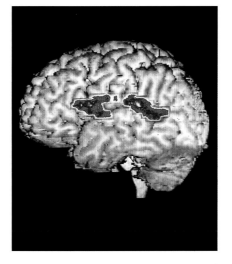

In verbal short-term memory there are two areas of high activity (shown in green/red): Broca's area (left) and the inferior parietal/ superior temporal cortex (right).

Remembering words

Verbal short-term memory involves several different components. When a person is trying to keep a string of letters in mind for a few seconds, at least two processes are active. The items are first circulated in a 'rehearsal system' (with associated activity in Broca's area), and then repeatedly put into a buffer store for verbal material (associated activity in the parietal lobe), which has a limited capacity and rapidly decays over a few seconds.

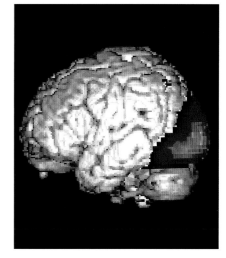

This PET scan of the left side of the brain shows the visual area of the occipital cortex being activated by visual stimuli (shown in red/orange).

Viewing images

The principal visual areas are in the occipital lobe at the back of the brain. PET scans have shown that the pattern of activation depends on the degree of complexity of the visual image. Simple white light activates only a limited area of the occipital lobes, while a more complicated visual stimulus activates a more extensive region. Colour perception involves a specific sub-region of the visual cortex, known as V4.

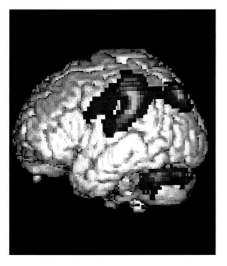

Tactile areas (upper) of the parietal cortex are activated as a blind person's fingers feel Braille dots. A cognitive area also becomes active (lower right).

Reading Braille

People who have been blind from birth show activation in the tactile areas of the parietal cortex as their fingers feel and make sense of the Braille dots. People with acquired blindness, however, show activity in the visual areas of the occipital lobe, as a sighted person would when reading a book. This suggests that they may be using visual imagery to interpret the touch sensations from their fingers as they use their newly acquired skill.

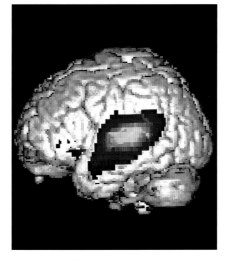

This PET scan of the left side of the brain shows the auditory area in the superior temporal lobe (part of the cerebrum) being activated by hearing.

Hearing sound

Listening to sound produces activation in the primary auditory cortex of the temporal lobes. Speech and non-speech sounds produce different patterns of activation. Hearing speech is associated with Wernicke's area in the left temporal lobe, while non-verbal sounds, such as a door slamming or the melody of music, produce activation in corresponding regions of the other side of the brain, in the right temporal lobe.

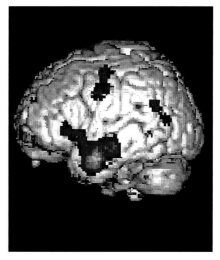

Looking at faces stimulates brain activity in an area of the occipital lobe. Face recognition, however, takes place mainly in the temporal lobe (orange/red).

Viewing faces

The perception of faces involves several different brain regions working together. A pathway running from the visual areas in the occipital lobe to the pre-frontal cortex is activated during facial perception, while an area known as the fusiform face area is activated during facial recognition.

Information also passes to the amygdala, a part of the limbic system concerned with emotion. This identifies the face as known or unknown, and as friend or foe.

Looking at the brain

Magnetic resonance (MR) imaging is the
'state of the art' method of revealing the complex structure
of the brain, and the conditions that may affect it.

Since the 1980s, magnetic resonance imaging (MR) has been used to visualize the anatomy of the human body in great detail. Magnetic resonance imaging does not use X-rays, but instead examines the behaviour of protons within the fat and water molecules of different body tissues. Protons become magnetized when placed in a magnetic field 15-20,000 times more powerful than the earth's magnetic field. Radio-frequency energy in the form of radio waves excites the protons, which emit very low power signals.

These signals are amplified and transformed into a digital images by a high-power computer. By altering the timing of the radio wave pulses, a series of image sequences in different planes is obtained. The magnetic resonance images are then systematically analyzed to assess the presence of disease or abnormalities.

APPLICATIONS

Although magnetic resonance imaging is costly when compared to plain X-ray, for example, the technique provides more information than any other type of radiological examination and is particularly useful in examining the most complex of the organs, the brain.

MR is particularly useful as it produces high-contrast images of soft tissues, which are not readily detected by X-rays or CT (computed tomography) scans. MR distinguishes tissues on the basis of their water content; in the brain it can differentiate between the relatively fatty white matter, the more watery grey matter and the more structured nerve fibres of the spinal cord.

Dense structures, such as bone, do not show up on MR scans, and therefore they are ideal for looking at and analysing the inside of the skull and vertebral column.

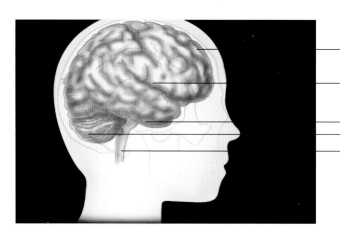

Frontal lobe

Position of pituatary gland

Pons
Cerebellum
Spinal cord

Arteriovenous malformation

An arteriovenous malformation (AVM) usually appears on the surface of the brain. Typically, the veins become very large because they are subjected to the high blood pressure normally only present in the arteries. The resulting vessels may compress vital areas of brain

giving rise to symptoms such as epilepsy. Haemorrhaging from the abnormal vessels into surrounding brain tissue may be catastrophic causing extensive brain damage – a 'stroke' is a more commonly used term for intracerebral bleeding.

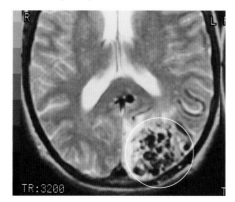

The two MR scans above have been taken in the transverse (left) and sagittal (right) planes. Multiple black voids are clearly visible – these are abnormally large blood vessels.

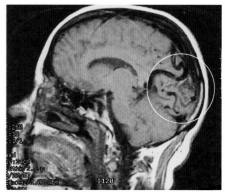

This can be treated by inserting a fine tube into an artery in the groin and threading it through the blood vessels to the brain – the vessel is then blocked using special glue.

Uses and applications

MR imaging, with its ability to distinguish soft tissues, lends itself particularly well to a number of neurological conditions. Neurological disorders often manifest themselves with symptoms such as headache, vertigo and stroke or transient (passing) attacks caused by obstructions to blood vessels. MR is particularly useful in visualizing the following problems:

■ **Lesions of the brain and spinal cord.** These include tumours such as meningioma, glioma and astrocytoma, brain

abscesses and cysts of the cerebellum
■ **Vascular and anatomical abnormalities** such as stroke, haemorrhages and hydrocephalus, where there is an excess of the fluid surrounding the brain.
■ **Myelin disorders** in which the fibres surrounding nerve cells are damaged, such as multiple sclerosis.

MR imaging uses magnetic fields many thousands of times stronger than that of the earth – this causes measurable changes in the body's hydrogen molecules.

Signals are amplified and transformed into digital images, which can be visualized directly by computer.

Infections and tumours

Before the advent of MR imaging, many tumours and infections of the brain were difficult to diagnose. MR scans are now a key diagnostic tool.

MR has significantly expanded the range of disorders and diseases of the brain that can be investigated. Previously, some brain tumours could not be visualized using, for example, CT scans. Cancerous tissue behaves differently to normal tissue in the magnetic fields utilized by MR, and is therefore easily visualized.

Similarly, abnormalities relating to infections, such as abscesses, meningitis and enchephalitis, can also be seen.

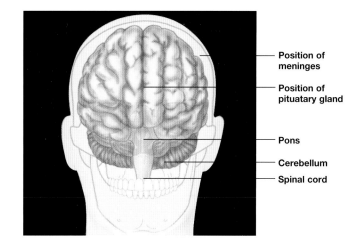

— Position of meninges

— Position of pituatary gland

— Pons

— Cerebellum

— Spinal cord

Acoustic neuroma

This is a tumour arising from the eighth cranial nerve, the nerve that transfers information from the inner ear (balance and hearing) to the brain. These small tumours are surrounded by bone in the base of the skull and were very difficult to diagnose prior to the development of MR. Using specific sequences, and occasionally an injection of a contrast agent containing gadolinium (a metallic element), even the smallest tumours may be clearly outlined.

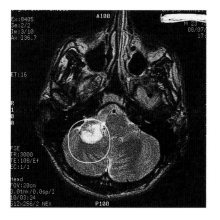

In this MR scan, a large, high signal (white) tumour is visible between the cerebellum and the pons, in a region called the cerebellopontine angle.

Intracranial infections

Bacterial infections of the outer lining of the brain result in meningitis. If the infection spreads to the brain substance, an abscess may result. In the case of tuberculosis, the focal area of infection (abscess) within the brain is known as a tuberculoma. It is most commonly seen in immunocompromised patients, such as people who have undergone organ transplant. The tuberculoma is often very slow to progress and may not become apparent until of significant size.

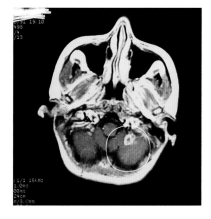

Here, an abnormally large vein has formed a complex tangle of enlarged blood vessels at the posterior aspect of this patient's brain.

Craniopharyngioma

This is a brain tumour that arises between the pituitary gland and the floor of the third ventricle. These tumours frequently have cystic areas and may contain cholesterol and keratin that will demonstrate different signal intensities on MR. The ability to show anatomy in multiple planes provides vital information to differentiate tumour extent from local oedema (swelling) caused by pressure on adjacent, normal brain tissue.

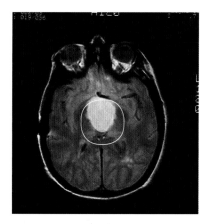

A large mass – the craniopharyngioma – appears as white (circled), in the midline and pushes up into the third ventricle of the brain.

Body planes

MR imaging allows direct assessment of the brain, not only in the transverse plane used by CT, but also in the sagittal and coronal planes. The unique ability of MR to provide images of the brain in three dimensions allows accurate diagnosis of disease and precise planning of treatment such as neurosurgery or radiotherapy. The physician may vary the width of a slice depending on what they are investigating, typically from 2–10 mm. Increasing the width necessitates a trade-off between picture quality and extraneous signal. It may require up to 30 slices to visualize the whole brain.

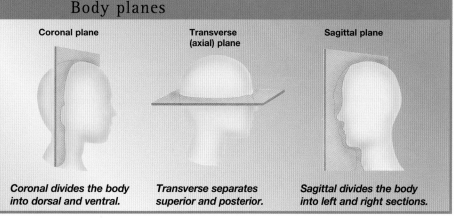

Coronal plane

Transverse (axial) plane

Sagittal plane

Coronal divides the body into dorsal and ventral.

Transverse separates superior and posterior.

Sagittal divides the body into left and right sections.

CT inside the head

Computed tomography (CT) scans are the most frequently requested hospital assessment of the brain and its immediate surroundings. They provide a rapid series of images and allow many neurological conditions to be diagnosed.

When a patient is suspected of having a serious head injury, CT scanning is the imaging procedure of choice. This is because of the speed with which images can be obtained, and the clarity on the images of brain tissue, blood and bone within the skull. This means that any damage is readily apparent. On a CT scan, the brain matter appears as mid-grey, the fluid-containing ventricles are the dark grey central structures and the skull appears white. The meninges do not show up.

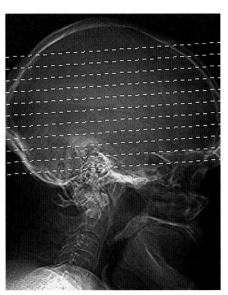

This X-ray is the initial planning, or 'scout', film taken before the series of scans for each patient. The dotted lines mark the levels of the planned CT slices, from the base of the skull up to the top of the cranium. In each of the scans, the front of the skull is at the top of the image and the patient's left is on the right of the scan.

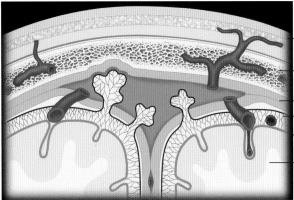

- Skin of scalp
- Skull bone
- Dura mater
- Arachnoid mater — Meninges
- Pia mater
- Cerebral hemisphere

A cross-section through the top of the skull shows the three layers of the meninges which surround the brain. Bleeding can occur within the cerebral hemispheres, or between the surrounding layers, depending on which blood vessels are involved.

A haemorrhage is bleeding from a ruptured blood vessel; a haematoma is a collection of blood that has clotted to form a solid mass.

The bleed is classified according to where it lies. For instance, a subdural haemorrhage lies beneath the dura mater.

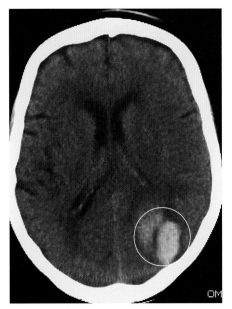

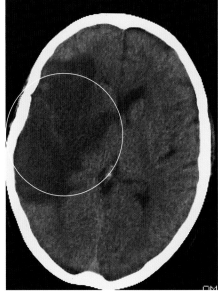

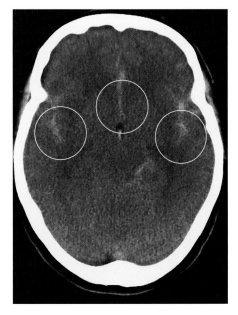

Acute intracerebral bleed

Bleeding within one or both of the cerebral hemispheres of the brain may occur in individuals with hypertension (high blood pressure) or as a result of trauma or a burst blood vessel. All patients with such bleeding will suffer a headache, and epilepsy is a possible long-term complication. Recently shed blood is high-density on the scan and appears white (circled).

Cerebral infarction

In this scan, a large part of the brain is much darker because the tissue on the patient's right side (circled) has died. As a result, this patient has left-sided paralysis. The dead brain area corresponds with the area served by the right middle cerebral artery. Narrowing of the right lateral ventricle is due to brain swelling. Multiple small infarcts are one cause of dementia.

Acute subarachnoid haemorrhage

The pia mater closely covers the surface of the brain, and bleeding can occur between it and the arachnoid. Blood then flows into the sulci (grooves) of the brain. In this scan, the cerebral sulci are white (circled), indicating the presence of fresh blood. Blood in the subarachnoid space is a profound irritant.

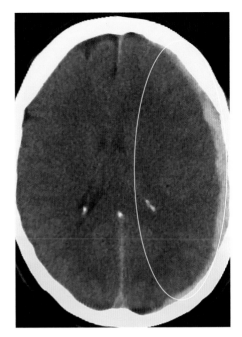

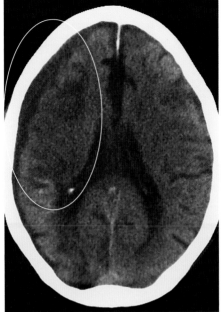

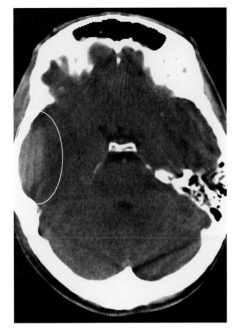

Acute subdural haematoma

In this scan, blood has passed over the surface of the brain, under the dura mater, but has not passed into the sulci, resulting in a semilunar haemorrhage. Fresh blood (white) is to the right of the brain, but is not entering the sulci. The gyri (ridges in the brain's surface) under the bleed are obliterated by pressure and a shift to the patient's left (right above) is visible. This injury initially rendered the patient unconscious, and in casualty, she was confused, restless and unco-operative.

Chronic subdural haematoma

Minor head injuries and falls may jar the brain and produce small tears in the veins that pass through the dura to the skull. The resulting long-term bleeding beneath the dura follows the contour of the brain. Here, the haemorrhage is semilunar in shape and acting as a mass, forcing the brain away from the skull.

Bleeding of this type may continue slowly for days or weeks, with the patient becoming more confused and unsteady. Over time, the blood becomes less dense on the scan.

Extradural haemorrhage

This scan reveals bleeding between the skull and the dura, resulting in a haemorrhage that is sharply localized. It may or may not be associated with an overlying fracture of the bone of the skull, perhaps from a blow to the head.

Extradural haemorrhage is characterized by a brief period of unconsciousness following a head injury. The patient may appear to recover fully and be able to carry out normal tasks, with only vague head discomfort. Later, consciousness is lost again.

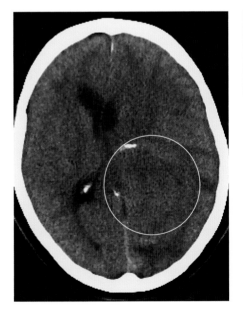

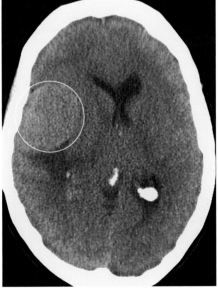

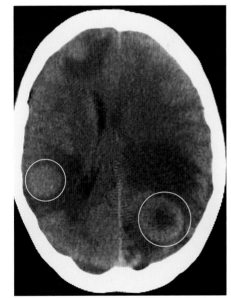

Cerebral glioma

Although brain tumours are rare, they can arise in the brain itself, in the meninges (the lining of the brain) or be a secondary spread from a cancer elsewhere. The edge of the tumour may absorb a contrast medium and appear white (circled). Patients with primary brain tumours have a long history of headaches, often in the mornings, and epilepsy may also develop.

Meningioma

The symptoms of a meningioma are similar to those of a primary brain tumour. This benign (non-malignant) tumour of the dura (the thickest of the three linings – meninges – surrounding the brain) takes up a great deal of contrast and becomes totally white. It can be seen (circled) adjacent to the skull, pushing the brain to the patient's left and deforming the right lateral ventricle.

Secondary brain tumours

When the patient has a known malignancy, alteration in behaviour, fits or headaches may indicate the spread of a cancer via the bloodstream into several areas of the brain. CT scanning will be used to identify this. The above scan has been enhanced by the administration of an intravenous contrast medium, and there are two obvious areas (circled) surrounded by swelling.

Cerebral hemispheres

The cerebral hemispheres are the largest part of the brain.
In humans, they have developed out of proportion to the other
regions, distinguishing our brains from those of other animals.

The left and right cerebral hemispheres are separated from each other by the longitudinal fissure that runs between them. Looking at the surface of the hemispheres from the top and side, there is a prominent groove running downwards, beginning about 1 cm behind the midpoint between the front and back of the brain.

This is the central sulcus or rolandic fissure. Further down on the side of the brain there is a second large groove, the lateral sulcus or sylvian fissure.

LOBES OF THE BRAIN
The cerebral hemispheres are divided into lobes, named after the bones of the skull that lie over them:
■ The frontal lobe lies in front of the rolandic fissure and above the sylvian fissure
■ The parietal lobe lies behind the rolandic fissure and above the back part of the sylvian fissure; it extends back as far as the parieto-occipital sulcus, a groove separating it from the occipital lobe, which is at the back of the brain
■ The temporal lobe is the area below the sylvian fissure and extends backward to meet the occipital lobe.

Lobes of the cerebral hemispheres

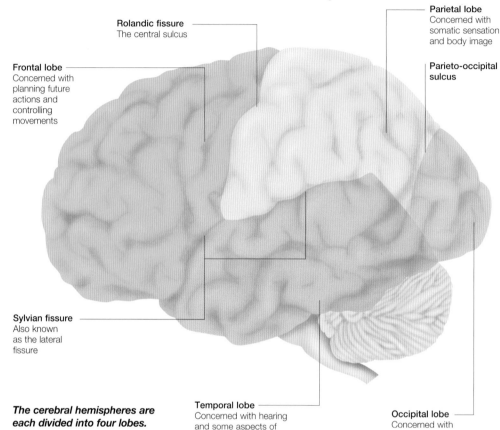

Rolandic fissure
The central sulcus

Parietal lobe
Concerned with
somatic sensation
and body image

**Parieto-occipital
sulcus**

Frontal lobe
Concerned with
planning future
actions and
controlling
movements

Sylvian fissure
Also known
as the lateral
fissure

Temporal lobe
Concerned with hearing
and some aspects of
learning, memory and emotion

Occipital lobe
Concerned with
interpreting the
visual scene

*The cerebral hemispheres are
each divided into four lobes.
They are named after the bones
of the skull which lie over them.*

Gyri and sulci

Gyrus
Elevated ridge
of cortical tissue

Sulcus
Shallow groove
of cortical tissue

Grey matter
Contains the cell bodies
of the nerve cells

White matter
Contains the axons
(nerve fibres) of nerve cells

*The human brain is highly
convoluted with many ridges
(gyri) and grooves (sulci)
across its surface.*

As the brain grows rapidly before birth, the cerebral cortex folds in on itself, producing the characteristic appearance that resembles a walnut. The folds are known as gyri and the shallow grooves between them are the sulci.

Certain sulci are found in the same position in all human brains and as a result are used as landmarks to divide the cortex into the four lobes.

DEVELOPMENT OF GYRI AND SULCI
Gyri and sulci begin to appear about the third or fourth month after conception. Before this time, the surface of the brain is smooth, like the brains of birds or reptiles. This complicated folding of its surface allows a larger area of cerebral cortex to be contained within the confined space of the skull.

Functions of the cerebral hemispheres

Different regions of the cortex have distinct and highly specialized functions.

The cerebral cortex is divided into:

■ Motor areas, which initiate and control movement. The primary motor cortex controls voluntary movement of the opposite side of the body. Just in front of the primary motor cortex is the pre-motor cortex and a third area, the supplementary motor area, lies on the inner surface of the frontal lobe. All of these areas work with the basal ganglia and cerebellum to allow us to perform complex sequences of finely controlled movements.

■ Sensory areas, which receive and integrate information from sensory receptors around the body. The primary somatosensory area receives information from sensory receptors on the opposite side of the body about touch, pain, temperature and the position of joints and muscles (proprioception).

■ Association areas, which are involved with the integration of more complex brain functions – the higher mental processes of learning, memory, language, judgment and reasoning, emotion and personality.

Primary motor cortex
Controls voluntary movement of the opposite side of the body; electrical stimulation in this area will produce movement of specific muscle groups

Primary somatosensory cortex
Receives information from sensory receptors on the opposite side of the body about touch, pain, temperature and the position of joints and muscles

Auditory association cortex
Concerned with the interpretation of the meaning and significance of sounds

Visual association area
Concerned with recognizing the meaning of visual information and relating it to previous experience

Broca's area
Concerned with the production of speech; in about 97 per cent of people this area is located on the left-hand side of the brain

Primary auditory cortex
Processes basic features of sound such as pitch and rhythm

Primary visual cortex
Receives visual information from the eyes relating to the opposite half of the field of vision

Some of the major functional areas of the cerebral cortex are mapped onto this side view of the human brain.

Motor and sensory body map

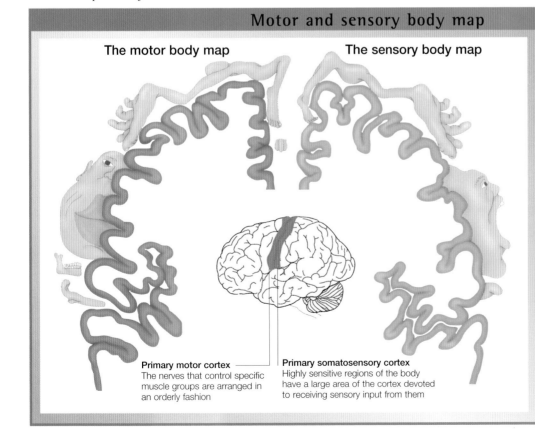

The motor body map

The sensory body map

The body surface is represented in the sensory and motor regions of the cerebral cortex in an orderly fashion.

A Canadian neurosurgeon called Wilder Penfield, working in the 1950s, mapped the regions of the sensory cortex that receive input from the different regions of the body. He stimulated the surface of the brain in locally anaesthetized patients and asked them to describe what they felt.

Penfield discovered that stimulation of regions of the postcentral gyrus produced tactile sensations in specific regions of the opposite side of the body.

Other research has shown that the volume of motor cortex devoted to different areas of the body is related to the degree of fine control and complexity of the movements involved, rather than the muscle bulk.

The cortex does not receive, or send out, the same amount of information from every region of the body.

Primary motor cortex
The nerves that control specific muscle groups are arranged in an orderly fashion

Primary somatosensory cortex
Highly sensitive regions of the body have a large area of the cortex devoted to receiving sensory input from them

Structure of the cerebral hemispheres

The cerebral cortex is made of two distinct layers: grey matter,
a thin layer of nerve and glial cells about 2-4 mm in thickness;
and white matter, consisting of nerve fibres (axons) and glial cells.

On the surface of the hemispheres is the grey matter, which ranges in thickness from about 2 to 4 mm. The grey matter is made up of nerve cells (neurones) together with supporting glial cells. In most parts of the cortex, six separate layers of cells can be distinguished under a microscope.

CORTICAL NEURONES
The cell bodies (which contain the cell's nucleus) of cortical neurones differ markedly in shape, although two main types of cell can be distinguished:
■ Pyramidal cells are so called because their cell body is shaped like a pyramid; their axons (nerve fibres) project out of the cortex, carrying information to other regions of the brain
■ Non-pyramidal cells, in contrast, have a smaller and rounder cell body and are involved in receiving and analyzing input from other sources.

The grey matter of the cerebral hemispheres can be subdivided into six layers of cells, based on the type of brain cell present.

The six layers of cells of the cortex

I: Molecular
Contains mostly axons that run laterally and glial cells

II: External granular
Contains mostly small pyramidal neurones

III: External pyramidal
Contains larger pyramidal cells that provide output to other cortical regions

IV: Internal granular
Rich in non-pyramidal cells that receive afferent input from the thalamus

V: Internal pyramidal
Contains the largest pyramidal cells whose long axons leave the cortex and descend to the brainstem and spinal cord

VI: Multiform
Contains pyramidal cells, some of which project back to the thalamus

Brodmann's area

The thickness of the six individual layers varies between different brain regions. A German neurologist called Korbinian Brodmann (1868–1918) examined these differences by staining nerve cells and looking at them under a microscope.

Brodmann was able to classify the cerebral cortex into over 50 distinct areas according to predefined anatomical criteria. Subsequent work has shown that each of Brodmann's anatomical areas has its own physiological function and characteristic pattern of connections.

This illustration represents functional areas of the left cerebral cortex, as plotted by the Brodmann system.

White matter

The white matter is composed of nerve fibres (axons) that connect different regions of brain.

Underneath the cerebral cortex (grey matter) is the white matter, which makes up the bulk of the inside of the cerebral hemispheres. It is arranged into bundles or tracts of three types:

■ **Commissural fibres**
These cross between the hemispheres, connecting corresponding regions on the two sides. The corpus callosum is the largest of these tracts.

■ **Association fibres**
These connect different areas within the same hemisphere. Short association fibres connect adjacent gyri and long association fibres interconnect more widely separated regions of the cortex.

■ **Projection fibres**
These connect the cerebral cortex with deeper underlying regions of the brain, the brainstem and the spinal cord. These fibres enable the cortex to receive incoming information from the rest of the body and to send out instructions controlling movement and other bodily functions.

Nerve bundles can be classified into three groups – commissural fibres (green), association fibres (blue) and projection fibres (red).

Distribution of the major nerve fibre tracts

Cingulum
Connects the frontal and parietal lobes with the parahippocampal and temporal gyri

Short association fibres
These U-shaped fibres link adjacent regions of cortex by arching beneath the sulci

Superior longitudinal fasciculus
Connects the frontal and occipital lobes

Level of sample
Coronal section through the brain to the right is at the level shown by the red line above

Internal capsule
Contains projection fibres that carry nerve impulses to and from the cortex

Grey matter
Composed of a thin layer of neurones and glial cells

Anterior commissure
Connects the olfactory regions on either side of the brain

Inferior longitudinal fasciculus
Connects the occipital to the temporal lobes – contributes to visual recognition

Brain damage and the case of Phineas Gage

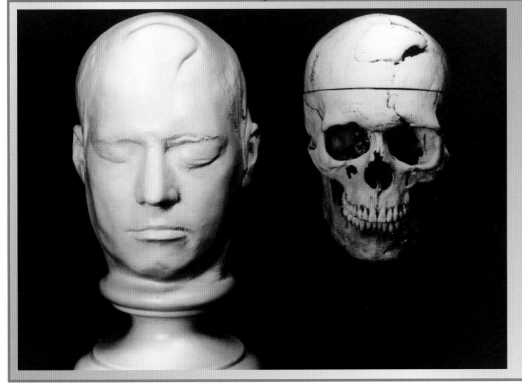

Neurologists have learnt a great deal about the brain by examining the behaviour of patients with brain damage.

One of the most notorious case histories was that of an American railway construction worker called Phineas Gage. Gage survived a blasting accident in 1848 in which a metal rod was driven through his left cheek and out of the top of his head.

After the accident, Gage's personality changed considerably – he became inconsiderate, moody, foul-mouthed and unable to plan ahead. This provided evidence that the frontal cortex, which was severely damaged during the accident, is involved in forward planning and self-image.

Phineas Gage's death mask and skull demonstrate the damage caused by the metre-long, 4 cm-wide metal rod.

Thalamus

The thalamus is a major sensory relay and integrating centre
in the brain, lying deep within its central core. It consists of two
halves and receives sensory inputs of all types, except smell.

The thalamus is made up of paired egg-shaped masses of grey matter (cell bodies of nerve cells) 3–4 cm long and 1.5 cm wide, located in the deep central core of the brain known as the diencephalon, or 'between brain'.

The thalamus makes up about 80 per cent of the diencephalon and lies on either side of the fluid-filled third ventricle. The right and left parts of the thalamus are connected to each other by a bridge of grey matter – the massa intermedia, or interthalamic adhesion.

NEUROANATOMY

The front end of the thalamus is rounded and is narrower than the back, which is expanded into the pulvinar. The upper surface of the thalamus is covered with a thin layer of white matter – the stratum zonale. A second layer of white matter – the external medullary lamina – covers the lateral surface.

Its structure is very complex and it contains more than 25 distinct nuclei (collections of nerve cells with a common function). These thalamic nuclear groups are separated by a vertical Y-shaped sheet of white matter – the internal medullary lamina. The anterior nucleus lies in the fork of the Y, and the tail divides the medial and lateral nuclei and splits to enclose the intralaminar nuclei.

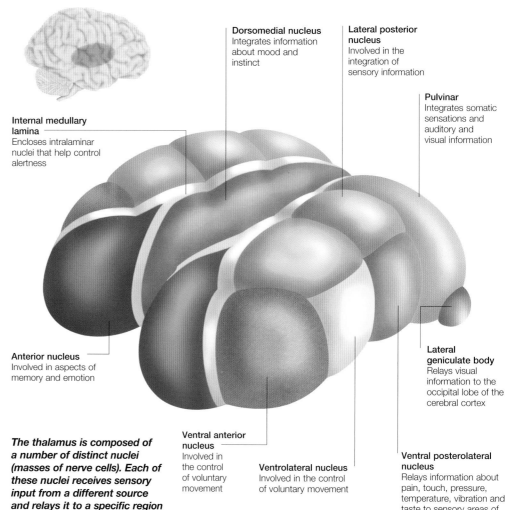

Dorsomedial nucleus
Integrates information about mood and instinct

Lateral posterior nucleus
Involved in the integration of sensory information

Pulvinar
Integrates somatic sensations and auditory and visual information

Internal medullary lamina
Encloses intralaminar nuclei that help control alertness

Anterior nucleus
Involved in aspects of memory and emotion

Lateral geniculate body
Relays visual information to the occipital lobe of the cerebral cortex

Ventral anterior nucleus
Involved in the control of voluntary movement

Ventrolateral nucleus
Involved in the control of voluntary movement

Ventral posterolateral nucleus
Relays information about pain, touch, pressure, temperature, vibration and taste to sensory areas of the cerebral cortex

The thalamus is composed of a number of distinct nuclei (masses of nerve cells). Each of these nuclei receives sensory input from a different source and relays it to a specific region of the brain.

Higher brain control

Side view of brain

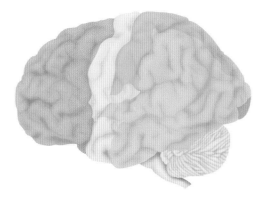

Internal view of brain

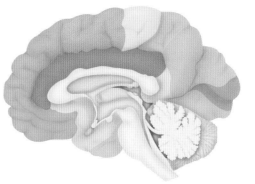

Each thalamic nucleus is connected to a specific region of the cerebral cortex (outer tissue of the brain). The two illustrations above are colour-coded to the artwork of the thalamus at the top of the page.

Each thalamic nucleus is linked to a distinct region of the cerebral cortex. These connections are made via a nerve fibre bundle called the internal capsule.

Some thalamic nuclei relay information received from different sensory modalities, including somatic (physical) sensation, vision and hearing, to the somatosensory cortex.

Others are involved in transmitting information about movement from the cerebellum and basal ganglia to the motor regions of the frontal cortex.

The thalamus is also involved in autonomic (unconscious) functions, including the maintenance of consciousness.

Hypothalamus

The hypothalamus is a complex structure located in the deep core of the brain. It regulates fundamental aspects of body function, and is critical for homeostasis – the maintenance of equilibrium in the body's internal environment.

The hypothalamus is a small region of the diencephalon; it is the size of a thumbnail and weighs only about four grams. It lies below the thalamus and is separated from it by a shallow groove, the hypothalamic sulcus. The hypothalamus is just behind the optic chiasm, the point where the two optic nerves cross over as they travel from the eyes towards the visual area at the back of the brain.

Several distinct structures stand out on its undersurface:
■ The mammillary bodies – two small, pea-like projections that are involved in the sense of smell
■ The infundibulum or pituitary stalk – a hollow structure connecting the hypothalamus with the posterior part of the pituitary gland (neurohypophysis) that lies below it
■ The tuber cinereum or median eminence – a greyish-blue, raised region surrounding the base of the infundibulum.

Hypothalamic nuclei

Paraventricular nucleus
Synthesizes the hormone oxytocin; in females, this causes milk production in the mammary glands and contraction of the uterine walls in childbirth

Corpus callosum
A band of nerve fibres that connects the left and right cerebral hemispheres

Suprachiasmatic nucleus
Concerned with controlling the sleep–wake cycle

Dorsomedial and ventromedial nucleus
Concerned with the control of hunger and thirst

Pituitary gland
Hormones released from this gland are under the direct control of the hypothalamus

Like the thalamus, the hypothalamus is composed of a number of nuclei. These nuclei are involved in the control of autonomic (unconscious) functions.

Supraoptic nucleus
Produces vasopressin (antidiuretic hormone), which increases water reabsorption in the kidneys

Hypothalamic control of other functions

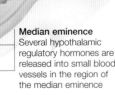

Hypothalamus

Anterior pituitary (AP)
The release of AP hormones is modulated by stimulatory factors released by the hypothalamus

Median eminence
Several hypothalamic regulatory hormones are released into small blood vessels in the region of the median eminence

Posterior pituitary (PP)
Hormones produced in the supraoptic and paraventricular nuclei in the hypothalamus are secreted into blood vessels here

The hypothalamus regulates a wide range of basic processes:
■ **The pituitary gland**
The hypothalamus is the main link between the central nervous system and the endocrine system, controlling pituitary gland function
■ **The autonomic nervous system**
Nerve fibres travel from the hypothalamus to the autonomic control centres in the brainstem. By this pathway, the hypothalamus can influence heart rate and blood pressure; contraction of the gut and bladder; sweating; and salivation
■ **Eating and drinking behaviour**
Stimulation of the lateral

The hypothalamus controls the pituitary gland via nerve fibres innervating the posterior pituitary, and blood capillaries supplying the anterior pituitary.

hypothalamus increases hunger and thirst. In contrast, activation of the ventromedial hypothalamus reduces hunger and food intake
■ **Body temperature**
Certain areas of the hypothalamus monitor the temperature of the blood and act as a thermostat
■ **Control of emotional behaviour**
The hypothalamus is involved, along with other brain regions, in the expression of fear and aggression, as well as in the control of sexual behaviour
■ **Control of sleep cycles**
The suprachiasmatic nucleus contributes to the daily patterns of sleeping and waking
■ **Memory**
Damage to the mammillary bodies is associated with impairment of the ability to learn and retain new information.

Limbic system

The limbic system is a ring of interconnected structures that lies deep within the brain. It makes connections with other parts of the brain, and is associated with mood and memory.

The limbic system is a collection of structures deep within the brain that is associated with the perception of emotions and the body's response to them.

The limbic system is not one, discrete part of the brain. Rather it is a ring of interconnected structures surrounding the top of the brainstem. The connections between these structures are complex, often forming loops o r circuits and, as with much of the brain, their exact role is not fully understood.

STRUCTURE

The limbic system is made up from all or parts of the following brain structures:
■ Amygdala – this almond-shaped nucleus appears to be linked to emotions, such as fear, aggression and pleasure
■ Hippocampus – this structure seems to play a part in learning and memory
■ Anterior thalamic nuclei – these collections of nerve cells form part of the thalamus. One of their roles seems to lie in the control of instinctive drives
■ Cingulate gyrus – this connects the limbic system to the cerebral cortex, the part of the brain that carries conscious thoughts
■ Hypothalamus – this regulates the body's internal environment, including blood pressure, heart rate and hormone levels. The limbic system generates its effects on the body by sending messages to the hypothalamus.

Medial view of the limbic system within the brain

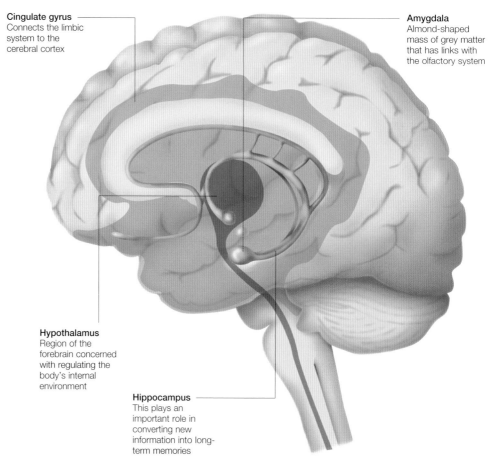

Cingulate gyrus
Connects the limbic system to the cerebral cortex

Amygdala
Almond-shaped mass of grey matter that has links with the olfactory system

Hypothalamus
Region of the forebrain concerned with regulating the body's internal environment

Hippocampus
This plays an important role in converting new information into long-term memories

The limbic system connections encircle the upper part of the brainstem. They link with other parts of the brain and are associated with emotion.

The limbic system and the sense of smell

Our sense of smell is strongly linked to memories of the past or emotions. For example, the smell of a new baby can trigger maternal affection.

The olfactory system (responsible for the sense of smell) is often included with the limbic system. There is certainly a close connection between the two.

EMOTIONS

Nerve fibres carrying information to the brain from the sensory receptors in the nose connect with structures in the limbic system, especially the amygdala. These connections mean that different smells are often associated with a variety of emotions and feelings. For example the scent of lavender is known to reduce tension, and the smell of baking bread or brewing coffee can lift the mood.

MEMORIES

Smell is also linked to memory; it is not uncommon for a passing scent to suddenly evoke memories that are believed to be long forgotten. This may be explained by the role of the limbic system, and especially the hippocampus, in learning and memory.

Connections of the limbic system

The limbic system has connections with the higher centres of the brain in the cortex, and with the more primitive brainstem. It not only allows the emotions to influence the body, but also enables the emotional response to be regulated.

The human brain can be considered to be made up of three parts. These parts have evolved one after another over the millennia.

BRAINSTEM
The 'oldest' part of the brain, in evolutionary terms, is the brainstem, which is concerned largely with unconscious control of the internal state of the body. The brainstem can be seen as a sort of 'life support system'.

LIMBIC SYSTEM
With the evolution of mammals came another 'layer' of brain, the limbic system. The limbic system allowed the development of feelings and emotions in response to sensory information. It is also associated with the development of newer – in evolutionary terms – behaviours, such as closeness to offspring (maternal bonding).

CEREBRAL CORTEX
The final layer of the human brain is shared to some extent with higher mammals. It is the cerebral cortex, the part of the brain that allows humans to think and reason. With this part of the brain, individuals perceive the outside world and make

The developing brain

The cerebral cortex
This outer layer of the brain evolved last, and is related to higher intellect

The brainstem
This part of the brain evolved first, and is responsible for self-preservation and aggression

The limbic system
This system developed secondly and enabled the emotions necessary for mammalian existence, which include caring for offspring

The three layers of the brain evolved one by one over thousands of years. Each is responsible for different bodily and intellectual functions.

conscious decisions about their behaviour and actions.

ROLE OF THE LIMBIC SYSTEM
The limbic system lies between the cortex and the brainstem and makes connections with both. Through its connections with the brainstem, the limbic system provides a way in which an individual's emotional state can influence the internal state of the body. This may prepare the body perhaps for an act of self-preservation such as running away in fear, or for a sexual encounter.

The extensive connections between the limbic system and the cerebral cortex allow human beings to use their knowledge of the outside world to regulate their response to emotions. The cerebral cortex can thus 'override' the more primitive limbic system when necessary.

Disorders associated with the limbic system

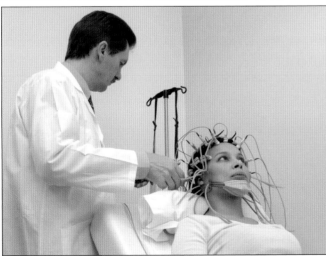

As the limbic system is associated with emotions, mood and memory, damage to the structures of this system may have effects in these areas.

ALZHEIMER'S DISEASE
It is thought that dementia, for example Alzheimer's disease, is associated with abnormalities of the limbic system. As the hippocampus (part of the limbic system) is involved with the

Temporal lobe epilepsy may involve the limbic system. Electroencephalography shows any abnormal electrical activity in particular areas of the brain.

processing of memory, and the amygdala for the experience and expression of emotions, this would explain why memory loss and personality changes are some of the earlier signs of Alzheimer's disease.

TEMPORAL LOBE EPILEPSY
In temporal lobe epilepsy, seizures arise in the temporal lobe of the brain, close to the limbic system. If the amygdala or hippocampus are involved, the patient may report complex experiences of smell, mood and memory during the seizure. These may even be severe enough to mimic schizophrenia.

Basal ganglia

The basal ganglia lie deep within the white matter of the cerebral hemispheres. They are collections of nerve cell bodies that are involved in the control of movement.

The common term basal ganglia is, in fact, a misnomer, as the term ganglion refers to a mass of nerve cells in the peripheral nervous system rather than the central nervous system, as here. The term basal nuclei is anatomically more appropriate.

COMPONENTS

There are a number of component parts to the basal nuclei that are all anatomically and functionally closely related to each other. The parts of the basal nuclei include:
- Putamen. Together with the caudate nucleus, the putamen receives input from the cortex
- Caudate nucleus. Named for its shape, as it has a long tail, this nucleus is continuous with the putamen at the anterior (front) end
- Globus pallidus. This nucleus relays information from the putamen to the pigmented area of the midbrain known as the substantia nigra, with which it bears many similarities.

GROUPING

Various names are associated with different groups of the basal nuclei. The term corpus striatum (striped body) refers to the whole group of basal nuclei, whereas the striatum includes only the putamen and caudate nuclei. Another term, the lentiform nucleus, refers to the putamen and the globus pallidus that, together, form a lens-shaped mass.

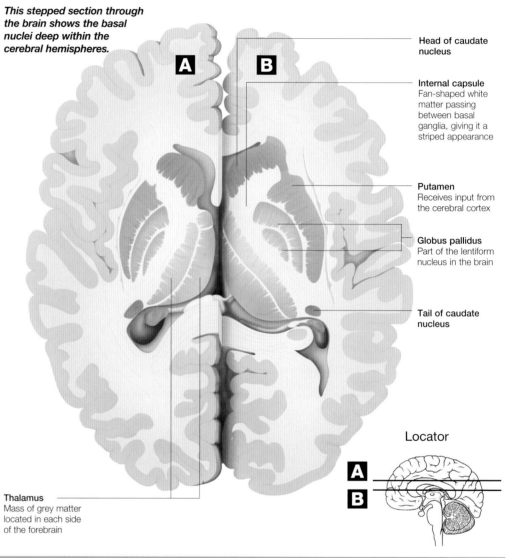

This stepped section through the brain shows the basal nuclei deep within the cerebral hemispheres.

Head of caudate nucleus

Internal capsule
Fan-shaped white matter passing between basal ganglia, giving it a striped appearance

Putamen
Receives input from the cerebral cortex

Globus pallidus
Part of the lentiform nucleus in the brain

Tail of caudate nucleus

Locator

Thalamus
Mass of grey matter located in each side of the forebrain

Coronal section through brain

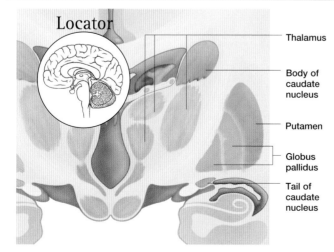

Locator

Thalamus

Body of caudate nucleus

Putamen

Globus pallidus

Tail of caudate nucleus

A coronal section through the brain reveals two anatomical factors: the shape of the basal ganglia and the location of the ganglia in relation to other structures in the area.

SHAPE OF GANGLIA

The coronal section shows that the lentiform nucleus is the shape of a brazil nut or an orange segment.

The putamen lies on the lateral (outer) side of the paler

A coronal section through the brain is shown. It reveals the relationship of the basal ganglia to other structures in the brain.

globus pallidus, which tapers to a blunt point. Just lateral to the putamen lies a streak of grey matter known as the claustrum (not shown), which is sometimes included under the heading of basal nuclei.

CAPSULE

The basal nuclei lie close to the thalamus, an important area of the brain, with which they make many connections. They are separated from the thalamus by the internal capsule, which is an area of white matter consisting of nerve fibres that pass from the cortex down to the spinal cord.

Structure and role of the basal ganglia

The overall shape of the basal ganglia (nuclei) is complex, and is hard to imagine by looking at two-dimensional cross-sections.

When seen in a three-dimensional view, the size and shape of the basal nuclei, together with their position within the brain as a whole, can be appreciated more easily.

In particular, the shape of the caudate nucleus can now be understood – it connects at its head with the putamen, then bends back to arch over the thalamus before turning forwards again. The tip of the tail of the caudate nucleus ends as it merges with the amygdala, part of the limbic system (concerned with unconscious, autonomic functions).

ROLE OF
THE BASAL NUCLEI

The functions of the basal nuclei have been difficult to study because they lie deep within the brain and are therefore relatively inaccessible. Much of what is known of their function derives from the study of those patients who have disorders of the basal nuclei that lead to particular disruptions of movement and posture, such as Parkinson's disease.

A summary of what is currently known about the function of the basal nuclei is that they help to produce movements that are appropriate; and they inhibit unwanted or inappropriate movements.

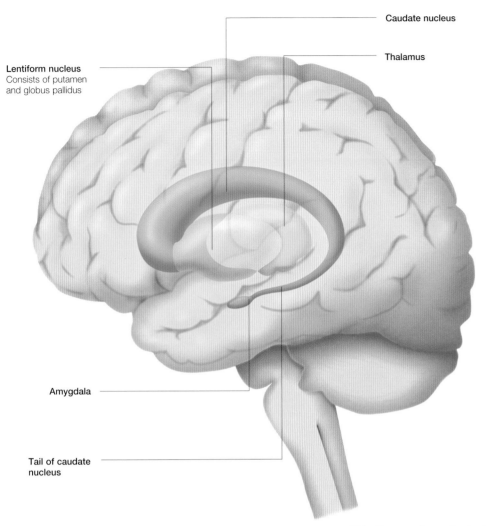

Caudate nucleus

Thalamus

Lentiform nucleus
Consists of putamen
and globus pallidus

Amygdala

Tail of caudate
nucleus

This diagram shows the brain in three dimensions. The size and shape of the basal ganglia can be seen in relation to other structures.

Disorders of basal ganglia

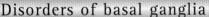

A range of movement disorders result from damage to the basal nuclei. These disorders include Parkinson's disease, Huntington's chorea and Wilson's disease.

MOVEMENT DISORDERS

Parkinson's disease is a disease of unknown cause that mainly affects people over the age of 50. It results in combinations of slowness of movement, increased muscle tone (rigidity), tremor and a bent posture. Affected individuals have difficulty in starting and finishing a

Parkinson's disease may result from damage to the basal nuclei. Symptoms of the disorder include a stooping posture, tremor and a shuffling walk.

movement and may also have a mask-like facial expression.

Studies of the basal nuclei of those individuals with Parkinson's disease have shown a lack of the chemical dopamine, a substance that allows neurones to communicate with each other.

Huntington's chorea is an inherited disease, which does not become apparent until an individual reaches mid life. It is associated with progressive degeneration of parts of the basal nuclei and cortex, leading to abnormal movements and dementia.

Wilson's disease is an inherited disorder associated with damage to the basal nuclei and progressive dementia in younger people.

Cerebellum

The cerebellum, which means 'little brain', lies under the occipital lobes of the cerebral cortex at the back of the brain. It is important to the subconscious control of movement.

The part of the brain known as the cerebellum lies under the occipital lobes of the cerebral cortex at the back of the head. The vital roles of the cerebellum include the co-ordination of movement and the maintenance of balance and posture. The cerebellum works subconsciously and so an individual is not aware of its functioning.

STRUCTURE
The cerebellum is composed of two hemispheres that are bridged in the midline by the vermis. The hemispheres extend laterally (sideways) and posteriorly (backwards) from the midline to form the bulk of the cerebellum.

The surface of the cerebellum has a very distinctive appearance. In contrast to the large folds of the cerebral hemispheres, the surface of the cerebellum is made up of numerous fine folds (folia).

LOBES
Between the folia of the cerebellar surface lie deep fissures that divide it into three lobes:
■ Anterior lobe
■ Posterior lobe
■ Flocculonodular lobe.

The cerebellum has two hemispheres, one on either side of the worm-like vermis. The surface of the cerebellum is made up of thin folds (folia).

Vermis
Central 'wormlike' portion of cerebellum which lies between two lateral hemispheres

Anterior lobe
Relatively small lobe, separated from posterior lobe by deep primary fissure

Posterior lobe
Largest of the three lobes, extending from primary fissure on upper surface of cerebellum to the posterolateral fissure on the underside

Pons
Part of the brainstem linking the medulla oblongata and the thalamus

Medulla oblongata
Upper end of the spinal cord and lowest part of the brainstem

Folia
Fine folds on surface of cerebellum, arranged transversely

Flocculonodular lobe
Small, propeller-shaped lobe that lies on the underside of the cerebellum; made up of flocculus and central nodule (part of the vermis)

Central canal of spinal cord

Cerebellar peduncles

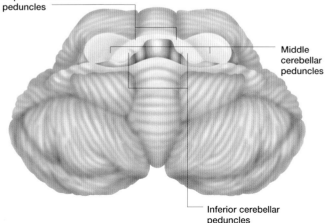

Superior cerebellar peduncles

Middle cerebellar peduncles

Inferior cerebellar peduncles

The cerebellum is connected to the brainstem, and thus to the rest of the brain, by three pairs of nerve fibre tracts that make up the cerebellar peduncles, or stalks. These can be seen on the inferior surface of the cerebellum, where they emerge together. The three tracts are:
■ The superior cerebellar peduncles, connecting the cerebellum to the midbrain
■ The middle cerebellar peduncles, connecting the

The three pairs of cerebellar peduncles serve to anchor the cerebellum to the brainstem. The peduncles consist of bundles of nerve fibres.

cerebellum to the pons
■ The inferior cerebellar peduncles, connecting the cerebellum to the medulla.

There are no direct connections between the cerebellum and the cerebral cortex. All information to and from the cerebellum goes through the peduncles.

Unlike the cerebral cortex, where each side controls the opposite (contralateral) side of the body, each half of the cerebellum controls the same (ipsilateral) side of the body. This means that any damage to one side of the cerebellum will cause symptoms in the same side of the body.

Internal structure of the cerebellum

The cerebellum has an outer grey cortex and a core of nerve fibres, or white matter. Deep within the white matter lie four pairs of cerebellar nuclei: the fastigial, globose, emboliform and dentate nuclei.

The cerebellum is composed of a surface layer of nerve cell bodies, or grey matter, which overlies a core of nerve fibres, or white matter. Deep within the white matter lie the cerebellar nuclei.

CEREBELLAR CORTEX

Due to the presence of the numerous fine folia (folds) in the surface of the cerebellum, the cortex is very extensive. It is made up of the cell bodies and dendrites (cell processes) of the vast majority of cerebellar neurones.

The cells of the cortex receive information from outside the cerebellum via the cerebellar peduncles and make frequent connections between themselves within the cortex.

SIGNALS

In most cases, signals from the cerebellar cortex are conveyed in the fibres of the white matter down to the cerebellar nuclei. It is from here that information leaves the cerebellum to be carried to the rest of the central nervous system.

CEREBELLAR NUCLEI

There are four pairs of cerebellar nuclei which, from the midline outwards, are known as the:
■ Fastigial nuclei
■ Globose nuclei
■ Emboliform nuclei
■ Dentate nuclei.

Cross-section through cerebellum

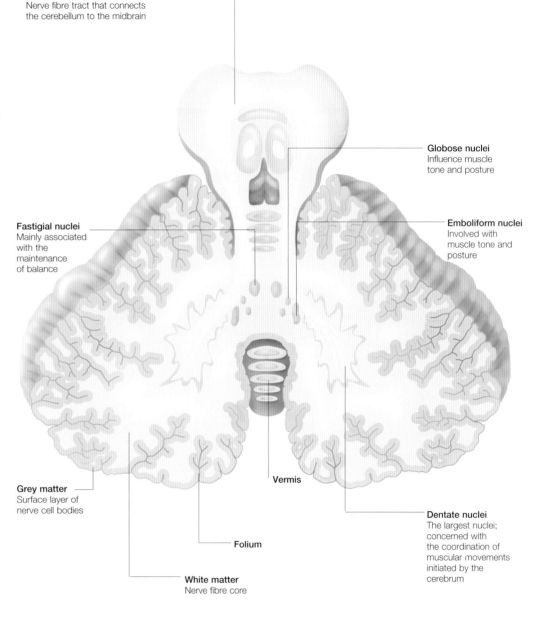

Superior cerebellar peduncle
Nerve fibre tract that connects the cerebellum to the midbrain

Globose nuclei
Influence muscle tone and posture

Emboliform nuclei
Involved with muscle tone and posture

Fastigial nuclei
Mainly associated with the maintenance of balance

Grey matter
Surface layer of nerve cell bodies

Vermis

Folium

White matter
Nerve fibre core

Dentate nuclei
The largest nuclei; concerned with the coordination of muscular movements initiated by the cerebrum

Layers of the cerebellar cortex

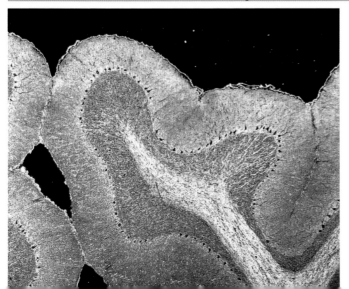

A micrograph of a stained section of the cerebellar cortex reveals its complex layered structure. Each layer contains distinctive cell types.

If the cerebellar cortex is stained and studied under the microscope, its structure can be seen to form a quite distinctive pattern of layers:
■ Molecular layer (the outermost layer) – contains nerve cell bodies and is rich in nerve fibres from the deeper layers of cells
■ Purkinje cell layer (the next layer) – although only one-cell

thick, this is relatively easy to visualize due to the size of the Purkinje cells. These specialized neurones are very important to cerebellar function. They receive signals via their dendrites which lie mainly in the layer above, and send information down to the cerebellar nuclei
■ Granular layer (the innermost layer) – this contains the cell bodies of numerous granule cells. These cells receive information via the peduncles and send signals themselves through their axons up into the molecular layer.

Brainstem

The brainstem lies at the junction of the brain and spinal cord.
It helps to regulate breathing and blood circulation as well as having
an effect upon a person's level of consciousness.

The brainstem is made up of three distinct parts: the midbrain, the pons and the medulla oblongata. The midbrain connects with the higher brain above; the medulla is continuous with the spinal cord below.

BRAINSTEM APPEARANCE
The three parts of the brainstem can be viewed from underneath:
■ The medulla oblongata – a bulge at the top of the spinal column. Pyramids, or columns, lie at either side of the mid-line. Nerve fibres within these columns carry messages from the cerebral cortex to the body. Raised areas known as the olives lie either side of the pyramids
■ The pons – contains a system of nerve fibres which originate in the nerve cell bodies deep within the substance of the pons
■ The midbrain – appears as two large columns, the cerebral crura, separated in the midline by a depression.

CRANIAL NERVES
Also present in the brainstem are some of the cranial nerves that supply much of the head. These nerves carry fibres that are associated with the cranial nerve nuclei, collections of grey matter, that lie inside the brainstem.

The brainstem connects the cerebral hemispheres with the spinal cord. There are three parts to the brain stem: the pons, medulla and the midbrain.

Ventral surface of the brainstem

Locator

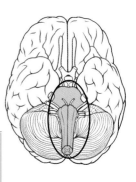

Midbrain

Pons
Extends from the medulla to the midbrain

Medulla oblongata
Extends from base of pons to just above nerve rootlets of the first spinal nerve

Cerebral crura
Cerebral crura are also known as cerebral peduncles, or 'little feet', as they appear to support the cerebral hemispheres

Middle cerebellar peduncle

Olives

Pyramids

Decussation of pyramids
Where nerve fibres cross over to the other side

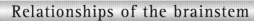

Relationships of the brainstem

Cerebral hemisphere

Thalamus

Brainstem

Midbrain

Pons

Medulla oblongata

Third ventricle

Pineal gland

Cerebral aqueduct

Fourth ventricle

Cerebellum

Spinal cord

A sagittal section through the brain shows the position of the brainstem in relation to the other parts of the brain and spinal cord:
■ The medulla oblongata – arises as a widening of the spinal cord at the level of the foramen magnum, the large hole in the bottom of the skull. The central canal of the spinal cord widens into the fourth ventricle allowing cerebrospinal fluid (CSF) to

A sagittal view of the brain and spinal cord shows the location of the various structures. The brainstem is located in front of the cerebellum.

circulate between brain and spinal cord.
■ The pons – lies above the medulla, at the level of the cerebellum with which it makes many connections. Above the pons lies the midbrain, encircling the cerebral aqueduct which connects the fourth ventricle to the third ventricle.
■ The midbrain – the shortest part of the brainstem lies under the thalamus, the central core of the brain, which is surrounded by the cerebral hemispheres. It thus lies below the thalamus and hypothalamus, and the tiny pineal gland.

Internal structure of the brainstem

The brainstem contains many areas of neural tissue that have a variety of functions vital to life and health. Responses to visual and auditory stimuli that influence head movement are also controlled here.

Cross sections through the brainstem reveal its internal structure, the arrangement of white and grey matter, which differs according to the level at which the section is taken.

MEDULLA
The features of a section through the medulla are:
■ The inferior olivary nucleus – a bag-like collection of grey matter which lies just under the olives. Other nuclei lying within the medulla include some belonging to the cranial nerves, such as the hypoglossal and the vagus nerves
■ The vestibular nuclear complex – an area that receives information from the ear and is concerned with balance and equilibrium
■ The reticular formation – a complex network of neurones, which is seen here and throughout the brainstem. It has a number of functions vital to life such as the control of respiration and circulation. The reticular formation is present in the midbrain as are several of the cranial nerve nuclei.

MIDBRAIN
A section through the midbrain shows the presence of:
■ The cerebral aqueduct – the

Cross sections of the brainstem

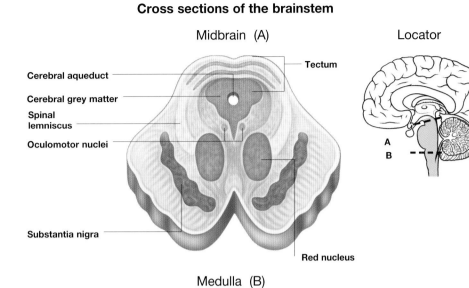

Midbrain (A)

Cerebral aqueduct
Cerebral grey matter
Spinal lemniscus
Oculomotor nuclei
Substantia nigra
Tectum
Red nucleus

Locator

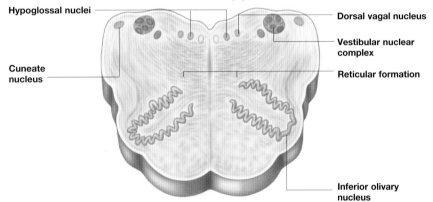

Medulla (B)

Hypoglossal nuclei
Cuneate nucleus
Dorsal vagal nucleus
Vestibular nuclear complex
Reticular formation
Inferior olivary nucleus

channel that connects the third and fourth ventricles. Above the aqueduct lies an area called the tectum, while below it lie the large cerebral peduncles
■ The cerebral peduncles – within these lie two structures on each side; the red nucleus and the substantia nigra. The red nucleus is involved in control of movement, while

damage to the substantia nigra is associated with Parkinson's disease.

PONS
The pons (not shown) is divided into upper and lower parts:
■ The lower part – mostly made up of transverse nerve fibres, running across from the nuclei of the pons to the cerebellum

The numerous nuclei and tracts that are within the brainstem can be seen in these cross sections. They are involved in most functions of the brain.

■ The upper portion – contains a number of cranial nerve nuclei. The pons also contains part of the reticular formation.

Brainstem death

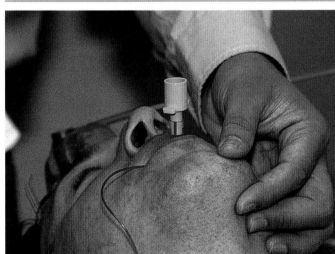

It is possible in some cases for life-support machines in intensive care units to maintain breathing and blood circulation in a patient who has suffered brainstem death.

CERTIFYING DEATH
In such cases doctors will certify death using a legally prescribed set of tests and observations. Many of these tests are designed to show death of the brainstem, the part of

Strict criteria exist when testing for brain stem death. One of these is the patient's ability to breathe independently when disconnected from a ventilator.

the brain that controls the vital functions of consciousness, breathing and circulation.

BRAIN STEM TESTING
Assessing the function of the brainstem includes looking for the following responses:
■ The ability to breathe without the help of a machine
■ Constriction of the pupil in response to light
■ Blinking of the eye when the cornea is touched
■ Eye movement when the ears are flushed with ice-water
■ Coughing or gagging when the airway is stimulated.
    The responses are absent if the brainstem is non-functioning.

Brain development

Childhood is a time of rapid brain development. In the first 10 years, connections are made between brain cells enabling children to learn complex skills and absorb vast amounts of information.

When a baby is born, the brainstem – a region of the brain situated just above the spinal cord controlling autonomic (unconscious) functions such as breathing and heart rate – is well developed. The brain is developed enough to allow a newborn baby to respond to stimuli with primitive 'survival' reflexes such as grasping, sucking and crying. It also enables the baby to hear, smell, taste and feel itself being touched.

Vision is not as well developed at birth, but the baby can focus on and follow the human face and interesting inanimate objects.

RAPID DEVELOPMENT

From birth, babies enter a period of extremely rapid brain development, notably in the cortex (the outermost area of the brain, associated with the 'higher' functions such as voluntary movement, problem solving and language). This period of intense brain development extends until about the age of three.

Information about the baby's world is processed by the cortex and stimulates development by making and reinforcing the connections between neurones (specialized brain cells). Without such stimulation, the brain cannot develop properly.

In their first 10 years, children's brains grow rapidly. This provides an ideal time for learning new skills and acquiring knowledge.

IMPORTANT MILESTONES

At this stage of development the brain enables babies to learn the skills for language and movement. The familiar milestones of childhood are achieved. For example, at six weeks babies will smile back in response to a parent; at three months they will reach out to grab a nearby object; at seven months they can sit up. Around the first year, babies take their first steps and speak their first words as those areas of the brain that control these abilities become sufficiently developed.

During these early years, the limbic system (part of the brain concerned with emotional

A newborn infant is able to respond to certain stimuli with primitive reflexes. For example, if a newborn's palm is touched it will automatically grasp.

expression) is also being stimulated. It is important that a baby receives love and warm personal attention, as this enables it first to learn to respond to affection, and then to give affection to others.

Although this rapid period of brain development is completed by the age of three or four, refinement and re-adjustment continues in the cortex during the rest of early childhood.

Physical growth of a child's brain

Although the number of neurones (nerve cells) in the brain does not increase after birth, the volume and thus weight of the brain does increase. This is due to the growth in size of the cells and the expansion of the brain's network of glial cells that surround, nourish and support the neurones. The brain grows to half its adult weight by the end of the first year and by the age of six, the brain is 90 per cent of its adult weight.

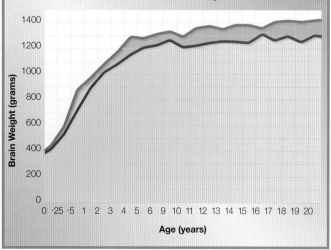

The red line represents the average brain weight for age for girls; the blue line for boys. The graph shows the massive brain growth in the first five years.

MAKING CONNECTIONS

The connections between neurones are repeatedly used and reinforced as a result of a child's activities and experiences. At this stage, the brain's abundance of connections and networks provide ample capacity for learning a range of complex new skills, such as reading and writing or learning to play a musical instrument.

As a child grows and its brain develops, the functions of the two hemispheres become better co-ordinated to support complex activities. The development of the frontal cortex also enables the child to understand abstract ideas and begin to think in a mature way. This consolidating phase continues until about the age of 10, by which time a child's brain has a complexity similar to that of an adult. After this, the brain starts to eliminate connections which are seldom or never used and so the abundant capacity for learning is rapidly diminished. It continues to make new connections during adulthood, but learning will never be as easy as in childhood.

A child's brain, with its multitude of connections and networks, makes learning new skills and absorbing information easy.

Physical co-ordination improves with practice as the connections needed to perform certain skills are reinforced in the brain.

Development of myelination

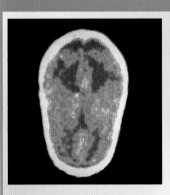

Newborn:
This coloured MR image shows a newborn's brain. An absence of myelin (the insulating sheath around nerve cells) is evident.

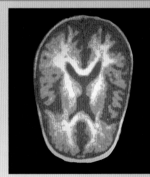

Six months old:
Myelin (white) is seen in the brain of a six-month-old baby. Myelinated nerves transmit images faster than other fibres.

Twenty months old:
More myelin is apparent in this scan. The developing ventricles of the brain (central purple edged areas) are also visible.

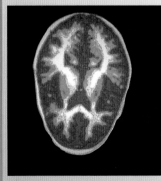

Five years old:
At this age, a child's brain is still growing rapidly. Much more of the brain is now myelinated (white).

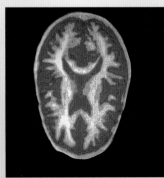

Nine years old:
A child is coming towards the end of its period of rapid brain development. Myelin will continue to be laid down.

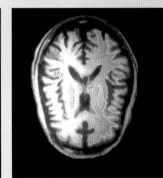

Adulthood:
Extensive myelination can be seen. The cortex has mature, irregular contours (unlike the smooth edges of a child's brain).

At birth, a human brain contains about one hundred billion neurones. Unlike most of the other cells in the body, neurones do not multiply; in fact the total number of neurones falls continuously throughout life.

However, it is not the number of neurones themselves, but rather the number and variety of connections between them that determines the brain's ability to function. Indeed, in adults a single neurone can connect with as many as fifteen thousand others.

Nerve communication

The speed at which nerve fibres conduct an impulse is directly related to the amount of insulating material (myelin) around the nerve fibre. Myelination of the nervous system takes several years to complete after birth. During this developmental phase of increasing neuronal communication, repeated activation of neuronal networks commits regions of the brain to specific functions.

Infrequent activation leads to the eventual loss of that connection (loss of plasticity). Indeed, there is considerable evidence to suggest that neurones that are not frequently used 'commit suicide', a process called apoptosis. This emphasizes the importance of keeping the brain active.

How the brain controls blood pressure

The medulla, a region of the brain situated just above the spinal cord, constantly monitors arterial pressure. It corrects changes in pressure by sending nervous signals to the heart and blood vessels.

The pressure of blood in the arteries is constantly measured by specialized pressure sensors called baroreceptors (baro- is a prefix for pressure). Baroreceptors are nerve endings contained within the walls of an artery that are able to detect even the smallest distension of the arterial wall. These pressure sensors are mainly found in the aortic arch and the carotid sinuses.

BARORECEPTOR NERVES

The baroreceptor endings are part of nerve fibres that travel up to a region of the brain called the medulla.

The afferent (from the Latin 'afferere' – to carry towards) fibres of the aortic baroreceptors form the aortic nerve, which joins the vagus (10th cranial) nerve before entering the medulla, where they terminate in a region called the nucleus tractus solitarii (NTS).

The afferent fibres of the carotid baroreceptors form the carotid sinus nerve, which joins the glossopharyngeal nerve (ninth cranial nerve) before also terminating in the NTS.

Anatomy of the baroreceptor reflex

Baroreceptors are found in two locations – the aortic arch and carotid sinus. They send nerve fibres (axons) to a region of the brain called the medulla.

Medulla
The medulla receives nervous input from a large number of sources, including baroreceptors

Vagus nerve
An extremely important nerve that carries a wide variety of information to and from the brain

Aortic nerve
Connects the aortic baroreceptors to the medulla

Aortic arch
Contains the aortic baroreceptors

Carotid sinus nerve
Carries information from the carotid baroreceptors to the medulla

Carotid sinus
Contains the carotid baroreceptors

Internal carotid artery
A major artery that carries oxygenated blood from the heart to the brain

Response of baroreceptors

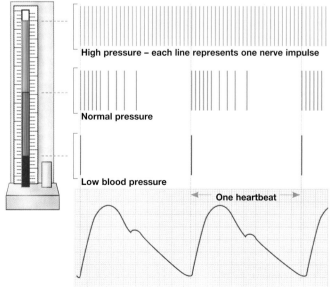

The response of baroreceptor nerves to increasing pressures

High pressure – each line represents one nerve impulse

Normal pressure

Low blood pressure

One heartbeat

Since blood moves through the arteries via pulsatile, rather than constant flow, the baroreceptor nerves do not 'fire' at a uniform rate.

This is because during systole (when the heart contracts and the pressure is highest) the arterial walls are distended causing the baroreceptor nerves to fire a volley of nervous impulses which travel up to the medulla. However, during diastole (when the heart is relaxed and the pressure is lowest) the arterial walls are not stretched, and this causes the baroreceptors to fall silent.

Arterial wall stretching is transformed into electrical activity in the baroreceptor nerve fibres. When pressure rises, nerve activity increases.

Importantly, many baroreceptors will be active at normal pressures; this allows them to inform the medulla when the pressure falls (by slowing the rate of nervous impulses), which would be impossible if the nerves were silent at rest.

BARORECEPTOR PROPERTIES

Not all baroreceptors have the same properties:
■ Some are responsive at low pressures, whereas others fire only when the arterial pressure has reached very high levels
■ The range of pressure over which they are sensitive also varies considerably
■ Baroreceptors vary in their sensitivity to the rate of change of arterial pressure – this parameter is thought to be very important, as it allows the brain to pre-empt changes in pressure.

Role of medulla

The baroreceptor nerves project to, and terminate in, a region of the medulla called the nucleus tractus solitarii (NTS). The NTS plays an important role in the control of autonomic (unconscious) functions, including, but not restricted to, the control of blood pressure. If it is damaged, for example following a stroke, the consequences can be fatal.

ROLE OF THE NTS

The NTS receives information not just from baroreceptors, but also from a large number of other sources including receptors found in the heart, gastro-intestinal tract, lungs, oesophagus and tongue. The NTS neurones do not act as a simple relay station for this diverse afferent input. Rather, they calculate what the correct blood pressure should be after taking into account information obtained from all the other sources.

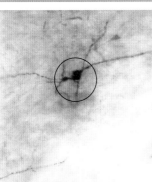

A micrograph of a neurone located in the NTS, which receives input from baroreceptors. The cell body, which contains the nucleus, is the dark oval (circled).

The top trace shows the electrical activity of a neurone located in the NTS. The neurone's rate of firing increases when arterial pressure is raised (bottom).

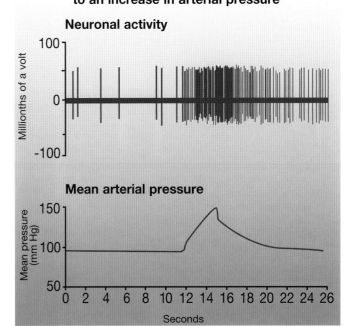

The response of an NTS neurone to an increase in arterial pressure

Neuronal activity

(y-axis: Millionths of a volt, 100, 0, -100)

Mean arterial pressure

(y-axis: Mean pressure (mm Hg), 150, 100, 50; x-axis: Seconds, 0 2 4 6 8 10 12 14 16 18 20 22 24 26)

The baroreceptor reflex pathway

The baroreceptor reflex pathway

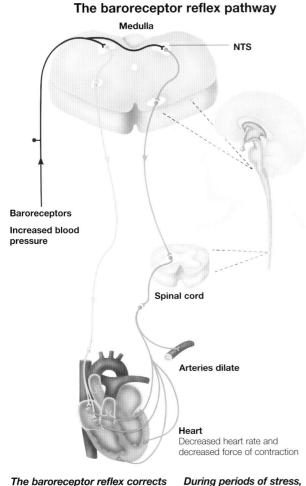

Medulla

NTS

Baroreceptors
Increased blood pressure

Spinal cord

Arteries dilate

Heart
Decreased heart rate and decreased force of contraction

The baroreceptor reflex corrects a rise in arterial pressure by reducing the rate and strength of the heartbeat, as well as causing the arteries to relax, so lowering blood pressure.

During periods of stress, the baroreceptor reflex is suppressed by nerves originating from the hypothalamus, this is one of the causes of hypertension.

If arterial pressure rises, baroreceptors respond to the distension of the arterial wall by sending a volley of nervous impulses to the NTS.

Under normal conditions, the NTS will try to correct this increase in pressure by sending nervous impulses to the heart, telling it to reduce its rate and strength of contraction; and to the arteries, telling them to become more elastic. This will have the effect of reducing both the cardiac output (the amount of blood that the heart pumps out each minute) and the resistance to blood flow in the arteries. These combined effects will act to lower blood pressure.

RESETTING THE BARORECEPTOR REFLEX

The baroreceptor reflex acts to maintain blood pressure at what physiologists call the 'set-point'. An analogy to the set-point

is the temperature setting of a central heating thermostat; the set-point of the baroreceptor reflex can be altered in the same way as a thermostat. The body does this either by affecting the threshold pressure at which the baroreceptors fire (peripheral resetting), or by altering the sensitivity of the neurones within the medulla (central resetting).

PERIPHERAL RESETTING

If pressure is maintained at a raised level for many minutes, the baroceptors become accustomed to the new pressure and 'think' that it is the correct level. Thus baroreceptors cannot accurately inform the brain about blood pressure levels over the long-term.

CENTRAL RESETTING

When we are exposed to a stressful situation, the neurones within the NTS that mediate the baroreceptor reflex are strongly suppressed, allowing blood pressure to rise. This was advantageous to our ancestors because it prepared them either to fight or to run away from their aggressors. However, this neural mechanism could be responsible for the high incidence of hypertension seen in modern Western society. The stress that we experience in our day-to-day lives, could, in some people at least, raise the set-point and so cause hypertension.

How the body feels pain

Pain is not just a signal that certain tissues in the body have been damaged – it also alerts the sufferer to danger. Painkillers can bring relief, but the body also has its own built-in pain inhibition system.

Any event that causes a degree of damage to the tissues of the body – be it mechanical (from pressure or a wound), chemical (exposure to acid, for example) or thermal (extreme heat or cold) – brings about the release of large amounts of chemicals, such as serotonin and histamine.

As well as producing reactions within the tissues, such as swelling and redness, these chemicals are detected by special sensory cells, called free nerve endings, which are found in the superficial layers of skin as well as in some of the internal organs. They are also known as nociceptors, because they react to noxious substances.

PAIN IMPULSES

In response to the chemical changes within the tissues, the sensory cells send nerve impulses to relay stations in the spinal cord. From here, they are passed through further relays in the lower part of the brain in the brainstem and the thalamus, and so on to the higher levels of the brain. There, the information is analyzed and perceived as pain. In most circumstances, a person will withdraw from the source of the pain.

Receptors in the skin

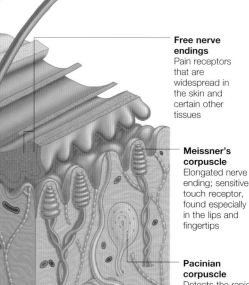

Hair shaft

Epidermis
Outer layer of skin

Merkel's disc
Senses continuous touch against the skin; signal is initially strong, then continues weaker

Dermis
Inner layer of skin; contains blood vessels, sweat glands and nerves

Ruffini's corpuscle
Located deeper in the skin; signals heavy, prolonged pressure

Free nerve endings
Pain receptors that are widespread in the skin and certain other tissues

Meissner's corpuscle
Elongated nerve ending; sensitive touch receptor, found especially in the lips and fingertips

Pacinian corpuscle
Detects the rapid movement of tissues

Classifying pain

There are two types of pain, distinguished according to the speed with which the sensations are felt. The first, which is felt as soon as tissue damage is sensed, is sharp and stabbing and is known as acute pain. Its impulses travel extremely quickly to the brain along special nerve fibres, called A-fibres, that have myelin sheaths to speed the impulses along.

The purpose of acute pain is to bring about an immediate, subconscious, reaction, to remove the body from the danger; A-fibre impulses cause a hand to be moved out of a flame, for example.

After some time, acute pain dies down and is replaced by the second type: the dull, throbbing, aching, persistent feeling that characterizes chronic pain. The impulses of chronic pain come from sensory receptors deeper in the tissues, and they travel 10 times more slowly that those of acute pain along unmyelinated nerve fibres called C-fibres.

People suffering from chronic pain, like this cancer patient, may need intravenous painkilling drugs that work by suppressing the C-fibre impulses.

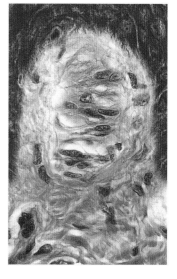

Meissner's corpuscles, one of which is shown here, transmit signals along myelinated nerve fibres. Acute pain signals also travel along myelinated fibres.

Pain inhibition

The body has three pain relief systems: each depends on
preventing nerve impulses from reaching the higher levels of the brain
by blocking them at the spinal relays or lower brain levels.

Two nerves join at the relay station in the spine, the junction of the two being called a synapse. One nerve carries signals from the sensory nerve endings, and the other carries them up the spine to the brain. Neurologists think of the synapse as a gate: normally it is shut, but strong impulses, as in acute pain, can force it open.

However, the synapse is only open to one type of pathway at a time. This is why A-fibre impulses, which travel faster, reach the synapse before C-fibre impulses and block them out until they have themselves died down. But if a painful area is rubbed vigorously, A-fibre

impulses are generated, and again they reach the synapse first, blocking out the slower C-fibre impulses. As a result, the aching, chronic pain is relieved.

CHEMICAL BLOCK
The second system depends on blocking the passage of nerve impulses by chemical means. In response to pain signals, the brain produces chemicals called endorphins. These are the body's own painkillers, and they block receptors in the brain stem and thalamus, and block the gates in the spinal relays. Morphine (a strong painkiller derived from opium) reduces pain because it blocks the same receptors.

SUPPRESSION
Finally, the brain can send impulses down the spinal cord to suppress pain signals at the spinal relay. This is most apparent when pain is extreme, when, for example, a soldier is fighting for his life or an athlete is pushed to the limits.

PAIN TOLERANCE
How much pain is felt is determined by the quantity of endorphins (pain-relieving chemicals in the brain). Exercise increases endorphin levels, as does relaxation, a positive mental

outlook and sleep. In contrast, fear, depression, anxiety, lack of exercise and concentrating on pain all reduce endorphin levels. The fewer endorphins there are, the more pain is felt.

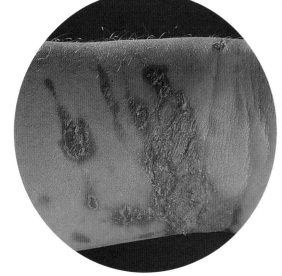

This second-degree burn was caused by boiling fat. Pain from such injuries is acute at first, becoming chronic for several days afterwards.

A natural and subconscious response is to rub a painful area, particularly when muscles are affected. Physiologically, the action of rubbing works effectively to ease discomfort.

Referred pain

Sometimes pain is felt in an area that is not in fact the source of the pain, and in such cases the sensation is called referred pain. Examples of this include pain from the area of the diaphragm, which can be felt at the tip of the shoulder, and pain from the heart – as in angina – which is felt across the chest, in the neck and along the inner side of the arm.

There are two explanations for this phenomenon. First, tissues that originate from

Referred pain that affects the ear is very common. The cause is often found to be tooth-related, such as abscesses or impaction, or associated with the larynx or pharynx (tonsillitis, for example).

the same embryological building block – that is, they come from the same area of basic tissue in a fetus as it develops inside the uterus – often share the same spinal relays, so activity in one part of the relay triggers activity in another part of the same relay. Second, there can be so many nerve impulses from an internal organ that they flood the pathways normally reserved for other areas of the body.

Doctors often check for referred pain as part of the diagnosis of a disorder that affects the internal organs. This is often somewhat of a surprise to the patient, who perhaps cannot understand why the main source of their discomfort (that is, the source of the pain) is being ignored during an investigation.

How memory works

Memory is the brain's ability to store and access information.
Short-term memory stores only small amounts of information, while
greater amounts of data are kept in long-term memory.

Memory is the ability to store and retrieve information. Remembering is a vital function, since learning, thought and reasoning could not occur without it. We learn not to touch hot objects, for example, from a very early age as we remember that they burn us, causing pain. In addition, our memories, the sum of our experiences, play a huge part in the development of our personalities.

BRAIN
Memory is regarded as a function of the brain, often likened to the way in which a computer stores and processes information.

Whereas a computer can only store one billion bits of information, however, the brain can store up to 100 trillion. Moreover, the word 'store' is misleading, as, unlike a computer, there is no single centre in which memories are filed away. Remembering appears to be a function of many parts of the brain, rather than any one structure.

MEMORY INPUT
The storage of memory is very complex, and our sensory experiences suggest that there may be many different kinds of memory: visual (sight),

auditory (hearing), olfactory (smell), gustatory (taste) and tactile (touch). Information is never presented in one simple form, but tends to be embedded in a complex context – we know from daily experience how important context and associations are for effective memorizing. For example, a

single item of information conveyed to us by speech will be set in the context of other data such as the speaker's face, voice and displays of emotion.

TWO FORMS
There are two forms of memory: short-term and long-term. Short-term memory stores small

Individuals carry with them a huge amount of information that has been amassed over the years. This data is stored in the long-term memory.

amounts of information and the contents are quickly lost. Long-term memory stores larger quantities of information.

Short-term memory

Research has shown that the short-term memory is able to hold around five to seven items at a time for a maximum of one minute.

For example, you are able to remember a telephone number while you dial the number. However, if the number is engaged and you redial, you will have to look up the number again – the result of having no memory trace for it in the brain.

The reason for this inability to remember in the short term is that complex data cannot be stored the moment it is perceived. It appears that some

If an individual is dialling a telephone number for the first time, they remember it only briefly. Short-term memory can only store a few items at a time.

form of analysis and selection process is necessary for the brain to determine which information is assimilated, and which is discarded. It seems that this process cannot occur without first storing the data temporarily.

CONSOLIDATION
To last, a memory has to be recorded via the short-term memory first, before being consolidated. This process requires repetition or study, and usually classification (organization into a category of related items).

Consolidation moves a fact from the short-term memory to long-term storage. Consolidation is believed to result in an alteration in the structure of the brain, as a memory trace is formed.

Long-term memory

Large amounts of information are carried in the long-term memory. This data is stored and accessed through large collections of nerve cells located within the brain – the amygdala and hippocampus.

Every individual carries an immeasurable amount of data, often preserved for life in the long-term memory. It is now known exactly where in the brain sensory data must pass in order to be stored in the memory.

CEREBRAL HEMISPHERES
The interface circuits, through which long-term memory is recorded and recalled, are located in large structures on the inner surfaces of the temporal lobes of each cerebral hemisphere of the brain.

These huge collections of nerve cells are known as the amygdala and the hippocampus, and together they make up the limbic system. Both structures are connected to all the sensory areas of the cortex (outer layer of the brain), and damage to these structures,

for example through a stroke or brain trauma, will lead to profound memory loss.

MEMORY SITES
The exact physical basis for the long-term memory is unknown. There is evidence, however, that the sites of memory are the same as the areas of the brain in which the corresponding sensory impressions are processed in the cortex.

It appears that, during recall, the amygdala and the hippocampus play back the neurological activity that occurs during sensory activity to the appropriate part of the cerebral cortex.

The amygdala and hippocampus are structures in the brain associated with memory. They convert new information into long-term memories.

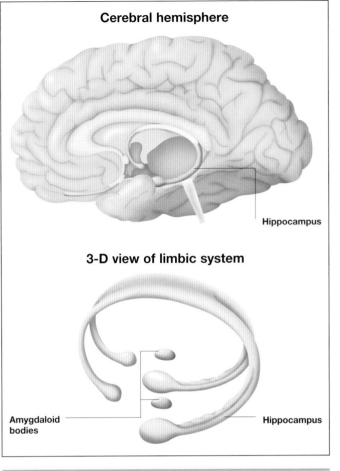

Cerebral hemisphere

Hippocampus

3-D view of limbic system

Amygdaloid bodies

Hippocampus

Amnesia

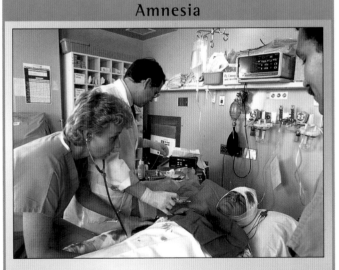

Amnesia is a failure to remember recent or past events. Most cases are caused by physical damage to the brain, although in rare instances it may be induced by emotional trauma, whereby an experience is too painful to remember.

Two types
Amnesia may take one of two forms:
■ Retrograde amnesia – this is most commonly caused by a blow to the head. The patient fails to remember what happened several hours prior to the accident, as the brain did

Patients with head injuries may experience amnesia. This can affect memories before (retrograde) or after (anterograde) the incident.

not have the chance to process that information.
■ Anterograde amnesia – this is caused by damage to the hippocampus, whereby memory of events occurring after the injury is impaired. Memory of the past remains intact, but everyday life becomes very difficult since the patient has no recollection of events from one moment to the next.

Memory loss

Most of us have no recollection of the first few years of our lives, after which time memories are fragmented and vague until we reach the age of around 10. This is probably because, in the first few years of life, the brain is not yet developed enough to process and store information.

DEGENERATION
Likewise, in the latter years of life, the brain undergoes a natural degeneration, and so memory may become impaired.

Interestingly, in older people, it is the short-term memory that is usually affected. For example, an older person may be able

to remember the exact details of a journey made 50 years before, but may be unable to recall what they did yesterday. This is because the ability to process new information often declines with age due to physical and chemical changes in the brain. Moreover, the regular recollection of long-term memories sharpens them, leaving a permanent memory trace in the brain.

Older people often have a good memory of past events, but have trouble recalling more recent memories. This is due to age-related changes in the brain.

How we feel emotion

External stimuli received through the senses arrive in the brain
as nervous impulses. Their emotional significance is determined by
the limbic system before producing a physiological response.

Experiencing an emotion involves a combination of physical and mental processes, which produce both physiological and psychological sensations.

RESPONDING TO STIMULI
To a large extent emotion is produced in response to external stimuli. The emotion experienced depends on the nature of stimuli and the individual's interpretation of those stimuli.

The physical aspects of emotional experience can be divided into two main elements:
■ The neurological processes produced by environmental or psychological stimuli
■ The physiological arousal that results from the stimuli.

ROLE OF THE AMYGDALA
Nervous impulses from the senses arrive in the brain at the thalamus, a mid-brain structure, where they are processed and passed on in a number of ways. Their emotional significance is believed to be determined by the limbic system within the brain, and in particular by the amygdala, an almond-shaped structure near the brainstem.

The amygdala assigns emotional content and value to incoming stimulus to provide a rapid initial assessment of its significance. This helps to determine quickly whether something is dangerous. The stimulus of encountering someone unexpectedly in a dark room, for instance, is labelled by the amygdala as a potential threat, and so produces an initial emotional response of fear.

ROLE OF THE CORTEX
Higher brain centres in the cortex can override the amygdala, integrating data from other sources, such as memory and context, to make a more accurate and considered determination of emotional significance.

In the example above, the cortex uses memory to identify the encountered person as a friend, and overrides the initial amygdala-produced emotion.

Emotional reactions may be complicated by culture or context. Emotions stimulated by fictional events, as in the theatre, produce real physical responses.

Physiology of emotion

Physiological processes are responsible for what are known as the visceral sensations involved in emotion. These include responses such as dry mouth, dilated pupils or unsettled stomach.

One purpose of emotion is to elicit an active response, and these visceral sensations are part of the process by which emotion readies the body for a physical response. For example, a stimulus that causes fear will also prepare the body to act on that fear.

THE ENDOCRINE SYSTEM
The level and type of physiological arousal is determined by the autonomic nervous system (ANS). This in turn is regulated by the

A lie detector test operates on the presumption that telling lies produces a stress response in the person talking. This can be identified by physical changes.

endocrine system as it releases hormones in response to emotional triggers. These hormones produce many of the visceral sensations associated with emotion. Two of the most important hormones in this context are adrenaline and noradrenaline, which set up the sympathetic division of the ANS for a 'fight or flight' response.

PATTERNS OF AROUSAL
Hormones produce widespread physiological sensations that are common to different types of emotion. Specific emotions, however, produce more specific patterns of physiological arousal according to their effect on another type of chemical messenger: neurotransmitters.

These work in conjunction with hormones to produce a range of distinctive response patterns, each with its own heart rate, finger temperature, galvanic skin response (electrical conductivity of skin) and so on.

Psychological and cultural factors

More complex emotions, such as shame, involve input from brain centres that control learning and memory. Cultural factors also affect the final response.

Emotion involves more than just visceral sensations. As a subjective experience, emotion is as much psychological as it is physiological. Experiments show that drugs or hormones can produce the physiological correlates of emotional arousal, without producing the conscious sensation of emotion.

In particular, more complex, less visceral emotions, such as guilt, involve more input from higher brain centres and processes such as learning, memory and self-image.

CONTEXT AND CULTURE

Factors that influence the psychology of emotion include context and culture. For instance, in the context of a theme-park ride, 'scary' stimuli can produce a mixture of terror and pleasure.

Cultural influence on emotions includes culture-specific emotions, such as the Chinese 'sad love'. Whereas in the West love is characterized as a positive emotion, in China love is not always positive and can be a negative or mixed emotion.

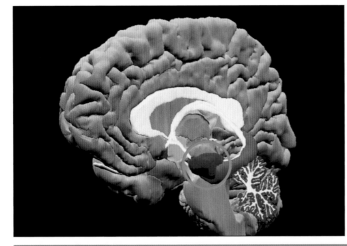

Nervous impulses send external stimuli from the senses to the brain. Part of the limbic system, the amygdala (circled), then determines the response.

A roller coaster ride produces a variety of emotional responses. Our higher brain centres intervene to determine whether it is fun or terrifying.

Expression of emotion

It has long been believed that some emotions are physically linked to the way they are expressed, especially in terms of the muscular activity of facial expression. To put it simply, some emotions and facial expressions are 'hard-wired' together.

This has led in turn to the belief that the process can be reversed, and that adopting an expression can induce a particular emotion.

For example, it has been found that smiling primes individuals to interpret stimuli as more positive. Suggested mechanisms to explain this finding include:
■ Smiling induces the release of endorphins (naturally occurring mood-enhancing opiates)
■ Some sort of feedback effect occurs with smiling that primes the brain centres involved with happiness and positive emotions.

Brain hemispheres
The two hemispheres of the brain play different roles in the recognition of faces, facial

expressions and even the recognition and experience of positive and negative emotions.
For instance:
■ Some areas of the left hemisphere are specialized for the recognition and processing of positive emotions, such as happiness
■ Some areas of the right hemisphere are specialized for

The face on the left is a mirror image of that on the right but is perceived as happier. This is because of the way that the hemispheres process emotion.

negative emotions, such as sadness and fear.

Brain damage can impair the experience of some emotions and exaggerate others. Left-hemisphere damage can produce excessive fear or depression, while on the right, damage can produce uncontrollable laughter or mania. Clinically depressed people may show reduced function in the left frontal lobe.

This hemispheric lateralization

can be demonstrated by looking at the picture below. Which face looks happier?

Most people choose the left-hand picture. This is because in the left-hand picture the smiley face appears in the left visual field of the observer, and is therefore processed primarily by the right hemisphere, where recognition of expression primarily occurs. The faces are actually mirror images of each other.

How laughter occurs

Laughter is the body's response to happiness and comprises both gestures and sound. Although laughter is not essential to survival, it is thought to act as a type of relief mechanism.

Laughter is a physiological response to happiness and humour and appears to be a distinctly human characteristic. It consists of two components: a set of gestures and the production of sound. When a person finds something humorous, the brain triggers both of these responses to occur simultaneously, at the same time causing changes to occur throughout the body.

FACIAL MUSCLES
Laughter involves the contraction of 15 facial muscles as well as stimulation of the zygomatic major muscle, which causes the upper lip to lift. Meanwhile, the epiglottis partially blocks the larynx, resulting in irregular air intake and causing a person to gasp. In extreme cases the tear ducts may be activated, causing tears of laughter to stream down the face. A person may even turn red in the face as they continue to gasp for air.

RANGE OF NOISES
A range of characteristic noises, which range from a gentle giggle to a loud guffaw, accompanies this response. In fact, research into the sonic structure of laughter (the pattern of sound waves produced when a person laughs) shows that all human laughter consists of varying patterns of a basic form, which is short vowel-like notes repeated every 210 milliseconds. It has also been revealed that laughter triggers other neural circuits in the brain, which in turn generate more laughter. This explains why it can be contagious.

The average person laughs around 17 times a day. Laughter clubs (one in Bombay shown) encourage people to get together and laugh.

The role of laughter

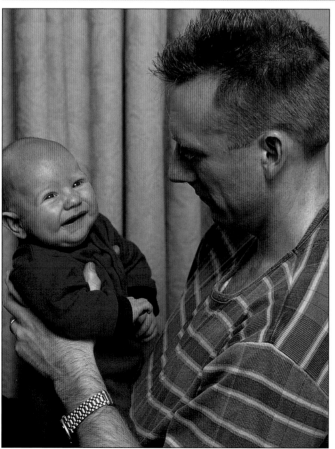

Smiling and laughter may be a sign of trust in a friend or relative. Babies often communicate with their parents by smiling and laughing.

As with much of human behaviour, it is difficult to determine the exact purpose of laughter, although there appear to be a variety of physical and psychological benefits. Many theories suggest that laughter may have evolved as a relief mechanism, whereby our ancestors would use it as a gesture of shared relief at the passing of danger. What is more, because laughter inhibits the 'fight or flight' response – designed to protect the body in danger – laughter may also indicate trust in a companion.

COMMUNICATION
In this way, many scientists believe that the purpose of laughter is one of communication, a social signal that strengthens human connections. Research by cultural anthropologists demonstrates that people tend to laugh together when they feel comfortable with each other, and that the more people laugh together, the greater the bonding between them. Interestingly, research shows that people are 30 times more likely to laugh in a group than when alone and that even the use of nitrous oxide (laughing gas) elicits less laughter when taken in solitude.

RESULTS OF STUDIES
Studies have also shown that laughter conforms to a social hierarchy whereby dominant individuals tend to use humour more than their subordinates; for example, when a boss laughs it is not uncommon for all his or her employees to laugh too. By controlling the emotional climate of the group, the boss exercises power.

In fact, it appears that laughter, like most human behaviour, has evolved as a means of influencing the behaviour of others. Studies have shown that in an embarrassing or threatening situation, laughter may serve as a conciliatory gesture and a means to deflect anger. If a threatening person can be made to laugh, then the risk of confrontation is reduced.

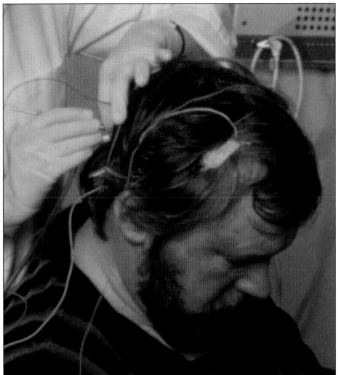

Gelotology is the study of the physiological responses that occur during laughter, and much research has been conducted to work out how laughter is triggered. While other emotional responses seem to be confined to one part of the brain (frontal lobe), laughter appears to involve a circuit running through several brain areas.

EEG RESEARCH
This has been demonstrated by research in which people were connected to an electroencephalograph (EEG) (an instrument that allows the electrical activity of the brain to be measured). The subjects were then told a joke and the consequent electrical activity of their brains was observed.

Within less than a second,

An EEG can help to study response to laughter. When subjects are connected to an EEG and told a joke, the brain's electrical activity is measured.

a wave of electrical activity was seen to pass through the cerebral cortex (the largest part of the brain). It was found that if this wave had a negative charge then laughter resulted, but if it was positive, laughter did not occur.

ELECTRICAL ACTIVITY
The electrical activity of the brain during laughter appears to take the following path:
1 The left side of the cortex (the layer of cells that covers the surface of the forebrain) is stimulated as the structure of the joke is analyzed
2 The frontal lobe, usually involved with emotional responses, is activated
3 The right hemisphere of the cortex is stimulated – intellectual analysis of the joke occurs here, determining whether or not the joke is funny
4 The sensory processing area of the occipital lobe (the area located at the back of the head that is associated with the processing of visual signals) is activated as nerve impulses from the right hemisphere are interpreted and converted into a sensory response

5 Various motor sections (responsible for movement) of the brain are stimulated causing a physical response to the joke.

THE LIMBIC SYSTEM
As with any emotional response, the limbic system in the brain appears to be central to laughter. The limbic system is a network of complex structures that lies beneath the cerebral cortex, and controls behaviour that is essential to survival.

While this area of the brain in other animals is heavily involved in defending territory and hunting, in humans it has evolved to become more involved in emotional behaviour and memory.

EMOTIONAL RESPONSE
Indeed, research has shown that the amygdala, which controls anxiety and fear, and the hippocampus, which plays a role in learning and memory, seem to be the main areas of the brain involved with emotional responses.

The amygdala interacts with the hippocampus and thalamus (the part of the brain that relays information from the senses to the cortex), playing a key role in the expression of emotions.

In addition, the hypothalamus has been identified by researchers as a major contributor to the production of loud, uncontrollable laughter.

The benefits of laughter

Laughter is more than an expression of happiness; it can actually promote health. Here, a stroke patient and speech therapist laugh together.

While people have always known that laughter makes them feel good, there is now scientific evidence that it promotes health in a number of ways.

Health benefits
Laughter has many benefits for the general health of an individual. These include:
■ Immune system – laughter inhibits the 'fight or flight' response, by reducing levels of certain stress hormones responsible. This is beneficial to health since these hormones suppress the immune system and raise blood pressure. Laughter actually boosts the immune system by causing an increase in white blood cells
■ Blood pressure – laughter lowers the blood pressure, while

increasing vascular blood flow and oxygenation of the blood. This in turn aids healing
■ Saliva – laughter leads to increased production of salivary immunoglobulin A, which helps to prevent pathogens (disease-causing organisms) invading the body via the respiratory tract
■ Exercise – it has been estimated that laughing 100 times is the equivalent of 15 minutes' workout on an exercise bike. Laughter exercises the diaphragm and abdominal, respiratory, facial, leg and back muscles, which explains why people often feel exhausted after laughing a lot
■ Mental health – laughter provides a way for negative emotions to be released. Ever since the pioneering work of Patch Adams (a physician who recognized the benefits of humour when treating patients), doctors have become increasingly aware of the therapeutic benefits of laughter.

How we sleep

The body enters an altered state of consciousness during sleep. While it used to be believed that the sole function of sleep was rest, studies show that the brain is far from inactive during this time.

Sleep is defined as a state of relative unconsciousness and reduced body movement. Unlike coma, subjects can be aroused from sleep by external stimulation. Relatively little is known as to the exact function of the phenomenon of sleep, despite the fact that the average person spends around a third of their lifetime asleep.

RESTORATIVE FUNCTION
In the past it was believed that sleep served a restorative function only. More recently, however, sleep studies with electroencephalography (using electrodes attached to the head that measure the electrical activity of the brain) suggest otherwise. While motor activity is inhibited by sleep, it seems the brain is far from inactive during this time. Although the functioning of the conscious part of the brain is depressed, brain stem functions such as control of respiration, heart rate and blood pressure are maintained.

PHYSIOLOGICAL CHANGES
While sleeping, humans close their eyes and adopt a sleeping posture – typically lying down. Hormonal changes cause heart, respiration and breathing rates to slow down. In addition, digestive activity is reduced and urine concentrated to allow a period of uninterrupted sleep.

In sleep the sensory part of the brain is depressed. However, we are still aware of external stimuli which is why we can be woken.

Types of sleep

By monitoring brain activity, scientists have identified two states of sleep. These are referred to as non-rapid eye movement (NREM) sleep and rapid eye movement (REM) sleep. These alternate throughout the night and serve very different roles.

NREM SLEEP
During the first 45 minutes of sleep, the body passes through four stages of deeper and deeper NREM sleep. This is seen as a decline in the frequency of brain waves, but an increase in their amplitude.

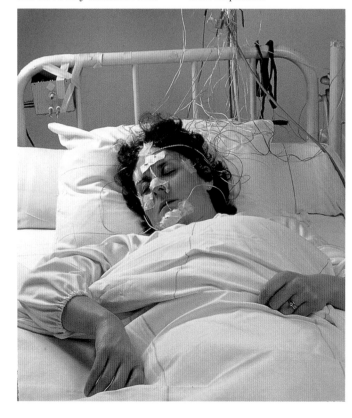

Studies of brain activity during sleep reveal two main stages. During REM sleep the brain is very active, and respiration rates increase.

The four stages of NREM sleep are:
■ First stage – the eyes are closed and relaxation begins. Conscious thoughts begin to drift; at this stage arousal is immediate if the body is stimulated
■ Second stage – the EEG becomes more irregular, and arousal becomes more difficult
■ Third stage – as the body slips into this stage the skeletal muscles begin to relax and dreaming is common
■ Fourth and final stage – (slow wave sleep) the body relaxes completely and arousal is difficult; bedwetting and sleepwalking may occur during this stage.

REM SLEEP
Around an hour after sleep begins the EEG pattern changes, becoming irregular and more frequent, indicating the onset of REM sleep. This change in brain activity is accompanied by an increase in body temperature, heart rate, respiratory rate and blood pressure, and a decrease in digestive activity. The brain pattern seen during this stage of sleep is more typical of the awake state, although the body actually respires more oxygen during this phase of sleep than when awake.

Typically during this phase, the eyes move rapidly beneath the eyelids, although the rest of the body muscles are inhibited and go limp, resulting in a temporary paralysis designed to prevent us from acting out our dreams. REM sleep makes up approximately 20 per cent of adult sleep.

DREAMS
Most dreaming occurs during REM sleep. It is hardest to wake somebody during this stage of sleep, although sleepers can wake spontaneously during this time – and will be more likely to remember the details of their dream if they do so.

CHEMICAL MESSENGERS
In addition to changes in brain wave patterns during sleep, there are changes in levels of neurotransmitters (the chemical messengers secreted by the brain). Noradrenaline levels decline and serotonin levels rise. This is because noradrenaline is responsible for maintaining alertness, while serotonin is thought to function as a sleep neurotransmitter.

The role of sleep

Sleep allows the skeletal muscles to relax and our energy levels to be replenished. The amount of sleep the body requires differs among individuals.

The most obvious role of sleep appears to be physical restoration. While we sleep, our muscles relax, allowing them to rest. The body requires more sleep after great physical exertion or illness.

BRAIN ACTIVITY

Slow wave sleep appears to be the restorative stage of sleep, when most neural mechanisms wind down. Sleep deprivation studies, in which subjects are woken each time they reach a certain stage of sleep, reveal that when continually deprived of REM sleep, subjects become moody and depressed, and exhibit personality disorders.

Many theories exist regarding the function of brain activity during sleep. The most likely theory is that REM sleep gives the brain the opportunity to analyze the day's events, discarding useless information, processing useful information and working through emotional problems in dream imagery.

During REM sleep, brain activity increases considerably. This is thought to be a time when the brain assimilates useful information learnt that day.

Sleep requirements

Sleep requirements and patterns change throughout our lives. While a baby can require as much as 16 hours sleep every day, the average adult will only require seven hours.

In old age, the amount of sleep required declines considerably, with people over 60 years requiring shorter spells of sleep, although these tend to be taken more frequently. Elderly people are more likely to take naps during the day.

SLEEP PATTERNS

Sleep patterns also change throughout life: the amount of REM sleep declines from birth, and often disappears completely in people over 60.

This is the reason why many older people sleep more lightly and commonly wake up more frequently in the night. This is because they are not able to attain the profound depths of REM sleep.

Sleep requirements vary from person to person, and with age. Elderly people require shorter, more frequent spells of sleep, and often nap during the day.

Sleep disorders

Although the exact role that sleep fulfils is not entirely known, it is clearly essential to our mental and physical well-being.

Insomnia

Insomniacs suffer from an inability to obtain a sufficient amount or quality of sleep needed to function adequately during the daytime. With prolonged lack of sleep, insomniacs show signs of fatigue, impaired ability to concentrate and carry out everyday tasks and, in some cases, paranoia.

Insomnia can be caused by unfavourable surroundings (noisy neighbours or an uncomfortable bed); physical ailments, such as those causing breathlessness or pain, or an irregular sleep pattern (caused by jet lag or working night shifts). The most common cause of insomnia, however, is psychological disturbance such as anxiety or depression.

Narcolepsy

Narcolepsy is the complete opposite of insomnia. Sufferers have little control over their sleep patterns, and can lapse into deep sleep spontaneously during waking hours. These episodes of unconsciousness last between 5 and 15 minutes and can occur without warning at any time.

This condition can be very hazardous, for example when the sufferer is taking a bath or operating machinery. The cause of narcolepsy is not understood, although it seems to arise from an inability to inhibit REM, or dreaming sleep. Most people sleep for some time before falling into a deep sleep, but narcoleptics appear to enter REM as soon as they close their eyes.

Insomnia is a condition in which the sufferer does not have enough quality sleep. The cause is often psychological.

How we dream

Around a fifth of time asleep is spent dreaming, although many people claim not to remember their dreams. The mental activity involved in dreaming is very different from that of waking thought.

Although many people claim not to dream, sleep studies have revealed that the average adult spends around 20 per cent of their sleep in a state of dream activity.

WHAT ARE DREAMS?
Dreams result from a form of mental activity that is very different from waking thought.

A dream is a series of images, thoughts and sensations conjured up by the mind during sleep. Dreams can take the form of pleasant fantasies, everyday scenarios or terrifying nightmares.

DREAM STUDIES
In-depth studies, in which subjects are monitored throughout sleep and woken during dreaming phases and questioned about their dreams, reveal much about the nature of dream activity.

It appears that most dreams are perceptual rather than conceptual – meaning that things are seen and heard rather than thought. In other words, in our dreams we often appear to be an onlooker witnessing events as opposed to conducting them and reflecting upon them.

SENSORY EXPERIENCE
In terms of the senses, visual experience is present in almost all dreams and auditory (hearing) experience in around 40 to 50 per cent of dreams. In comparison the remaining senses – touch, taste and smell – feature in only a small percentage of dreams.

EMOTIONS
The overriding feature of all dreams tends to be a single and strong emotion such as fear, anger or joy, rather than the integrated range of subtle emotions experienced during the waking state.

Most dreams are composed of interrupted stories, partly made up from memories and fragmented scenes. Dreams can range from the very mundane to the truly bizarre.

During sleep the brain conjures up the scenarios we know as dreams. They tend to be composed of vivid visual images and, often, strong emotions.

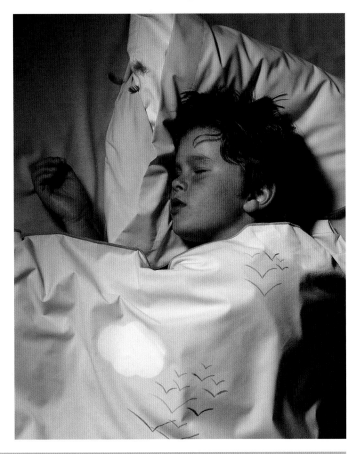

When do dreams occur?

Research in recent years has revealed that two clearly distinguishable states of sleep exist: non-rapid eye movement sleep (NREM) and rapid eye movement sleep (REM).

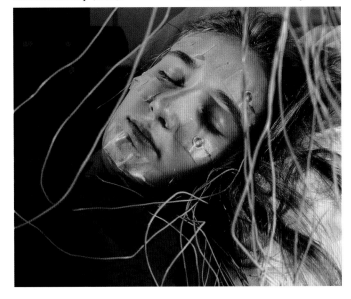

NREM sleep makes up the greater part of our sleeping time, and is associated with a relatively low pulse and blood pressure and little activation of the autonomic nervous system.

Very few dreams are reported during this state of sleep, and tend to be more like thoughts rather than vivid images.

REM sleep occurs cyclically during the sleep period and is characterized by increased conscious brain activity, the eyes moving rapidly from side to side

Sleep studies reveal that most dreams occur during the REM stage of sleep. This stage is associated with rapid movement of the eyes beneath the lids.

beneath the eyelids, and frequent reports of dreams.

Typically a person will have four or five periods of REM sleep during the night, although usually only a single dream may be remembered the following morning if at all.

REM sleep occurs at intervals of about 90 minutes and makes up around 20 per cent of the night's sleep. Evidence from dream studies suggests that dream periods last for around five to 20 minutes.

Sleepwalking

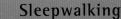

When we sleep, our muscles become very relaxed, with the result that the body becomes temporarily paralyzed. This is designed to prevent the body from acting out our dreams.

In some people this mechanism does not work quite so effectively and sleepers can become active while dreaming, sometimes to the point of walking in a semi-conscious state. This phenomenon is known as somnambulism, or sleepwalking.

Sleepwalkers can often perform tasks and even hold conversations. Very often they will have no recollection at all of what happened during the night.

Brain activity while dreaming

When we dream, the limbic system (the part of the brain associated with emotions, senses and long-term memory) is active, while the forebrain (associated with short-term memory and intelligence) is inactive. This may explain the nature of our dreams.

Recent studies using positron emission tomography (PET) scanning, which can be used to measure blood flow to the brain, indicate that different parts of the brain are active when we dream and when we are awake.

PREFRONTAL CORTEX
During the normal waking state the prefrontal cortex – the front part of the brain – is the most active (indicated by increased blood flow to this area on a PET scan). This part of the brain is responsible for our conscious thought, intelligence, reasoning and short-term memory.

LIMBIC SYSTEM
Studies show that during REM sleep the prefrontal cortex of the brain is completely inactive, while the limbic system – the part of the brain that controls emotions, senses and long-term memory – is most active.

It appears that this could account for the heightened emotions experienced during REM dreams, as well as the retrieval of long-term memories (often our dreams can transport us back to events that occurred some time ago).

The fact that short-term memory is de-activated may also account for the bizarre content of dreams – the scene changes, fragmented narratives and people's identities that seemingly melt into one another. It may also account for the fact that many people cannot remember their dreams once they awake.

VISUAL IMAGES
PET studies have also revealed that the primary visual cortex – the part of the brain used to see when we are awake – is inactive during sleep. Instead a different visual area, called the extrastriate, is active.

The extrastriate is the visual area that is responsible for the recognition of complex objects like faces and emotions. This could explain the vivid visual images typical of most dreams.

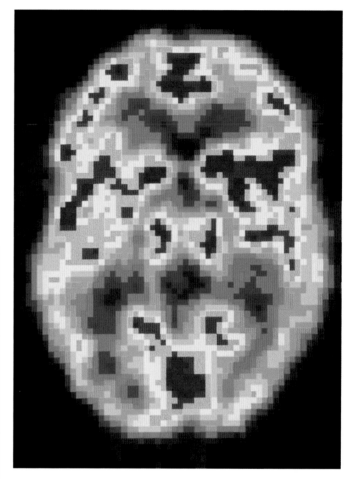

The content of our dreams often seems utterly disconnected from the real world. We dream about situations and scenarios that could never occur in real life.

PET studies reveal that different parts of the brain are active during dreaming and when awake. This may explain the strange nature of many dreams.

Role of dreams

Throughout history the role of dreams has attracted many different theories. Ancient cultures placed much importance on dreams, believing that they were spiritual in origin and could even predict the future.

Subconscious expression
The psychologist Sigmund Freud believed that dreams represented a 'road to the subconscious' and were an expression of repressed (usually sexual) desires.

Today, many psychoanalysts use the recounting of dreams as a part of clinical treatment.

It has long been thought that dreams are an expression of the subconscious. Analysis of dreams is often used as a technique by psychoanalysts.

Dreams may express important wishes or fears of the dreamer, and the analysis of dreams can provide great insight into a person's mental functioning.

Dreams and brain function
A more recent theory suggests that dreams are directly linked to the long-term memory system. Research has been carried out in which subjects who were deprived of REM sleep found it more difficult to learn new information, which appears to support this theory.

Also some studies show that REM sleep increases when we are trying to learn a new or difficult task. This suggests that information in the short-term memory is transferred to the long-term memory as we dream.

How we smell

The nostrils carry air towards specialized cells located just
below the front of the skull. These cells are able to detect thousands
of different types of odours at very low concentrations.

Our sense of smell is in many ways similar to our sense of taste. This is because both taste and smell rely on the ability of specialized cells to detect and respond to the presence of many different chemicals.

The olfactory (smell) receptors present in the nose 'transduce' (convert) these chemical signals into electrical signals that travel along nerve fibres to the brain.

OLFACTORY RECEPTORS

Odours are carried into the nose when we inhale, and dissolve in the mucus-coated interior of the nasal cavity. This mucus acts as a solvent, 'capturing' the gaseous odour molecules. It is continuously renewed, ensuring that odour molecules inhaled in each breath have full access to the olfactory receptor cells.

A small patch of mucous membrane located on the roof of the nasal sinuses, just under the base of the brain, contains around 40 million olfactory receptor cells. These are specialized nerve cells that are responsive to odours at concentrations of a few parts per trillion. The tip of each olfactory cell contains up to 20 'hairs', known as cilia, which float in the nasal mucus; these greatly increase the surface area of the cell, thereby enhancing its ability to detect chemicals.

When odour molecules bind to receptor proteins on an olfactory cell they initiate a series of nerve

The olfactory system

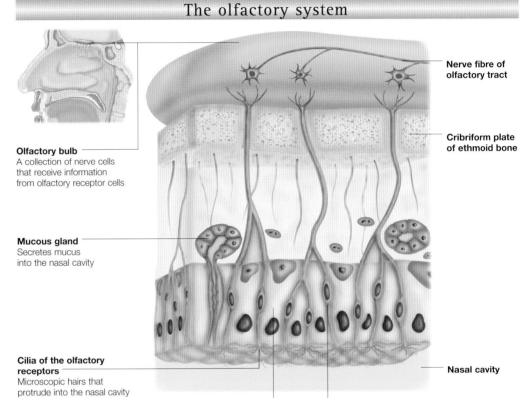

Olfactory bulb
A collection of nerve cells that receive information from olfactory receptor cells

Mucous gland
Secretes mucus into the nasal cavity

Cilia of the olfactory receptors
Microscopic hairs that protrude into the nasal cavity

Nerve fibre of olfactory tract

Cribriform plate of ethmoid bone

Nasal cavity

Supporting cell
The olfactory receptor cells are embedded in supporting cells

Olfactory receptor cell
Responsive to the presence of odour molecules

impulses. These impulses travel along the cell's axon (a nerve fibre that projects from the nerve cell body), which projects through the cribriform plate, the thin layer of skull immediately above the olfactory epithelia.

The olfactory cells in turn communicate with other nerve cells, located in the olfactory bulb, which carry information, via the olfactory nerves (also known as cranial nerve I), to the rest of the brain.

Odour molecules dissolve in mucus secreted into the nasal cavity. Specialized receptors respond to odour molecules by sending nervous impulses to the brain via a structure called the olfactory bulb.

Dimensions of odour

An experienced wine taster can distinguish between numerous odours. Even an untrained nose is thought to be able to detect 20,000 different smells.

Receptors in the retina at the back of the eye are responsive to three colours (red, blue and green). Taste receptors respond to seven modalities. In contrast, there are thought to be hundreds (if not thousands – scientists are not entirely sure) of different types of olfactory receptor.

However, since most of us can differentiate between around 20,000 different odours, it seems unlikely that there is an individual receptor dedicated to

each odour molecule. Rather, it is thought that an odour molecule activates many different types of receptor with varying degrees of success; some receptors are very responsive to a specific odour, whereas other respond only weakly. This pattern of activity is interpreted by the brain to represent a specific smell.

When an odour molecule binds to an olfactory receptor, a complex cascade of chemical reactions is initiated inside the olfactory cell. This has the effect of amplifying the original signal; thus the brain can become aware of odours at remarkably low concentrations.

The way the brain interprets smell is different from the way it interprets other senses (for example, vision) – some branches of the olfactory nerves project directly to the areas of the brain that control emotions and memory, without first travelling to the cortex, the region responsible for the development of conscious experience.

In contrast, visual input is first relayed to the visual cortex, an area involved in the conscious perception of vision, before being relayed to the emotion and memory areas.

EFFECT ON MEMORY
The neuroanatomy of the olfactory pathway means that smells can have a very profound effect on our memory. Re-exposure to an odour that was first smelt during childhood, for example, can bring back a flood of memories of that period.

This PET scan of the brain shows olfactory (smell) activity. Areas of low activity are purple; highly active areas are yellow.

Smells first experienced during childhood can evoke strong and intense memories when they are re-encountered in later life.

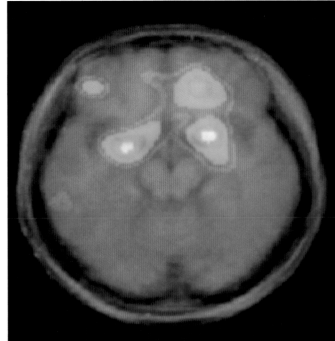

The role of pheromones

Some animals release special types of chemicals, called pheromones, into the air, water or ground in order to influence the behaviour or physiology of other members of their species. There is currently much debate as to the degree that humans use pheromones to unconsciously communicate with each other.

Research suggests that humans do respond to pheromones to some degree. For example, one study showed

It has been suggested that humans unconsciously react to pheromones released by potential sexual partners, but no firm evidence exists to prove this.

that some mothers are able to discriminate between a T-shirt worn by their child and one worn by another child of the same age.

MENSTRUAL SYNCHRONY
Over the past 30 years, a research group in the US has provided much evidence to suggest that the menstrual cycles of female flat-mates tend to converge with time.

A recent study, in which underarm body odour was collected on cotton pads from female donors and then wiped under the noses of recipient women, demonstrated that this is because women are responsive to each others' pheromones.

How good is our sense of smell?

Compared to other animals, humans have very poor smell. To take an extreme example, a dog has 25 times as many olfactory cells as a human, with 30 per cent of its cortex devoted to smell, compared to only five per cent in humans. This explains why trained sniffer dogs can detect odours at concentrations 10,000 times weaker than we can smell.

The evolution of a bipedal gait, which resulted in the nose being raised far from the ground, may have reduced Homo sapiens' reliance on olfaction.

Our sense of smell seems to have been blunted during the process of evolution. One possible explanation for this is that the development of a bipedal gait led to the nose being raised further from the ground; thus there was less advantage, evolutionarily speaking, in having a large

area of the cortex devoted to detecting odours.

The development of higher cognitive functions, such as language – which require considerable cortical processing power – may have also contributed to the reduced reliance on olfaction.

Losing smell

Anosmia ('without smell') is a term used to describe the sudden loss of the sensation of smell. It often occurs after a blow to the head injures the olfactory nerves, but may also be the result of a nasal infection affecting the olfactory receptors.

Disorders of the brain can also affect the sense of smell. For example, some epileptics may experience an 'olfactory aura' before they have a seizure. Other disorders include olfactory hallucinations in which the affected individual experiences a specific odour, which is usually unpleasant.

How the brain processes sound

Sound hitting the inner ear is converted into neuronal (nerve) signals. This is a complex and subtle process, which enables the brain to interpret and understand a wide range of sound.

The cochlea – the organ of hearing located in the inner ear – is a coiled bony structure containing a fluid-filled system of cavities.

The central cavity, or cochlear duct, contains the specific structure for hearing, called the spiral organ of Corti. Located on the basilar membrane, this spiral organ contains the thousands of sensory hair cells that convert mechanical movement (caused by sound vibrations resonating through the fluid) into electrical nerve impulses which are then transmitted to the brain.

PATHWAYS TO BRAIN
The neuronal pathways of the auditory system are composed of sequences of neurones arranged in series and parallel. The impulses begin in the organ of Corti and ultimately reach the auditory areas of the cerebral cortex known as the transverse temporal gyri of Heschl.

TRANSIT STATIONS
As neuronal activity is transmitted towards the brain it goes through several 'transit stations'. Some of these transit stations respond in particular

ways to various aspects of the auditory signal thus giving the brain more context to the sound. For example, some cochlear neurones have a sharp burst of activity at the start of a sound, called a primary-like response pattern; this informs the auditory cortex of the start of a sound sequence.

The neurones, transit stations and various brain auditory centres are found on both sides of the body. The auditory centres in the brain receive sound from the opposite ear.

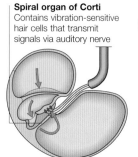

Spiral organ of Corti
Contains vibration-sensitive hair cells that transmit signals via auditory nerve

This cross-section of the cochlea shows how vibrations are transmitted across membranous divisions between the chambers to the organ of Corti hair cells.

Pathway of signals to the brain

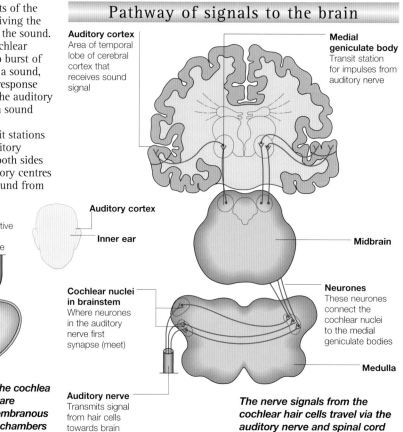

Auditory cortex
Area of temporal lobe of cerebral cortex that receives sound signal

Medial geniculate body
Transit station for impulses from auditory nerve

Auditory cortex

Inner ear

Midbrain

Cochlear nuclei in brainstem
Where neurones in the auditory nerve first synapse (meet)

Neurones
These neurones connect the cochlear nuclei to the medial geniculate bodies

Medulla

Auditory nerve
Transmits signal from hair cells towards brain

The nerve signals from the cochlear hair cells travel via the auditory nerve and spinal cord to the auditory cortex.

Interpreting pitch of sound

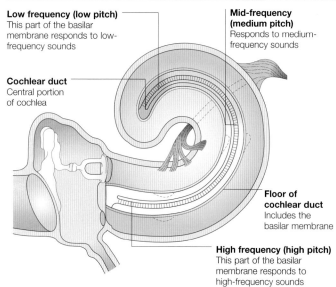

Low frequency (low pitch)
This part of the basilar membrane responds to low-frequency sounds

Mid-frequency (medium pitch)
Responds to medium-frequency sounds

Cochlear duct
Central portion of cochlea

Floor of cochlear duct
Includes the basilar membrane

High frequency (high pitch)
This part of the basilar membrane responds to high-frequency sounds

The stimulation of groups of hair cells at specific locations along the basilar membrane allows the brain to differentiate sounds of different frequencies or pitch.

The hair cells in the spiral organ of Corti are able to convey different tones by responding to different frequencies at different locations along the basilar membrane, thereby contributing to the sound-filtering process.

THE BASILAR MEMBRANE
Cells at the base of the basilar membrane respond more readily to high-frequency sound waves, while those at the tip are more sensitive to low-frequency sounds. This is equivalent to how a grand piano emits

sounds, with one end producing high notes and the other low ones.

However, there are additional subtleties used to transduce the different tones.

Imagine a tuning fork that emits the note 'A' is struck. The sound waves reaching the cochlea will all resonate at a frequency of 440 cycles per second (Hertz). This triggers the basilar membrane to vibrate at 440 times a second. However, there is a particular section of the basilar membrane, that is constructed in such a way that it will vibrate with the largest amplitude at 440 times a second. This will then set the neurones from that region signalling at 440 times a second.

How the brain interprets sound signals

Once nerve impulses are transmitted to the auditory cortex, several areas of the brain are responsible for interpreting the signals.

There is still much to be learned about how the brain interprets sound and language. We know that there are several areas of the temporal lobe on both sides of the brain responsible for interpreting different aspects of sound. We also know that these areas receive a lot of additional contextual information from the various staging posts as the basic neuronal signals make their way to the auditory cortex.

IDENTIFYING SOUNDS

The brain identifies sounds by recognizing essential features of each sound – such as volume, pitch, duration and intervals between sounds. From those elements, the brain creates a unique acoustic 'picture' of each sound, in much the same way that a colour television can reproduce the whole spectrum of colours on a screen using dots of just three colours.

The auditory cortex also has to separate many different sounds arriving at the same time, filtering and analyzing them to produce meaningful information. Of course, the brain uses the context in which sound is received to make certain assumptions about what it it will hear. For instance if the visual cortex tells it that a young girl is speaking it will expect speech of a certain pitch to arrive.

AUDITORY ASSOCIATION CORTEX

The auditory association cortex is used to process complex sounds whereby many sound waves arrive at the same time. This is particularly important in language recognition, and damage to this area results in a person detecting sounds without being able to distinguish between them.

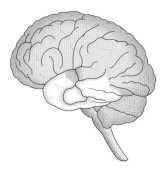

The auditory cortex (pink) recognizes and analyzes sounds. The association cortex (yellow) acts to distinguish more complex features of the sounds.

The visual cortex influences the context in which sound is interpreted. When using a phone we have no visual clues and rely solely on auditory input.

Locating sound

Listening to sound from behind

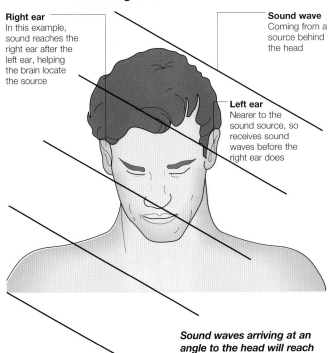

Right ear
In this example, sound reaches the right ear after the left ear, helping the brain locate the source

Sound wave
Coming from a source behind the head

Left ear
Nearer to the sound source, so receives sound waves before the right ear does

Sound waves arriving at an angle to the head will reach each ear at a different time. This allows us to detect the direction from which the sound is coming.

The brain is very accurate at integrating information to locate sound.

The two main ways it does this are by picking up the minute difference in timing and intensity of the sound reaching the two ears.

A sound wave will reach the ear that is closer to the source of the sound a fraction of a second before it reaches the other ear. The brain can interpret the time difference to distinguish the direction of the sound.

In addition to this, if sound is coming from the side, the head causes a 'sound shadow' screening one ear, such that it receives less sound than the other ear. Often, our response is to turn our head in the direction

of the sound, evening up the sound to both ears.

However, even with only one ear we would still be able to locate a sound source. This is because small details of the sound we hear, caused by waves deflecting off the irregular surface of the pinna, vary with the angle at which the sound approaches the ear. As we develop, we learn that particular sound differences are associated with particular directions, and from this we can detect the direction of a sound source.

From an early age, babies learn to recognize typical details of sounds coming from different directions. They can then use the information as a reference.

How ageing affects the brain

During the average person's lifetime, a small percentage
of brain cells die and are never replaced. This cell loss hardly affects
function, but degenerative disorders have more serious effects.

By the time people reach 80, their brains weigh about seven to eight per cent less than they did in their 20s. The reason for this is that brain cells, or neurons, are not replaced when they die.

LOSS OF BRAIN CELLS
The rate of loss varies between different areas of the cerebral cortex (grey matter). But since we are born with 100 billion neurons and a lifetime's loss represents only about three per cent of the total, this does not present a significant problem.

It has also been suggested that it is the number of interconnections between the cells, rather than the number of cells, which is important for cognitive function.

WASTE MATERIAL
Another change in the ageing brain is that granules of a yellowish-brown pigment called lipofuscin accumulate in the neuronal cell bodies. This material is thought to represent waste production. At around the age of 60, microscopic examination of the brain will reveal senile plaques of degenerated cells and other waste material scattered throughout the cortex.

At a day centre, carers can offer help and support to elderly people. They can help them to deal with everyday problems such as paying household bills.

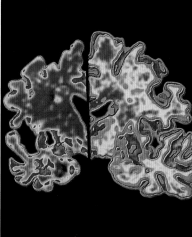

Alzheimer's disease can cause the death of brain cells and a reduction in brain size. These scans show an affected brain (left) and a normal brain (right).

DELAYED REACTIONS
Blood flow through the brain is reduced between the ages of 30 and 70. Nerve impulses travel at a slower speed with age. Conduction of impulses along nerve fibres is thought to be 15 per cent lower in a person of 80 than in someone of 30.

The result is that overall reaction times are longer in an older brain. This may be particularly significant when it comes to braking times when driving a car, or reaction times in order to break a fall.

DEMENTIA
Degenerative brain disorders usually occur in old age but are by no means an inevitable part of ageing. Dementia is a progressive loss of mental functioning, which can result in forgetfulness, impaired speech and mobility, an inability to carry out basic tasks, changes in behaviour and incontinence. There are

about 8 million new cases of dementia worldwide every year and the numbers are going to increase as the world's population ages. Dementia is also caused by blood circulation problems. These include multiple small strokes and arteriosclerosis (hardening of the arteries), which reduce the flow of blood to the brain. Dementia is also present in Huntington's chorea, an inherited progressive, degenerative brain disease.

ALZHEIMER'S
Alzheimer's disease is the leading cause of dementia and accounts for more than half of all cases in the over-65 population. Alzheimer's rarely occurs before the age of 60, but has been known to affect people under 50 years old.

In Alzheimer's, a protein called beta-amyloid accumulates in the tissues of an affected person's brain, causing cells to die.

In elderly people, nerve impulses take longer to travel through the brain. This can make them slower to react in certain situations, such as driving a car.

People with Alzheimer's disease can feel isolated and confused. Affected people may also appear to be suffering from severe depression.

Local care homes can offer respite for relatives of elderly people. However, close relatives may feel guilty that they are no longer the primary carers.

In healthy people beta-amyloid is processed and rendered ineffective by the immune system. However, in people with Alzheimer's this protective sequence of events has started to break down.

SYMPTOMS OF ALZHEIMER'S

The first signs of Alzheimer's disease are failure of short-term memory and confusion about time and place.

In the later stages of Alzheimer's, affected people can develop forms of antisocial behaviour and, if the disease is severe, adopt obsessive rituals such as constant hand washing or touching of door knobs. Once these symptoms become obvious, the decline may be either slow or rapid, but it is always irreversible.

PERSONALITY CHANGES

Eventually, individuals can develop a change in personality and forget the names and faces of the most familiar friends and relatives.

In the declining stages of Alzheimer's disease, some elderly people may be unable to carry out a conversation or be no longer able to read a newspaper or listen to the radio or television. Some people can live for many years in this condition and eventually die not because of the Alzheimer's disease but due to a completely unrelated illness.

THE CARER'S ROLE

Dementia can be a burden for carers and loved ones. Throughout the illness, carers are faced with many difficult decisions. For example in the early stages of the condition, they have to decide whether or not they tell their loved one that he or she has Alzheimer's.

Carers live with the constant uncertainty of the illness. They can never be sure what the next stage will bring since everyone with dementia responds in a different way. For relatives, one of the saddest aspects of the disease is that their loved one

will not get better, but will only deteriorate further.

The structure of the household may change, with the healthy partner having to take on practical tasks, such as cooking or management of financial affairs, which were once the spouse's responsibility.

MAKING CARE DECISIONS

As the person becomes more confused, their ability to make important legal and financial decisions diminishes and it is usually necessary for the carer or other family members to assume these responsibilities on their behalf by gaining power of attorney. Later, when a relative needs round the clock attention,

a decision may have to be made about whether the individual would be more effectively cared for in a nursing home.

NURSING HOMES

Some people believe that permitting their loved one to go into a home is a mark of failure, and they may feel that they have let their relative down. On the other hand, it can be a relief to know that he or she is receiving the necessary care and attention. For these reasons, the experience is often an emotional one.

The financial burden of paying for a nursing home is an additional factor to consider. Local authorities and support groups can offer advice, and financial assistance may be available in certain cases.

MAINTAINING MENTAL AGILITY

Although dementia does affect many elderly people, senility is not an inevitable consequence of ageing. Research has shown that the effects of ageing on the brain can be countered, to a certain extent, by keeping the brain active.

As with any muscle of the body, the brain needs to be exercised. Activities such as doing crosswords or reading combined with a healthy lifestyle (good diet, regular exercise and not smoking) help to maintain mental agility.

A residential home can offer elderly people happiness and security. However, they will probably experience mixed emotions as they settle in.

How caffeine affects the body

Caffeine, found in a range of products, has a powerful stimulant action on the body. As a result, it can adversely affect sleep patterns and may become addictive in the long term.

Caffeine is the most widely used drug in the world – most people consume it in some form every day. Although caffeine is usually associated with coffee, it actually occurs naturally in many plants, including tea leaves and cocoa nuts, and is contained in many drinks. In fact, many people consume up to a gram of caffeine a day without even knowing it.

SOURCES
The most common sources of caffeine include:
■ Fresh coffee – a single cup can contain up to 200 mg
■ Tea – a cup of tea can contain as much as 70 mg of caffeine
■ Cola – a can may contain around 50 mg
■ Chocolate – milk chocolate can contain up to 6 mg per 28 g. Dark chocolate contains more cocoa and thus more caffeine
■ Painkillers – certain headache tablets can contain as much as 200 mg per tablet.

STIMULANT
Recreationally, caffeine is enjoyed by many people who find that it gives them an energy boost and a feeling of heightened alertness. Many people drink coffee to help them wake up in the morning or to remain alert during the day.

Medically, caffeine is used in some migraine and headache drugs, and is a component of certain over-the-counter cold and flu remedies.

Coffee beans are the seeds of coffee fruits. Coffee contains caffeine, which is a stimulant, boosting energy and increasing mental activity.

Short-term effects

Adenosine is a chemical secreted by the brain. Levels of this chemical build up throughout the day and bind to specialized adenosine receptors in the brain, causing nervous activity to slow down, blood vessels to dilate and drowsiness to occur.

In terms of its chemical make-up, caffeine looks very similar to adenosine. Caffeine is thus able to bind to the same receptors in place of adenosine. However, caffeine does not slow down the activity of a nerve cell as adenosine would, but has the opposite effect, causing nerve cell activity to speed up.

Moreover, because caffeine blocks the ability of adenosine to dilate blood vessels, the blood vessels of the brain constrict. This is the reason why some headache tablets contain caffeine (constriction of the brain's blood vessels can help to relieve certain types of headache).

ADRENALINE
When a person takes caffeine, the pituitary gland responds to the increased brain cell activity. It does this by acting as though the body were facing an emergency situation, and releases hormones that stimulate the adrenal glands to produce adrenaline.

The release of adrenaline (the 'fight or flight' hormone) has the following effects, explaining why, after a cup of coffee, a person might experience tense muscles, cold, clammy hands

A dose of caffeine has an instant effect on the nervous system. Brain cell activity is increased, resulting in release of the hormone adrenaline.

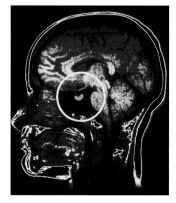

Caffeine stimulates the pituitary gland in the brain, shown on this scan circled. The gland triggers the releases of 'fight and flight' hormones from the adrenals.

and a feeling of excitement:
■ Pupils and airways dilate
■ Heart rate increases
■ Blood pressure rises, as blood vessels close to the surface of the skin constrict
■ Blood flow to the stomach is reduced
■ The liver releases sugar into the bloodstream to provide extra energy.

Addictive properties

Many people become addicted to caffeine. Not only is it a stimulant, but it raises the levels of dopamine in the brain, which increases feelings of pleasure.

Caffeine is an addictive drug. It belongs to a drug group known as stimulants, so called because of their excitatory effect on the brain. Other stimulants include amphetamines and cocaine.

BRAIN CHANNELS

Although the effects of caffeine are less powerful than those of other stimulants, the drug operates in a similar way and, because it manipulates the same channels in the brain, it is just as addictive.

In the short term, caffeine is a harmless substance, but the long-term consumption of caffeine can be a problem. Once the adrenaline released by ingesting caffeine wears off, a person may feel tired and mildly depressed and so may reach for another cup of coffee.

It is in this way that many people become addicted to caffeine without even realizing it. It is not healthy for the body to be in a constant state of emergency and many people become jumpy and irritable.

PLEASURE

Like other stimulants, caffeine raises levels of dopamine, a neurotransmitter that activates the pleasure centre of the brain. It is suspected that this action is a contributory factor to the addictive nature of caffeine.

For years, scientists have studied the behaviour of neuro-transmitters – chemicals in the brain. Caffeine raises the level of the neurotransmitter dopamine.

Effect on sleep

Caffeine has a significant effect on sleep. It takes around 12 hours for caffeine to leave the body's system. This means that if a person has a cup of coffee containing 200 mg of caffeine at around 4 pm, then by 10 pm there will still be 100 mg of caffeine in their bloodstream.

LACK OF DEEP SLEEP

Although the person may be able to fall asleep, they will not be able to attain the deep sleep that the body requires. As a result, they will wake feeling tired, and may instinctively pour themselves a cup of coffee to help wake them up.

And so the cycle continues.

If a person tries to break this cycle, they may find that they feel very tired and mildly depressed. They may also experience headaches due to dilation of the blood vessels in the brain.

Caffeine may hinder deep sleep. A person is therefore likely to wake feeling tired and repeat the cycle by drinking coffee to help them wake up.

It takes around 12 hours for caffeine to leave the body after consumption. If caffeine remains in the bloodstream, it can adversely affect sleep.

Decaffeinated drinks

With increasing awareness of the harmful effects that caffeine can have on the body, decaffeinated drinks are growing in popularity. These provide the taste of coffee, tea and cola, but without the detrimental effects.

Filtration

Decaffeination of coffee involves treating the coffee beans with a solvent that absorbs the caffeine. This is then filtered from the solution, leaving only the coffee oils (vital to flavour). This solution is then added back to the coffee beans, which are roasted and processed as normal.

Research has shown

Decaffeinated coffee, which has no harmful effects, is very popular. Removing caffeine from coffee beans, however, is a complex process.

that people suffering from hypertension benefit from cutting caffeine out of their diets.

How the body responds to stress

When we perceive a threat our sympathetic nervous system triggers a widespread response known as 'fight or flight'. The role of this reflex is to enable the body to react effectively to danger.

The autonomic nervous system regulates the body's basic processes (such as heart rate and breathing) in order to maintain homeostasis (normal functioning of internal bodily processes).

Humans have no voluntary control over this aspect of the nervous system, although certain events, such as emotional stress or fear, can bring about a change in the level of autonomic activity.

OPPOSING EFFECTS

The autonomic nervous system is divided into two parts: the sympathetic and parasympathetic nervous systems. Both generally serve the same organs, but cause opposite effects. In this way, the two divisions counterbalance each other's activities to keep the body's systems operating smoothly.

Under normal circumstances, the parasympathetic nervous system stimulates activities such as digestion, defecation and urination, as well as slowing heart rate and respiration.

The sympathetic nervous system, on the other hand, functions to produce localized adjustments (such as sweating) and reflex adjustments of the cardiovascular system (such as an increase in heart rate).

'FIGHT OR FLIGHT'

Under conditions of stress – such as those caused by fear or rage – however, the entire sympathetic nervous system is activated. This produces an immediate, widespread ('fight or flight') response. The overall effect is to prepare the body to react effectively to danger, whether to defend itself or to flee from a dangerous situation.

The sympathetic nervous system exerts control over a number of organs. In stressful conditions, all of these organs are stimulated simultaneously.

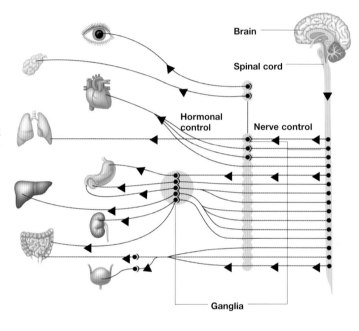

The sympathetic nervous system

Brain

Spinal cord

Hormonal control

Nerve control

Ganglia

Role of chemical messengers

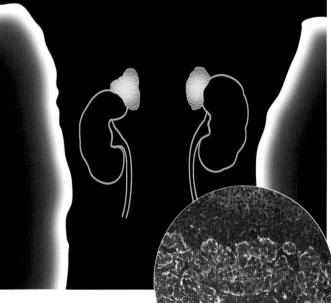

The adrenal glands are located on the upper surface of each kidney. In stressful situations these glands are stimulated to produce a surge of hormones.

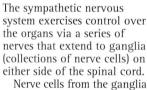

The medulla of the adrenal gland, seen on this micrograph, secretes adrenaline and noradrenaline. These hormones are vital for 'fight or flight'.

The sympathetic nervous system exercises control over the organs via a series of nerves that extend to ganglia (collections of nerve cells) on either side of the spinal cord.

Nerve cells from the ganglia project to target tissues such as glands, smooth muscles or cardiac muscle.

NORMAL RESPONSE

Under normal circumstances, nerve impulses from the brain stimulate the ends of the sympathetic nerve fibres to secrete the chemical messengers adrenaline and noradrenaline.

These hormones stimulate the target organs, and in this way act as chemical mediators for conveying the nerve impulses to the target organs.

STRESSFUL STIMULI

In stressful situations, the whole of the sympathetic nervous system is activated at once. Adrenaline and noradrenaline are immediately secreted from the adrenal medulla (inner portion of the adrenal gland). These hormones are carried in the bloodstream, reinforcing the effects of the sympathetic nervous system.

Meanwhile, the hypothalamus (part of the forebrain) stimulates the pituitary gland to secrete adrenocorticotrophic hormone (ACTH). This triggers the adrenal cortex (the outer portion of the adrenal gland) to release the hormone cortisol into the bloodstream).

Cortisol prepares the body for danger by stabilizing membranes and increasing blood sugar. Stored amino acids are rapidly transported to the liver and converted into glucose, the fuel necessary for the production of energy.

Response to fear

The sympathetic nervous system triggers the characteristic symptoms of fear. These enable the body to achieve a heightened performance under stress.

The surge in levels of adrenaline and noradrenaline from both the nerve endings and the adrenal medulla causes an immediate reaction throughout the body, giving rise to a number of responses that are characteristic of fear.

The aim of these responses is to enable the body to respond effectively to danger, whether it be to run, see better, think more clearly or to stay and fight.

BODY RESPONSES

Fear responses include:
■ Rapid, deep breathing – the airways enlarge and breathing becomes more efficient to allow an increased intake of oxygen into the body

Under stressful situations, such as during an examination, there is an increase in blood flow to the brain. This enables us to think more clearly.

■ Pounding heart – the heart beats harder and faster and blood pressure rises considerably.
Vasodilatation (increase in diameter of blood vessels) occurs within the vessels of those organs essential for emergency reaction, such as the brain, heart and limbs. This allows more blood to reach the organs, providing more oxygen and essential nutrients necessary for heightened performance
■ Pale skin – the effects of the sympathetic nervous system cause vasoconstriction (contraction in the walls of the blood vessels supplying the skin). As a result, blood flow is greatly reduced. This means that blood loss from superficial wounds is decreased should the body be required to fight. It also explains why people can literally go white with fear
■ A surge in energy – the body's metabolism is increased by as much as 100 per cent in order to maintain heightened responses. To compensate, the liver produces more glucose, which is rapidly respired to produce extra energy. This explains why a cup of sweet tea may be helpful after a stressful event

■ Increased physical strength – as a result of increased blood flow and energy levels, the strength of muscular contraction increases. This is why people can perform great feats of strength when they are in danger, for example lifting a very heavy weight, such as a human body
■ Resistance to pain – the secretion of endorphins (natural painkillers) from the brain increases the body's resistance to pain, enabling an individual to remain active despite injury
■ Hair shafts – hairs stand on end as part of a primitive reflex, similar to hair ruffling in cats and dogs

Stressful stimuli, such as a confrontation with danger, activates the entire sympathetic nervous system. This triggers a number of fear responses.

■ Pupils dilate – this sharpens the vision
■ Sweating of the skin – perspiration increases to keep the body cool
■ 'Butterflies' in the stomach – this is caused by decreased blood flow to the stomach (in favour of the vital organs). Urinary tract mobility is also suspended as blood is diverted away from the kidneys.

Effects of long-term stress

Prolonged stress can be damaging to health. The effects can render individuals more susceptible to infection and stress-related illness.

The fear responses are designed to help the body in threatening situations, such as those of immediate and physical danger.

Relaxation
As soon as a threat has passed, the body gradually reverts back to normal as the parasympathetic nervous system is activated.

The muscles begin to relax, heart rate and blood pressure decrease, breathing becomes more regular and deeper and the stomach relaxes as blood flow returns. The emotional state changes from one of anger and

fear to a more calm and peaceful condition.

Prolonged stress
However, in stressful conditions that are socially generated, such as those caused by a heavy workload or financial worries, the fear response can exist on a long-term basis – in other words, there is no relaxation in the body's response to stress.

If there is no outlet for this tension, the effects of stress can have a detrimental effect on the body. An individual may suffer symptoms such as headaches, abdominal pain, weight loss (due to the constantly raised metabolic rate), fatigue and high blood pressure, which may lead to damage to the heart, blood vessels and kidneys.

How alcohol affects the body

Alcohol is appreciated in modern society for the pleasurable effects it can have on the body. In excess however, alcohol is an intoxicating substance and can be detrimental to health.

Alcohol (otherwise known as ethyl alcohol, or ethanol) has long been exploited for its pleasurable effects on the body. Historical archives record the use of alcohol in ancient civilizations, in a number of religious and social rituals.

FERMENTATION
Alcohol is an organic substance, produced by a natural process known as fermentation.

Sugars present in fruits or grains undergo a reaction with enzymes to form alcohol – a process exploited artificially by breweries and distilleries worldwide.

ALCOHOL CONCENTRATION
The concentration of alcohol varies with different drinks, from around four per cent in most beers and 12 per cent in wine, to 40 per cent in spirits such as vodka or whisky.

Today the consumption of alcohol plays a major role in society, and still features in many religious practices.

DETRIMENTAL EFFECTS
Ever since ancient times, however, the perils of this intoxicating substance have been preached about, and strict laws exist in order to regulate alcohol consumption.

Although in moderation, the effects of alcohol on the body are usually minimal, it is an addictive substance and excessive intake, particularly for prolonged periods, can have a serious impact upon health.

Alcohol plays an important role in social gatherings. People drink together in pubs and bars, enjoying the relaxing effects that alcohol can have.

Path of alcohol through the body

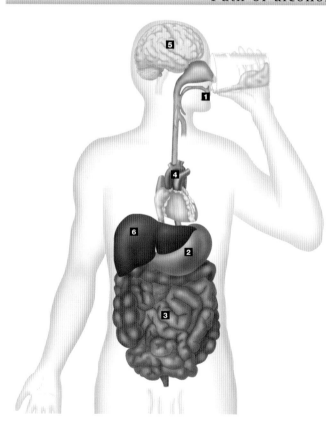

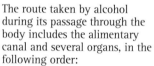

The route taken by alcohol during its passage through the body includes the alimentary canal and several organs, in the following order:

1 Mouth – alcohol may be diluted by saliva before it is swallowed

2 Stomach – alcohol passes via the oesophagus into the stomach where it is further diluted by gastric juices. Some alcohol is absorbed into the bloodstream here, but most passes into the small intestine. The rate of absorption will depend upon the strength of the alcohol and the presence of food in the stomach

3 Small intestine – this is supplied by a dense network of small blood vessels, and is the site of most of the absorption of alcohol into the bloodstream

4 Bloodstream – once in the bloodstream, alcohol is circulated

Alcohol is absorbed into the bloodstream as it passes down the alimentary canal. Once it reaches the liver, alcohol is metabolized to release energy.

around the body and taken up by the cells of various tissues

5 Brain – once alcohol reaches the brain it has an immediate intoxicating effect. Alcohol acts on many sites of the central nervous system including the reticular formation (responsible for consciousness), the spinal cord, cerebellum and cerebral cortex

6 Liver – absorbed alcohol quickly passes to the liver, where it is metabolized to water, carbon dioxide and energy at a rate of around 16 grams of alcohol (two units; for example two small glasses of wine) per hour. This rate varies however, depending upon the build of the individual.

OTHER SITES OF EXCRETION
A small proportion of alcohol goes to the lungs, and is excreted in exhaled air (allowing levels of intoxication to be calculated by the use of a breathalyzer). Some alcohol is disposed of in the urine, and a tinier amount still is excreted in the sweat.

Effects of alcohol

Once absorbed into the bloodstream, alcohol has an immediate effect on the central nervous system. This results in symptoms characteristic of drunkenness.

In general, alcohol reaches the bloodstream within five minutes of ingestion.

IMPAIRED JUDGEMENT
The most immediate effect of alcohol is that drinkers become relaxed and more sociable.

After a single unit of alcohol, the activity of the brain is slowed down, with the result that judgement may be impaired and reaction times slower.

LOSS OF CO-ORDINATION
Muscle co-ordination is increasingly reduced as the relevant control centres of the brain become intoxicated. This can result in clumsiness, staggering and slurred speech.

As the levels of alcohol in the blood rise, the pain centre of the brain is numbed, and the body becomes desensitized.

If the individual continues to drink, their vision may become blurred as the visual cortex is affected.

DRUNKEN BEHAVIOUR
A person is said to be 'drunk' when they no longer have control over their actions.

If sufficient alcohol is consumed the individual may fall into a deep sleep, or even lose consciousness. Extreme quantities of alcohol effectively anaesthetize certain centres of the brain, causing breathing or heart beat to cease, resulting in death.

MEMORY LOSS
Excessive measures of alcohol can affect the short-term memory, and thus actions carried out when drunk may not be recalled the following day.

As blood alcohol levels rise, the brain becomes increasingly intoxicated. The drinker may lose consciousness as certain brain centres are affected.

Long-term effects

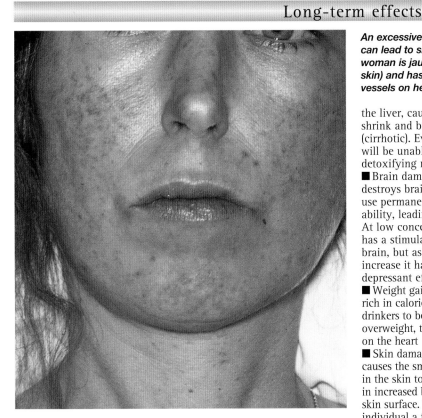

An excessive intake of alcohol can lead to skin changes. This woman is jaundiced (yellowed skin) and has tiny broken blood vessels on her face and neck.

If the body is subjected to excessive alcohol intake for prolonged periods, the effects can be extremely serious. These include:
- Tissue damage – as an irritant, alcohol, especially in purer forms, damages the tissues of the mouth, throat, gullet and stomach, causing increased

susceptibility to cancer
- Loss of appetite – large quantities of alcohol affect the stomach and appetite; thus heavy drinkers tend to neglect their diet. Alcohol is calorific but it does not contain any useful nutrients or vitamins
- Liver damage – excessive quantities of alcohol damage

the liver, causing it to shrink and become defective (cirrhotic). Eventually the organ will be unable to carry out its detoxifying role
- Brain damage – as alcohol destroys brain cells, prolonged use permanently reduces mental ability, leading to dementia. At low concentrations alcohol has a stimulatory effect on the brain, but as concentrations increase it has a more depressant effect
- Weight gain – alcohol is rich in calories, causing heavy drinkers to become bloated and overweight, thus putting a strain on the heart
- Skin damage – alcohol causes the small blood vessels in the skin to dilate, resulting in increased blood flow to the skin surface. This will give the individual a flushed appearance, and a false feeling of being hot. The capillaries in the skin eventually rupture, giving the skin a permanently ruddy and unsightly appearance
- Accidental injury – fatal injury is more likely in heavy drinkers. Alcoholics are seven times as liable to be victims of serious accidents as non-alcoholics.

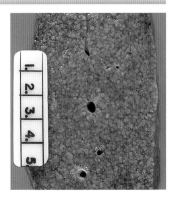

Alcohol is an addictive substance. Long-term abuse can lead to serious health problems such as cirrhosis of the liver (shown here).

Withdrawal

Heavy drinking may be followed by a headache, nausea and fatigue, otherwise known as a hangover. This is due to the dehydrating effect of alcohol, which effectively starves the body's cells of water.

Prolonged alcohol abuse can lead to dependence, and so withdrawal may result in DTs (or delirium tremens), causing shaking, loss of appetite, inability to digest food, sweating, insomnia and seizures. In severe cases, people may hallucinate.

Giant cell arteritis

Symptoms

Giant cell arteritis (also known as temporal arteritis) causes inflammation of the medium-sized blood vessels that supply the head and neck. The condition often affects the arteries in the temples. If it is widespread, it is known as giant cell arteritis or cranial arteritis.

CLINICAL FEATURES
Symptoms of giant cell arteritis:
- Headache
- Intermittent impaired vision, such as double vision
- Sudden vision loss in one eye
- Jaw claudication (cramp) – affects 50 per cent of patients
- Tenderness of the scalp.

A quarter of patients also suffer from polymyalgia rheumatica (PMR), a condition that causes symmetrical pain and stiffness in the shoulders and hips.

Sometimes, patients with giant cell arteritis have vague symptoms, such as tiredness, depression, prolonged fever, weight loss and reduced appetite.

Giant cell arteritis causes headache and tenderness on one side of the scalp above the ear, in the region of the temporal artery.

Diagnosis

It is essential to diagnose giant cell arteritis as promptly as possible in order to reduce the risk of blindness. A medical history, an examination of the patient and a simple blood test are usually used to help diagnose giant cell arteritis.

During the examination the physician will check whether there is any tenderness over the superficial artery in the temple, and whether there is any loss of pulsation in the artery.

FURTHER TESTS
- An eye examination
- Blood tests – these will show mild anaemia and a raised platelet count if the disease is present. The most important indicator of giant cell arteritis is a raised ESR (erythrocyte sedimentation rate). The ESR is markedly raised – above 50 mm/hr – in giant cell arteritis. However, in around 10 per cent of affected patients, the ESR may be normal; this complicates the diagnosis.

ARTERY BIOPSY
It is useful to perform a temporal artery biopsy to confirm the diagnosis. This procedure entails the removal of a segment of the artery, which lies just under the skin. It is performed under a local anaesthetic.

The biopsy will be analyzed to see whether there is an inflammatory arteritis along with the presence of multinucleated giant cells (hence the name giant cell arteritis). The biopsies of the temporal arteries of up to 20 per cent of patients

with polymyalgia rheumatica are similar to those of patients with giant cell arteritis.

Sometimes, biopsies are falsely negative in giant cell arteritis due to 'skip lesions' with areas of normal artery or because steroid treatment is already well established.

Swelling of the optic disc at the back of the eye may indicate giant cell arteritis. This is detected by examination utilizing an ophthalmoscope.

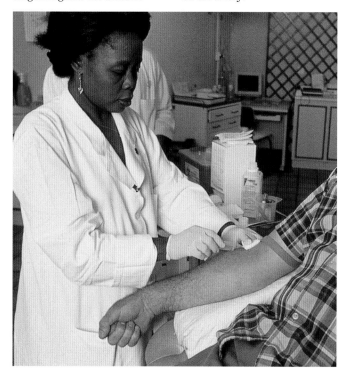

Blood tests may be used to confirm the diagnosis of giant cell arteritis. Affected patients will have mild anaemia.

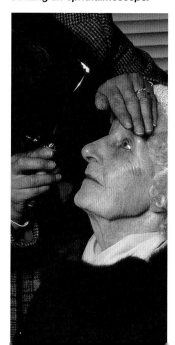

Causes

The cause of giant cell arteritis is unknown, but the disease is thought to be due to an abnormal immune response within the wall of arteries. The same pathology is thought to cause polymyalgia rheumatica.

The loss of vision in giant cell arteritis is caused by thrombosis (blood clots) in the blood vessels that supply the retina at the back of the eye.

Intermittent symptoms of visual impairment or jaw pain are caused by partial blockage of blood vessels. There is no evidence to suggest that the condition is infectious.

Giant cell arteritis is not a directly inherited condition, but variations in its incidence between different races suggests that genetic predisposition may play a part in the aetiology (origin) of the condition.

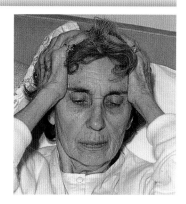

Giant cell arteritis is rare in the under 50s. The headaches are a result of inflammation of the arterial walls.

Superficial temporal artery (parietal branch)

Superficial temporal artery (frontal branch)

The arteries most often affected are the two main branches of the superficial temporal artery, which supply the scalp.

Treatment

Giant cell arteritis responds within two to three days to treatment with large doses of steroids. Some physicians advocate initially administrating it intravenously (directly into the vein) if they believe that vision may be threatened.

If there are visual symptoms, then oral doses of at least 60 mg of prednisolone a day are recommended.

It is important that treatment is not delayed until a temporal artery biopsy has been carried out. The biopsy should be organized as soon as possible. It may still be positive for more than a week after starting steroids.

The progress of patients diagnosed with giant cell arteritis is monitored by regular checks on their erythrocyte sedimentation rate (ESR).

LONG-TERM CONTROL

Once the disease has come under control, the physician will gradually reduce the intake of steroid tablets to a lower maintenance dose – 7.5 mg to 10 mg a day. The lowest possible dose is used to minimize the risk of the side effects of steroids, such as osteoporosis and infection.

Immunosuppressant drugs – such as azathioprine and methotrexate – are occasionally used as a substitute for steroids in patients who have difficulty coming off steroids.

Treatment needs to be continued for around two years in order to prevent relapse.

The progress of patients is monitored by:
■ Checking how much the patient's symptoms have come under control
■ Monitoring the patient's ESR.

Prognosis and incidence

The prognosis for giant cell arteritis depends on the promptness of treatment. If sight is already severely affected, it is unlikely to completely return to normal. However, there may be partial improvement, and the disease is unlikely to get worse once the patient is on steroid treatment.

Lowering the dose of the steroid administered may trigger a relapse, but this is less likely after the first 18 months of treatment or over a year after stopping treatment. Typically, complete remission occurs after about two years.

INCIDENCE

Giant cell arteritis almost always affects people over 50 years of age, with the average age of onset around 70 years. It is at least twice as common in women than in men. The incidence of giant cell arteritis varies in different areas of the world. In northern Europe, the incidence of the condition is up to 20 cases per 100,000 in people aged over 50.

If giant cell arteritis remains untreated, 50 per cent of patients may experience vision loss in one eye.

Headaches

Symptoms

Headaches are common – surveys suggest that 80 per cent of the population suffer from headaches in any one year. Although usually harmless, they are frequently painful and restrictive.

OCCURRENCE
About 15 per cent of women and six per cent of men suffer from migraine, a condition resulting from spasm and overdilation of certain arteries in the brain, which results in a throbbing headache affecting one side of the head. On average, each migraine sufferer loses six to nine working days every year. This adds up to 18 million working days lost each year from this disorder alone.

Symptoms associated with a migraine include nausea. Before the onset of a headache, a warning sensation may occur in the form of visual disturbance.

Causes and diagnosis

There are many different causes and types of headaches. For example, any virus infection can be associated with headache.

DIAGNOSIS
In order to make a diagnosis a doctor will need to find out certain details regarding the headache, such as the time of occurrence, the exact location, the intensity, the duration and the general effect.

CLASSIFICATION
The most significant types of headache can be classified under the following headings:
■ Tension headaches. These are by far the most common type of headache; they are mild to moderate and are felt on both sides of the head. They often feel like a tight band of pressure around the head. They can last for days and can worsen during the day.

Men seem to suffer from cluster headaches more than women. This type of headache can cause severe pain and last for up to 60 minutes.

■ Cluster headaches. These are more common in men. The pain is severe and usually one-sided. They last for 20–60 minutes and may wake the sufferer several times at night. The headaches come in clusters and may be seasonal. There may be watering and reddening of the eyes and the nose may feel blocked
■ Chronic daily headaches. These occur more than two weeks in every month. Tension or migraine headaches may also occur. They can be associated with taking too many opiate-based tablets
■ Migraines. These come in attacks lasting 4–72 hours. They may be preceded by an aura and are described as moderate to severe. The sufferer feels a throbbing pain on one side and may experience nausea and vomiting. Migraines may be made worse by light, noise or simple daily activities.

Migraine often causes a one-sided throbbing headache: the red-shaded area shows a typical pattern of pain distribution.

SERIOUS CONDITIONS
People with persistent headaches worry that there may be a serious cause such as a brain haemorrhage or tumour. Possible warning signs of these serious conditions are:
■ Vomiting that does not relieve the headache
■ Neurological disturbances (including seizures).
Other signs that may provide a cause for concern are:
■ Persistent headaches in children
■ Pain on touching the temple area, which is a feature of giant cell arteritis (an inflamed blood vessel at the side of the head above the ear). This invariably responds to steroid treatment.

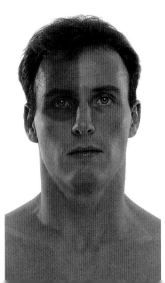

Treatment

Most headache sufferers manage themselves. They know what causes them and how to make the appropriate lifestyle changes that help to avoid them. They usually have a headache remedy that works for them and rarely visit the doctor.

The most popular remedies include aspirin, paracetamol and ibuprofen. Combination remedies, such as those containing codeine, are more expensive and, when taken too often, are known to be associated with chronic daily headaches. Appropriate lifestyle changes may include:

■ Diet
■ Regular meals
■ Regular sleep patterns
■ Reducing stress factors.

PAIN-REDUCING DRUGS

Headaches may be difficult to control with the use of normal painkillers, such as paracetamol, especially if the pattern of attacks keeps changing. There are certain drugs that doctors can prescribe such as:

■ Domperidone – which will diminish nausea
■ Amitryptyline – an antidepressant particularly used in tension headaches
■ Sodium valproate – an anti-epileptic drug that is also used in tension headaches.

There are certain migraine-specific drugs such as:

■ Ergotamine – this is a 5HT agonist, and should not be taken by patients with ischaemic heart disease or uncontrolled blood pressure.

Cluster headaches can be treated by:

■ A 5HT agonist nasal spray or injection
■ Oral steroids (60 mg) – taken daily for two weeks, these will abort a cluster headache.

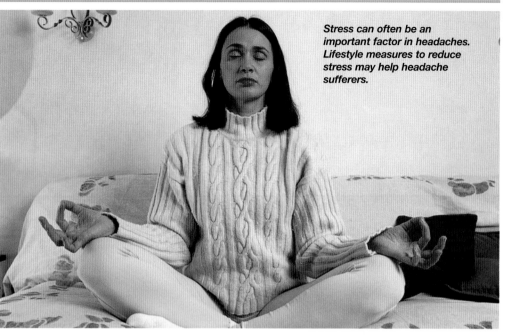

Stress can often be an important factor in headaches. Lifestyle measures to reduce stress may help headache sufferers.

OTHER THERAPIES

Complementary therapies, such as osteopathy, acupuncture, aromatherapy, massage and homeopathy, have all been tried by headache sufferers.

Hormone replacement therapy (HRT) can also be useful in cases of migraine associated with the menstrual cycle (14 per cent of women with migraine have attacks only around the time of menstruation).

However, hormone-based therapies such as the oral contraceptive pill or HRT are used cautiously in migraine sufferers as they are three times more likely to develop a stroke, especially if there is a family history of the condition.

Alternative therapies, such as head massage, have been known to help headache sufferers. Massage aids relaxation and relieves pain.

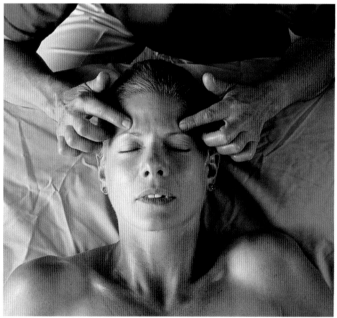

Prognosis

The outlook for people with chronic headache is difficult to predict. The good news is that they can almost always be helped by treatment, but the headaches may flare up again. For instance, migraine can be active for up to 20 years during a person's life. Women seem to be particularly vulnerable to headaches at certain stages of their lives, namely puberty, pregnancy and the menopause.

Girls going through puberty may be particularly susceptible to headaches. This may be due to hormones that are released during the menstrual cycle.

Prevention

If attacks of migraine are occurring frequently, not responding well to treatment or interfering with quality of life, tablets may be taken regularly to reduce the frequency of these attacks. Propranolol, atenolol and pizotifen are commonly used. About half of all patients taking such drugs respond significantly. Cluster headaches can be reduced in frequency by verapamil, a calcium-channel blocker.

Regular headaches can have an impact on a person's quality of life. Certain types of medication can reduce the frequency of attacks.

Migraine

Approximately 1 in 10 people in the UK suffer from migraine, although 60 per cent never consult their GP about managing their condition. An attack can last for between 3 and 72 hours.

Migraine is a common condition in which recurrent headaches are accompanied by symptoms such as nausea and vomiting and, in some people, other neurological disturbances. It occurs more often in women, with an estimated prevalence of about 16 per cent, compared with 6 per cent in men. Over 60 per cent of sufferers have affected relatives, suggesting that there may be an inherited factor.

The maximum incidence is in the 20–30 age group; it is unusual for migraine to begin beyond the age of 40. Migraine-like symptoms starting after this time need to be investigated thoroughly to exclude more serious causes.

Migraines can be extremely distressing for the sufferer. Little is known about the causes, but understanding is increasing.

Migraine triggers

Red wine is a common trigger for many migraine sufferers. Avoidance of these 'triggers' may lessen migraine attacks.

Cheese is implicated in migraines. This may be because it contains tyramine, an amine that has effects similar to those of adrenaline.

A number of people who suffer from migraine are aware of certain triggers that can lead to an attack. These include:
■ **Diet**
Common food triggers include chocolate, cheese, food containing monosodium glutamate, fruit and alcohol, especially red wine. Chemicals contained in these foods appear to be a migraine trigger.

Chocolate is a well-known trigger of migraine, but the attack may depend on the amount ingested or the purity of the product.

■ **Hypoglycaemia (low blood sugar)** Poorly controlled diabetics liable to hypoglycaemia who have migraine suffer more migraine attacks than well-controlled diabetics. Non-diabetics may find that missing meals can provoke a migraine attack, although this may not be due directly to hypoglycaemia.
■ **Hypertension and stress**
Stress may affect emotions, connected with anxiety, or be linked with fatigue and lack of sleep. Many patients notice that their attacks recur on a sudden release from stress.
■ **Exertion**
Strenuous exercise may be a factor influencing the onset of migraine.
■ **Hormonal influences**
Female sex hormones can have a marked but variable influence on migraine attacks. Many women suffer migraine attacks at the beginning of a menstrual period or, more rarely, mid-cycle around the time of ovulation.
■ **Change in sleep pattern**
Either lack of sleep or sleeping

longer than usual can trigger a migraine attack.
■ **Drugs**
As well as oral contraceptives, a number of other drugs, such as nitroglycerine used to treat angina, may bring on attacks.
■ **Smells**
Strong odours, such as perfume, cigarette smoke or certain foods, can provoke migraine.
■ **Bright light**
Bright sunlight or artificial light.

Migraine sufferers with diabetes are prone to more attacks if their diabetes is poorly controlled. The attacks appear to be triggered by low blood sugar levels.

Types of migraines

Over 66 per cent of migraine sufferers are able to identify factors that can trigger an attack. The majority of migraine sufferers have headache, but a few have a rarer form of the condition.

Common features of a migraine attack

Other than pain in the head, there are a number of features that typically characterize a migraine attack.

PRODROME
A prodrome is a forewarning of an attack. There may be a characteristic mood disturbance with depression or euphoria, and thirst and food cravings can occur. Bowel function may be disordered, with diarrhoea or constipation, and urine output may increase. The sufferer may feel generally ill at ease, tired and look pale.

AURA
An aura is a temporary disturbance of brain function that usually lasts for about 15–45 minutes before the headache itself begins. About 10–15 per cent of migraine sufferers have an aura at the beginning of an attack.

In the International Headache Society's classification of the different varieties of migraine, the main distinction is between those with aura (formerly referred to as classical migraine) and those without aura (formerly referred to as common migraine).

The most common type of aura involves disturbance of vision. There may be a loss or interruption of part of the normal field of vision, which is replaced by sparkling or twinkling patterns with zig-zags and whorls. There may be flashes of light or a shimmering effect, like a heat haze. Occasionally, there are more complex visual hallucinations involving objects or people.

Less often, the aura involves other neurological symptoms, such as numbness, tingling or pins and needles, often starting on one side of the face or in one hand and gradually spreading. There may be speech disturbance, and dizziness is common.

OTHER COMMON FEATURES
■ Nausea/vomiting
■ Diarrhoea
■ Intolerance of bright light (photophobia)
■ Intolerance of noise (phonophobia)
■ Sensitivity to smells, such as from food, perfume or cigarettes
■ Extreme fatigue
■ Irritability
■ Giddiness.

Headache

The headache in migraine is often one-sided and commonly centred around the forehead, but it can affect both sides and may affect any part of the head. It has a throbbing or pulsating quality and may be very severe.

The headache usually lasts between 4 and 72 hours, and is often worse with movement; it may be relieved by sleep or vomiting. When the acute symptoms have settled, there is often a period of feeling exhausted and lethargic.

The red-shaded area on this man's head represents the common distribution of pain in migraine. This is known as hemicranial pain.

The visual disturbances associated with migraine can be hard to describe. Some migraine sufferers draw or paint what they experience in order to communicate the sensations.

Less common types of migraine

Although relatively rare, several other varieties of migraine are well-recognized:

■ **Basilar migraine**
More common in children and young adults, it is associated with some disturbance of brainstem and cerebellar function, including double vision (diplopia), unsteadiness of walking (ataxia) and slurred speech (dysarthria). Occasionally, consciousness may be altered with sleepiness, confusion or even coma. A severe headache may follow, often at the back of the head. Although complete recovery is usual, attacks can be alarming.

■ **Hemiplegic migraine**
Numbness and weakness develop on one side of the body, often beginning in one hand or arm and spreading. If the left side of the brain is involved, speech may also be disturbed.

Within an hour, a typical migrainous headache usually develops. The weakness and numbness normally disappear completely within a few hours or days. Very rarely (fewer than 1.5 per 100,000 cases each year), a stroke may occur in association with such a migraine attack.

■ **Ophthalmoplegic migraine**
Paralysis of muscles controlling the movement of one eye produces a squint and double vision, with vomiting and a severe headache, often behind the affected eye. The eye muscle paralysis outlasts the headache and may persist for several days.

■ **Status migrainosus**
This is a migraine attack in which headache persists for more than 72 hours. Hospital admission is usually needed.

Migraine affects more women than men. Usually sufferers are aged 20–30 years. Typical migraine attacks are associated with incapacitating headache.

Managing migraines

On average, migraine sufferers experience 13 attacks each year. There is no miracle cure for the condition, but the onset of an attack can be recognized and the pain managed.

The current medical consensus on the causes of migraine is that it is due to biochemical disturbances in the brain, involving the chemical messenger (neurotransmitter) serotonin. A disturbance of transmission through certain pathways in the brain that involve serotonin is believed to underlie the headache and other features seen in a migraine attack. Several of the drugs that are helpful in the treatment of migraine are now known to block serotonin receptors.

ORIGIN OF THE AURA

One popular theory concerning the origin of the aura is that during the experience, blood vessels in the brain became narrowed (vasoconstriction), leading to a reduction in blood flow. This is thought to cause symptoms such as visual disturbance. It is believed that there is then a second stage in which branches of the external carotid artery in the scalp became stretched and dilated (vasodilatation), and that this produces the characteristic throbbing headache.

REDUCED BLOOD FLOW

A reduction in blood flow beginning in the occipital region at the back of the brain (which is involved with vision) has been demonstrated during the aura phase of a migraine attack. However, it is now believed that this is in fact not the actual cause of the attack, but the consequence of other changes in the brain which are responsible for causing migraine.

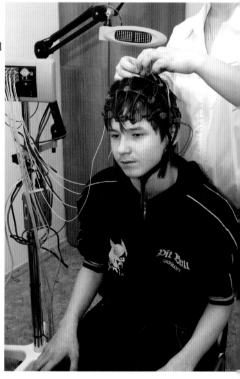

The two arrows represent the direction of the spread of pain. The blue area is the maximal extent of depressed cerebral blood flow in classical migraine.

Investigating migraines

The diagnosis of migraine is usually clear from the patient's history. If a sufferer is well between attacks and their physical examination is normal, no further investigation is needed to confirm that the patient is suffering from migraines.

However, when migraine-like attacks begin in middle age, if there is anything unusual about

MR brain scanning may be utilized if a patient's headaches do not follow the typical course of recurrent migraine.

the attacks or if the neurological examination is not normal, then further investigation will be needed. This is to exclude other conditions that may produce symptoms resembling some of the features of migraine.

EPILEPSY

Occasionally in migraine attacks, there may be some alteration in awareness, or the aura may occur without progressing to a headache, and so epilepsy, which may cause similar symptoms, will need to be ruled out.

TRANSIENT ISCHAEMIC ATTACK (TIA)

TIAs are brief episodes of disturbed blood supply to a local area of the brain or brainstem. They may produce a variety of temporary neurological symptoms that can resemble some of the features of a migraine aura, such as tingling in the face or hand. If there is a migraine aura that is not followed by the characteristic headache, the possibility of a TIA will need to be considered, particularly in an older person.

ARTERIOVENOUS MALFORMATION

A cluster of abnormal blood vessels in the brain or brainstem may, rarely, produce symptoms that could be confused with migraine. If there is doubt, a CT or MR scan may be needed to exclude any abnormality in the brain.

An electro-encephalogram (EEG) may also help to distinguish migraine from epilepsy. In fact, the MR scan or EEG may show some minor abnormalities in migraine sufferers, but these are usually distinguishable from the signs of more serious brain disease.

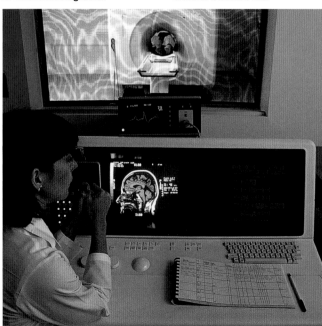

Electro-encephalography (EEG) records the electrical activity of the brain. In migraine sufferers, an EEG may be carried out to determine whether epilepsy is a possible factor in the attacks.

Treating and preventing migraines

It is estimated that migraine costs the UK £750 million a year in lost productivity. However, there is a wide range of treatments available, and most sufferers will be able to manage their symptoms.

The first step in treatment of migraine is to identify obvious triggers for the attacks. Sufferers may find it useful to keep a 'headache diary' to record the dates and severity of attacks, allowing any pattern to be identified, such as a relationship to the menstrual cycle, stress or a particular food or drink.

Sometimes a diary reveals previously unsuspected trigger factors, and may also help to assess whether particular treatments are working. Once identified, fairly simple changes in diet or lifestyle may help reduce the number of attacks.

MEDICATION

A wide range of drugs, including simple painkillers (analgesics) available over the counter are the mainstay of treatment for most migraine sufferers. Other, more powerful prescription drugs need to be used with supervision.

Drugs may be taken either during an attack to try and abort it or reduce its severity, or on a regular basis to try and reduce the frequency of attacks. Simple analgesics, such as aspirin or paracetamol, are first-line treatments, usually taken in combination with an anti-emetic drug, such as metoclopramide.

It is thought that emotional stress and anxiety can be factors in provoking migraines. Therefore, managing stress may help to alleviate migraines.

Using drugs to treat migraine attacks

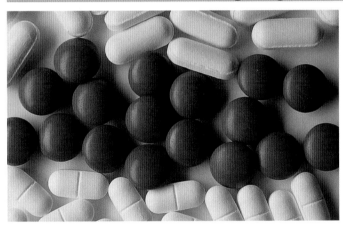

Three serotonin agonists are licensed in the UK for migraine treatment: sumatriptan (most commonly prescribed, available as self-administered subcutaneous injection, tablets and intra-nasal spray), zolmitriptan and naratriptan (tablets only).

These new drugs act on and stimulate the serotonin

Acute migraines may respond to simple painkillers, such as paracetamol, ibuprofen and aspirin, shown here. Anti-emetic drugs help to control nausea.

receptors in the brain and in blood vessels (thought to be significant in the aetiology of migraine), and have revolutionized the lives of many migraine sufferers. They quickly relieve the migraine headache and are potent vasoconstrictors.

All three drugs have a number of unwanted side effects, including malaise, dizziness, nausea and a feeling of heaviness in the chest. They are contraindicated in patients with ischaemic heart disease and high blood pressure, due to their potent vasoconstrictive action.

Prevention of migraine

Migraine sufferers who have frequent attacks may be given regular medication. Beta-blockers, for example, are widely used for the treatment of high blood pressure (where this is thought to be a causative factor); propranolol may be helpful for prevention in up to 70 per cent of migraine sufferers. Unfortunately, they cannot be used in people with asthma and heart failure.

Tricyclic antidepressants, such as amitriptyline and imipramine, are often tried in the prevention of migraine. It is believed their

Beta-blockers have been found to be effective in the prevention of migraine. However, there are some limitations to their use.

mechanism of action against migraine is not simply by virtue of the antidepressant effects. Side effects, such as dry mouth, constipation and sedation may be troublesome in some people.

Pizotifen inhibits the effects of serotonin, and is similar in some ways to the tricyclic antidepressants. It is generally quite well tolerated, but may cause drowsiness and weight gain. Several anti-epileptic drugs may also be helpful for migraine sufferers.

The localized, crushing pain of migraine is represented in this sufferer's painting. The symptoms of an attack can, however, be different for each affected individual.

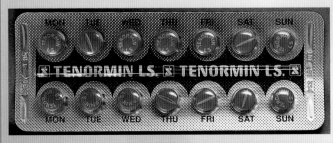

Epilepsy

Symptoms

Epilepsy is a relatively common brain disorder that has a complex collection of symptoms. People with epilepsy have a continuing tendency to have seizures in which there is a sudden electrical discharge from some brain cells. The seizures cause disturbances in mental function, consciousness, sensory perception and body movements.

A person has to have had more than one seizure to be classified as having epilepsy.

CLASSIFYING EPILEPSY
Classification of epilepsy depends on what form the seizure takes, whether an electroencephalogram (EEG) reveals any changes in the brain, where in the brain the seizures originate, if there is any trigger or cause and the patient's age.

The electrical activity of the brain is recorded using electroencephalography. It is important for diagnosing epilepsy.

Types of seizure

Epileptic seizures can be divided into generalized seizures and partial seizures.

Generalized seizures (primary epilepsy)
These affect the whole brain, although there is no detectable abnormality. They include:
- Tonic-clonic seizures (formerly called *grand mal*) – patients suffering from these seizures lose consciousness completely. They also become stiff and then jerk rhythmically. They may also lose bowel or bladder control
- Absence seizures (formerly called *petit mal*) – abrupt lapses of consciousness that may only last a few seconds and might go unnoticed. They occur mainly in children, who may appear to be daydreaming
- Atonic seizures – usually occur in children, who fall suddenly to the ground
- Status epilepticus – seizures occur successively with no intervals of consciousness, and can be fatal.

Partial seizures (secondary epilepsy)
These affect only one part of the brain and are due to a structural abnormality. They sometimes progress to generalized seizures. They may be:
- Simple seizures – patients experience unusual sensations with no loss of consciousness
- Complex seizures – same as above, but patients lose consciousness.

Diagnosis

An EEG can be taken as one way of diagnosing epilepsy. Electrodes placed over the patient's scalp record electrical impulses generated by part of the brain called the cerebral

This EEG shows the electrical activity in a healthy person's brain. An EEG of a patient with epilepsy may reveal an abnormal rhythm of brainwaves.

cortex. This will show the functional behaviour of the cells. Abnormalities in the brain tend to occur when cells fail to work together.

A routine EEG lasts about 15 minutes but can often miss characteristic changes associated with epilepsy. For this reason several EEG tests may be needed before conclusive results are obtained.

The symptoms of epilepsy range from headaches to convulsions. Observation of symptoms by a friend or relative may help in diagnosing the disease.

MEDICAL HISTORY
A full medical history should be taken, along with a description of the seizure characteristics and frequency. The exact nature of a seizure will help to identify the type of epilepsy and where the electrical discharge arises.

In some types of seizure a warning 'aura' may precede a seizure and afterwards the individual may be confused, have a headache and/or have sore muscles. A reliable eyewitness account of this is invaluable.

FURTHER INVESTIGATION
Further investigation may be needed to ensure that there has been a seizure, to clarify what

kind of seizure it was, and to find what (if anything) caused the seizure. Such investigation may include:
- Blood tests – to identify any abnormal levels of chemicals in the blood
- Magnetic resonance imaging (MRI) – this is a useful tool for identifying any structural problems within the brain.

Treatment

Once a diagnosis has been made, the patient is started on an anticonvulsant medication. There are many anticonvulsants available – including carbamazepine and sodium valproate – but no single one is suitable for all forms of epilepsy. Which one is used will depend on the type of epilepsy, the patient's age and whether there are any other limiting factors, such as pregnancy.

A low dose is given initially, and then increased until control is achieved. If too high a dose is used, the patient is likely to experience unwanted side-effects, ranging from drowsiness to excess body hair. Repeated testing to find the correct level of drug is sometimes necessary, since the same dose can lead to different effects in different people.

SURGERY
Surgical treatment is today reserved for rare cases when drugs fail and a specific identifiable point in the brain is causing the stimulus.

A person who has lost consciousness during a seizure but is still breathing should be placed in the recovery position. This will prevent the patient from choking.

First aid

The first-aid procedure for an tonic-clonic epileptic seizure is as follows:
■ The area around the person is made safe for both the first-aider and the person
■ Any tight clothing on the person is loosened
■ The person's head is cushioned
■ Artificial respiration is given if the person stops breathing
■ When the limbs have stopped jerking, the person is put in the recovery position.
    Nothing should be put in the person's mouth, and an ambulance needs to be called only if the seizure is the person's first, if there is any injury or if the seizure has lasted over three minutes.

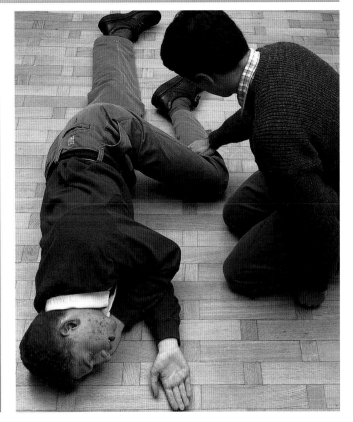

Prognosis

Most people with epilepsy are able to live a normal life. It is important that possible trigger factors, such as strobe lights and loud music, are avoided.

The prognosis for children with epilepsy is generally good. As a precaution, children who have epilepsy should always bathe or swim under adult supervision.

Most patients who experience a seizure will have a second one within two years. This usually occurs in the first few weeks after the initial attack.

The decision to opt for treatment before the second seizure takes place will depend on whether it is thought that recurrent seizures are likely to seriously affect a patient's life and work.

DRUG TREATMENT
Drug treatment completely controls seizures in a third of patients with epilepsy and greatly reduces their frequency in another third.

About two-thirds of people with epilepsy whose seizures are controlled will eventually be able to discontinue treatment. However, this will need to be carried out very slowly as seizures can recur as the drug levels fall.

SOCIAL ASPECTS
Epilepsy still has a certain stigma. In fact, some patients do not tell their friends, work-mates or even employers of their condition for fear of negative consequences.

RESTRICTIONS
A seizure-free period of one year is required before a driving licence can be granted in the UK. This restriction also applies to people with epilepsy who are on drug treatment.

Children should not bathe or ride a bicycle unsupervised.

With the correct diagnosis, treatment, and commonsense precautions, most patients will be able to control their condition.

Attention deficit hyperactivity disorder

Children with attention deficit hyperactivity disorder (ADHD) have a limited attention span, which makes it difficult for them to complete tasks. They are also distractable, impulsive and overactive.

Attention deficit hyperactivity disorder (ADHD) refers to a pattern of difficulties with some aspects of thinking – including paying attention, concentration and organization – and behavioural difficulties, such as being overactive and impulsive.

These behaviours are all very common among typical children, and therefore the diagnosis of ADHD is only given when the difficulties are so severe that they have disrupted the child's life in more than one area, such as recreational activity, school work, getting on with his or her peers and with life at home.

DIAGNOSIS

ADHD is usually identified in early childhood and is generally diagnosed by a mental health professional such as a psychiatrist, although paediatricians, particularly those working in the community, may also diagnose the condition.

More boys are diagnosed with ADHD than girls, although the reasons for this are not clear. It has also been suggested that ADHD is more common in socially deprived areas.

About 33 per cent of children who are diagnosed with ADHD have reading problems. They are also likely to have difficulties in mixing with other children, often because they are aggressive.

PREVALENCE

It is difficult to say exactly how common ADHD actually is. This is because over time people are becoming more aware of it, and therefore the condition is now being recognized more readily. Estimates of the prevalence of ADHD among children range from about 0.5 to 1.5 per cent.

Children with ADHD may have difficulty carrying out everyday tasks such as washing, despite being intellectually and physically capable of doing so.

ADHD is only diagnosed when a child demonstrates severe difficulty in thinking or behaviour. This may affect peer relationships and school work.

What causes ADHD?

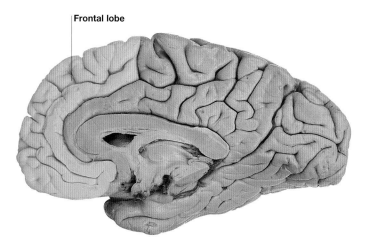

Frontal lobe

There is much debate as to what causes ADHD, although it is almost certain that it results from a combination of both environmental and genetic factors. However, any parent will recognize that some children are more difficult to parent than others. Children who have a diagnosis of ADHD are generally described as being difficult to soothe as babies.

ADHD may arise from a number of complications during the antenatal and post-natal periods. As a result, children

One theory for ADHD suggests that it may arise as a result of very subtle damage to the frontal lobes of the brain.

with a diagnosis of ADHD have difficulties in regulating and organizing their behaviour. These are high-level skills that are controlled by the frontal areas of the brain, and it is thought that in ADHD these areas are not working properly. However, any damage is believed to be so subtle that it is unlikely to be picked up on brain scans.

It is likely that the development of these high-level skills is also influenced by factors in the child's environment. A child's ability to learn is influenced by stresses in the home, such as those caused by illnesses and the wider circumstances in which the child lives.

Treating ADHD

ADHD is commonly treated with medication to improve the child's attention span and alertness. Children with ADHD may also be taught techniques that enable them to change their behaviour and to identify and avoid problematic situations.

A child with ADHD is often treated with a combination of therapy and medication. The most common types of medication used are stimulants such as methylphenidate (Ritalin) and amphetamines. These drugs stimulate the parts of the brain that regulate attention and focused behaviour, and therefore improve the ability to concentrate.

Ritalin may be used as part of a treatment programme for ADHD. It is only used under strict supervision, and is not suitable for children under six.

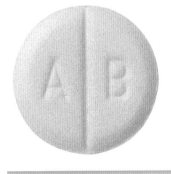

The drug selected is usually taken in several doses throughout the day. It starts working about 30–60 minutes after being taken and lasts for about three to five hours. The effects of the medication wear off very quickly.

SUCCESS RATE
Estimates suggest that medication works to some extent in about 90 per cent of cases of ADHD. Children undergoing such drug therapy often report that it gives them more 'thinking time'. As a result, they find that they are more likely to be able to work at school and to think before acting. In the long term, however, it is difficult to know how helpful medication is in terms of social and academic adjustment.

Children with ADHD may act aggressively in certain situations. Medication can help an affected child modify its unacceptable behaviour.

Other treatment approaches

It is known that children with a diagnosis of ADHD have difficulties getting on with other children of their age and with family members. It is generally helpful, therefore, to use other forms of intervention alongside medication.

There are a number of approaches that are beginning to emerge. These approaches include techniques that mental health professionals may use with children themselves, parent training techniques and techniques to be employed by educators.

CHANGING BEHAVIOUR
A 'cognitive behavioural' approach to modifying a child's behaviour is employed by a child psychologist. The idea is that the therapist helps the child to identify situations where a certain behaviour, such as aggression, is unhelpful for the child. These techniques would generally be used with older children.

With pre-school children, the therapist aims to help the parents. The techniques employed usually take the form of some sort of parent training. In particular, parents are helped to focus on and reward the child's positive behaviour rather than reprimanding negative behaviours, which tends to reinforce them, exacerbating the problem. This is also the approach favoured in the classroom.

LONG-TERM OUTLOOK
The symptoms that are part of ADHD are more common in all pre-school children and decrease over the course of development. However, the symptom patterns consistent with the diagnosis of ADHD tend to persist into

One approach to managing ADHD is to help the child work out what triggers problem behaviour. This may motivate the child to change its conduct.

Parents will be encouraged to focus on their child's positive behaviour and to offer rewards when they act appropriately.

adolescence and beyond.

A child is more likely to continue to have difficulties into adulthood if it also has verbal deficits combined with learning and behavioural problems and poor family management practices. Children who have problems with aggression are the most likely to do poorly, both academically and socially.

Autism

Autism is a behavioural syndrome caused by an abnormality in developmental processes early in life. It is a condition that occurs in one in 100 children.

Autism develops within the first 30 months of life. Although abnormalities are generally apparent from birth, the condition is often not diagnosed until age four or five. Autism is a spectrum condition, which means that it affects different children in different ways – some are only mildly affected whereas others may have severe behavioural problems.

All children with autism will show the following difficulties to varying degrees:
■ Language
■ Getting on with others
■ Behaviour patterns.

COMMUNICATION
In all children with autism there is a delay in the acquisition of language, and language difficulties manifest themselves early in life. Fifty per cent of autistic children never develop useful expressive language.

An autistic baby is unlikely to make attempts to communicate, such as through babbling. Some speech may develop but it is likely to be preservative – the child will go off on rambled tangents – or it might be echolalic, repeating what

another person says without understanding the meaning.

Due to language difficulties, autistic children are likely to confuse personal pronouns, for example talking about the self in the third person, and may have problems with taking turns in conversation. Finally, children with autism will have difficulties in terms of their play, which lacks creativity and imagination.

Autistic children tend to play alone and have a limited range of interests. They may find it difficult to interact with others.

Many children with autism will display repetitive or obsessive behaviours. Much of their behaviour is routine-led.

Social development and behaviour patterns

Autistic children have significant problems in terms of getting on with others. For example:
■ They are averse to affection, particularly of a physical kind
■ They will not naturally show an understanding of how another person feels or thinks
■ Even if hurt, they tend not to seek comfort
■ They will avoid looking another person in the eye.

As a result of these difficulties, autistic children will not show any interest in having relationships with others and will be very solitary.

BEHAVIOUR PATTERNS
Autistic children tend to organize themselves and the world around them very tightly and will become extremely distressed

One of the features of autism is an avoidance of eye contact. This can make communicating with an autistic child difficult.

if their routine is broken. This is because they are unable to extract meaning from their experiences and therefore fail to anticipate what will happen next; routines are therefore a means of avoiding surprises that might be distressing to them.

Autistic children may also have a restricted range of interests and often have attachments to unusual objects rather than people or other living things. Autistic children tend to play in repetitive ways, and their play will lack a story. They may have repetitive mannerisms, such as twirling around or circling their hands.

ABNORMAL RESPONSES
As well as these features, some children also have unusual responses to smells, sights and sounds. Some individuals might not respond to pain or might gain pleasure from inflicting pain on themselves.

Managing autism

Autism is a life-long condition, and once diagnosed the child
will need to be educated in a suitable setting with the help of a multidisciplinary team.
Behavioural therapy may be needed to manage difficult or obsessive behaviours.

Autism is three to four times more common in boys than in girls. The sex difference is most marked in those individuals who have a higher IQ; in children with a low IQ the numbers of boys and girls are more equal.

Fifty per cent of the autistic population have an IQ in the moderate to profoundly learning disabled range. Only 10-20 per cent have an IQ in the normal range. Autism is not linked to socio-economic status.

SPECIAL ABILITY

Overall, autism is much more common in children who have learning disabilities. However, in a minority of autistic individuals there may be areas of special ability, such as an exceptional rote memory. Asperger syndrome is a type of autism that is linked to above average intelligence and fewer speech problems.

Autistic children are socially withdrawn and have difficulties with language. They often have learning disabilities as well.

Coping with autism

Once the diagnosis of autism is made, it is essential that professionals are involved in helping families to understand and cope better with the autistic family member.

It is essential that children with autism are educated in a setting that is right for them. This is often at a special school with a structured curriculum and an emphasis on promoting language and communication skills.

THERAPY APPROACHES

Behavioural interventions are often used to help promote adaptive behaviours and to reduce behaviour that might get in the way of the child's learning, such as self-injurious or obsessional behaviour.

Medication is used in some instances, but only to a limited degree: fenfluramine is used to

Many children with autism have other learning difficulties associated with a low IQ that may complicate their schooling.

The Higashi approach to teaching children with autism uses music and art in its teaching practices.

control repetitive mannerisms; haloperidol or pimozide are used for excitability.

A technique known as the Higashi approach, also called daily life therapy, uses movement, music and art to enable children with autism to learn through imitation in a structured environment.

Speech and language therapy play an important role in treatment. For individuals who do not use speech, communication can be taught using other strategies, and the co-operative aspects of communication might thus be facilitated.

Causes of autism

Owing to the fact that autism is heavily associated with learning difficulties and epilepsy, it is thought that the cause is biological.

However, at present no-one has been able to pinpoint for certain what has gone wrong in the brains of children with autism. It is suggested that it might be to do with higher levels of blood and platelet-bound serotonin, but the mechanisms are yet to be fully understood.

Although in any one case it may be difficult to ascertain a cause, there is evidence to suggest that autism is linked with a number of perinatal injuries, congenital rubella, phenylketonuria and infantile spasms.

'Theory of mind'

At the level of thinking, it is believed that autistic individuals have difficulties in terms of what has been called 'theory of mind'. What this means is that these individuals are unable to anticipate or think about what another person is thinking or feeling.

Down's syndrome

Down's syndrome is a genetic abnormality caused by the presence of
an extra chromosome. One in 1000 babies has the condition, which
can have serious health implications.

Down's syndrome is a genetic
condition that causes varying
levels of learning disability, some
chronic health problems and a
distinct physical appearance. The
syndrome can occur in anyone
but the risk increases with
maternal age.

The genetic basis for the
abnormality was not discovered
until the mid 20th century.
The human body has 23 pairs
chromosomes (structures in
the nucleus of cells that carry
hereditary information), a pair
inherited from each parent. In
1959, researchers linked Down's
syndrome to the presence of an
extra chromosome 21.

MAIN FEATURES

The main features of Down's
syndrome evident at birth are:
- Floppiness due to reduced
muscle tone
- Eyes that slant outwards
- Palms with a single crease
Later, as a child develops
and grows, learning disability
may become evident, but most
children are able to live an
ordinary home and school life.

ASSOCIATED CONDITIONS

There are some health problems
that are more likely to develop in
these children, but some people
will have no associated health
problems and others will have
several. These problems include
heart and bowel disorders as
well as hearing and vision
impairments, an increased

susceptibility to infections and
thyroid dysfunction. Adults with
Down's syndrome may develop
dementia at a younger age than
is usual. Leukaemia is more
common in people with Down's
syndrome than in the general
population, about one in 100
children will develop it.

The outcome for people with
Down's syndrome has greatly
improved over the years as
medical advances have improved
life expectancy.

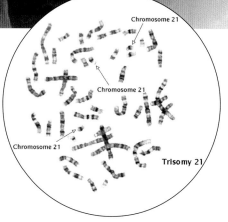

*Learning disabilities are the
major feature associated with
Down's syndrome, but the
degree of this is extremely
variable. However, children
with the condition can be very
cheerful, affectionate and lively.*

*Three copies (instead of two) of
chromosome 21 are evident in
this cell from an amniocentesis
sample. Down's syndrome
results from this genetic
abnormality.*

Chromosome 21

Chromosome 21

Chromosome 21

Trisomy 21

Physical features of Down's syndrome

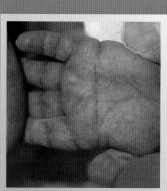

**Babies with Down's syndrome
may have hands that are broad
and short-fingered, with a
single crease across the palm.**

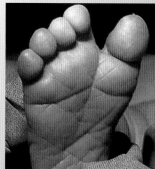

**There is often a large gap
between the big toe and the
second toe. This is sometimes
known as the 'sandal gap'.**

**Baby's with Down's
syndrome have eyes that
characteristically slant
upwards and outwards.**

The clinical features of Down's
syndrome vary from slight
abnormalities to serious medical
problems. These include a large
tongue, a gap between the big
and second toe, problems with
the gastrointestinal tract (such
as constipation or occasionally,
obstruction of the small bowel).
About half of people with the
syndrome have a congenital
heart defect, for example,
affected the blood vessels or a
'hole in the heart'. Fifty per cent
of children will have hearing
impairment and eye problems;
these include 'glue ear', squint
and cataracts.

Genetic causes

Down's syndrome is caused by an extra (third) copy of chromosome 21. The extra copy can only be acquired at certain points in the cycle of cell division.

The failure of chromosomes to separate properly during meiotic cell division is termed meiotic non-disjunction. This can occur during the formation of germ cells (the precursors for sperm and ova) in either parent, and can lead to an unequal number of chromosomes in the daughter cells.

A small fraction (one per cent) of Down's syndrome cases are due to non-disjunction of mitotic (non-sex) cells, which results in a mosaic karyotype. This means that while some cells have a normal set of 46 chromosomes, a proportion of cells have 47 chromosomes. The phenotype is variable, depending on the proportion of normal cells and the tissues affected.

TRANSLOCATION

Four per cent of Down's syndrome cases are due to unbalanced rearrangements of chromosome 21, where genetic material is exchanged between chromosomes. These are known as Robertsonian, or reciprocal,

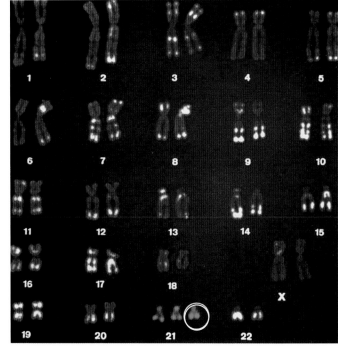

This karyotype (diagram of a chromosome set) shows the extra copy of chromosome 21 found in Down's syndrome. This abnormality can be detected by prenatal diagnosis.

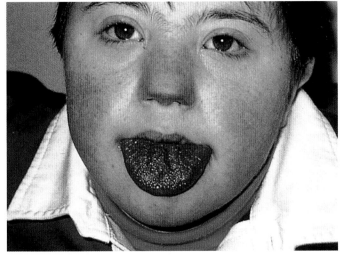

translocations. The 14/21 Robertsonian translocation is the most common rearrangement.

MATERNAL AGE

Although women of any age can, and do, have a child with Down's syndrome, it seems that the risk of having an affected baby increases with maternal

As a result of the genetic causes of Down's syndrome, children often have heart disorders. This child's tongue is cyanosed (blue) due to a lack of blood oxygen.

age. A 25 year old mother has a one in 1250 risk of having a baby with Down's syndrome and a woman of 35 has a one in 400 risk. It is not yet known exactly what causes the extra chromosome that can be passed to the child by either parent.

Screening and prenatal diagnosis

Amniocentesis is the ultimate diagnostic test for Down's syndrome. It is usually performed in the second trimester of pregnancy.

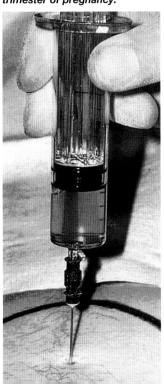

This ultrasound scan shows the face of a fetus with Down's syndrome in profile. The face is seen looking up with the typical short nose visible (circled).

ASSESSING RISK

All pregnant women are now offered screening for Down's syndrome regardless of age. Initial screening is done with a blood sample from the mother and a nuchal scan of the baby around 11 weeks into the pregnancy. This specialized scan measures the thickness of the skin at the back of the baby's neck – the nuchal translucency. The results of the blood test, the mother's age and the nuchal translucency measurement are used together to calculate the individual risk of having a baby with Down's syndrome. If these tests indicate high risk, then further testing with amniocentesis or chorionic villus sampling will be recommended.

FURTHER SCREENING

Both amniocentesis and chorionic villus sampling are carried out using ultrasound as a guide, and both involve passing a fine needle through a woman's abdominal wall into the uterus. During amniocentesis, a sample of the

amniotic fluid that surrounds the fetus is withdrawn in order to detect chromosomal abnormalities. In chorionic villus sampling, a tiny piece of the placenta is removed for examination. Both these procedures carry a small risk of miscarriage.

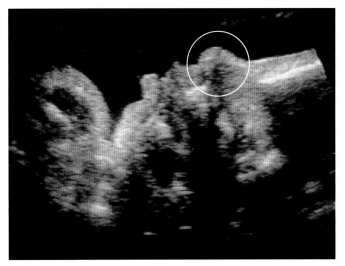

Viral encephalitis

Encephalitis is inflammation of the brain, and is often caused by a virus. This uncommon condition can affect all ages, but can affect children as a complication of childhood infections.

Encephalitis is a serious neurological condition, which can be caused by a virus that spreads to the brain through the nerves or the blood. It causes inflammation of the brain tissue itself, as opposed to inflammation of the meninges (the membranes that surround the brain), which occurs in meningitis. Sometimes, both the brain and the meninges become inflamed and this is known as meningoencephalitis.

CAUSES OF ENCEPHALITIS
The main viruses that cause encephalitis in the UK include:
■ Herpes simplex virus (types I and II) – the virus can be passed to the baby by a mother during delivery (if she has genital herpes). Encephalitis can also be a complication of herpes simplex skin infection
■ Measles virus – about 1 in 5,000 children with measles develop encephalitis as a complication. The condition usually develops a few days after the rash becomes obvious
■ Mumps virus – this is a less

common cause of encephalitis
■ Varicella virus (chickenpox) – this is usually a comparatively mild form of the illness
■ Influenza viruses
■ Tick/mosquito-borne viruses – in some countries, particular types of viral encephalitis can be transmitted to humans via tick and mosquito bites.

Encephalitis involves inflammation and wasting of brain tissue. This can be identified through magnetic resonance imaging of the brain.

The herpes simplex virus (shown below) is a common cause of encephalitis in Europe. This form of the disease responds well to anti-viral therapy.

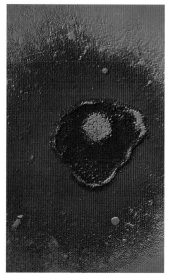

Recognizing the symptoms

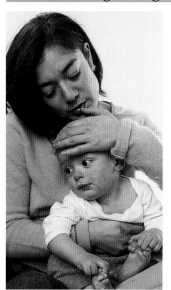

INITIAL SYMPTOMS
The symptoms of viral encephalitis develop in stages:
■ Initial symptoms are a high fever and a headache, nausea and vomiting and also pain in the joints

Babies suffering from viral encephalitis may slowly develop a high fever and become drowsy and floppy, or experience the sudden onset of convulsions.

■ Over a period of hours or days an affected person may develop: confusion, drowsiness or even loss of consciousness, seizures or a change in personality
■ Eventually other neurological symptoms may occur such as slurring of speech, difficulty moving and vision problems. Symptoms are often mild to begin with but then become progessively more serious. Encephalitis is a medical emergency and an affected person should be taken to hospital as soon as possible. In babies or very young children, symptoms are not easily identified as they are unable to articulate pain, but drowsiness and a very high fever as well as irritability may be present

Reye's syndrome

This is a very rare condition that may occur following a viral infection. It has been associated with taking aspirin in children under 12 years of age.

Reye's syndrome causes an encephalopathy (clinically similar to encephalitis although there is no actual inflammation of the brain cells) and liver failure. Symptoms initially include vomiting, drowsiness and convulsions. As the disease progresses the child may lose consciousness and fall into a coma.

If doctors suspect Reye's syndrome the child will undergo blood tests to assess liver function and a CT scan or MRI of the brain to look for oedema (swelling). A liver biopsy may also be taken. There is no actual treatment for the condition itself, but artificial ventilation may help to reduce pressure in the brain.

Reye's syndrome is a very rare, potentially fatal condition. It shares many of the symptoms of encephalitis and may confuse diagnosis.

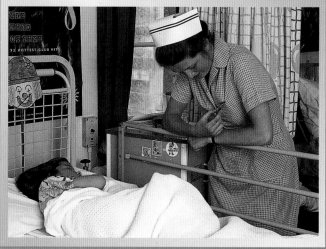

Confirming the diagnosis

Several diseases have similar symptoms of encephalitis, preventing diagnosis on clinical examination alone. MR imaging and a lumbar puncture may be necessary.

If the doctor suspects that a person has viral encephalitis, prompt admission to hospital is necessary as the condition is serious and requires expert nursing and medical care.

Unfortunately the symptoms could apply to a range of diseases that affect the brain, from infections to tumours, and investigations must be carried out to exclude other possibilities. After admission, doctors will carry out several tests both to confirm the diagnosis and to discover the cause of the inflammation.

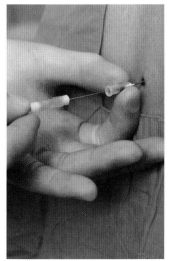

A lumbar puncture may be done to exclude bacterial meningitis. A hollow needle is used to obtain cerebrospinal fluid from around the spinal cord.

HOSPITAL TESTS

Initially doctors perform clinical examinations, such as testing reflex reactions, to assess the nervous system.

Other tests will include the following:
■ Scans of the brain are often carried out – both MRI (magnetic resonance imaging) and CT (computed tomography) scanning can reveal any swelling of the brain tissue or temporal lobe abnormalities, such as atrophy (wasting away) from loss of neural (nerve cell) tissue
■ In most cases, a lumbar puncture is carried out. This can distinguish between a viral and bacterial infection, and will therefore exclude bacterial meningitis as the cause of the symptoms. A small sample of cerebrospinal fluid is removed from around the spinal cord, under local anaesthetic. A narrow needle is inserted through the space between the vertebrae in the lower back and fluid is allowed to drip out. The sample is examined for signs of inflammation or infection

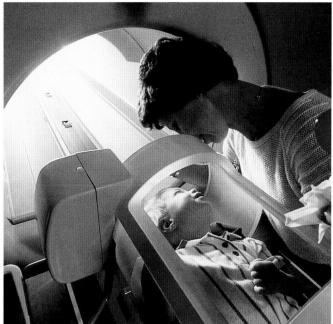

■ Blood and urine samples are taken to look for abnormalities and to look for alternative causes for the symptoms
■ An electroencephalogram (EEG) is performed – this shows the brain's activity as waves on a graph. In some types of encephalitis, particularly herpes simplex encephalitis, the results show slow-wave abnormalities over one or other brain hemisphere
■ Scans of the brain are often carried out – both MRI and CT scanning can reveal any swelling of the brain tissue or temporal

MR images provide the clearest pictures of the brain abnormalities associated with encephalitis. Rapid diagnosis of the disease is essential.

lobe abnormalities, such as atrophy (wasting away) from loss of neural (nerve cell) tissue
■ Very rarely, a brain biopsy may be performed – this enables laboratory technicians to check for the herpes simplex virus, which is one of the common causes of viral encephalitis. The virus can be cultured from the biopsy specimen.

Treating encephalitis

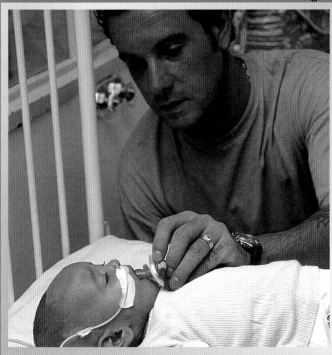

After a few days, children suffering from encephalitis may need to be fed through a naso-gastric tube. Their condition requires constant monitoring.

Affected people are usually nursed in an intensive care unit. The treatment has two aims:
■ Treating the specific cause of the inflammation
■ Treating the effects of the encephalitis.

Treating the cause
A rapid diagnosis is essential, as early treatment can make an enormous difference to the prognosis. Diagnosing infection with the herpes simplex virus is particularly important, as this is the most common form of viral encephalitis in the UK and the only one that responds to treatment with anti-viral therapy (intravenous injections of the anti-viral drug acyclovir).

Treating the effects
It is important to monitor a person's consciousness and, if he or she is drowsy or unresponsive, to make sure that the airway is kept clear. The following steps might be taken to ease symptoms:
■ Rehydrating with intravenous fluid therapy may also re-balance the body's chemical levels
■ If the illness persists for more than a few days, the person may be fed via a nasogastric tube
■ If there is increased pressure within the skull, artificial ventilation can reduce it.

Response to treatment may not be rapid, even in those cases where anti-viral therapy is appropriate. Some people recover fully but others may need physiotherapy or speech therapy for several months to fully regain motor skills. There may be permanent neurological damage in some people.

Hydrocephalus

Hydrocephalus is an abnormal increase in the amount of fluid in
the ventricles of the brain. Symptoms are variable, and treatment is
aimed at minimizing damage to the affected child's brain tissue.

Hydrocephalus is an uncommon condition, in which there is an abnormal increase in the volume of cerebrospinal fluid (CSF) within the ventricles (cavities) of the brain.

Hydrocephalus has three causes:
■ A blockage in the flow of CSF from the ventricles to the subarachnoid space (the space between two of the three membranes that surround and protect the brain)
■ Reduced reabsorption of CSF
■ Excess CSF production.

ASSOCIATED CONDITIONS
Blockage and reduced reabsorption of CSF may be associated with a number of conditions present at birth, most

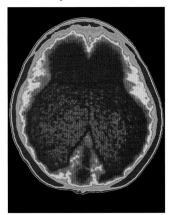

commonly spina bifida – an abnormality of the spinal cord. Congenital abnormalities of the brain itself, in particular a narrowing in the system around which the CSF circulates, may also result in hydrocephalus.

Alternatively, a blockage in the flow of CSF or reduced uptake may follow an intracranial haemorrhage (bleeding within the skull), an infection such as meningitis, in which the membranes covering the brain become infected and inflamed, or a brain tumour. Premature babies who have an intracranial haemorrhage are particularly at risk of developing this condition.

Excess production of CSF may occasionally occur in infancy as a result of a choroid plexus papilloma. This is a small tumour in the choroid plexus (a rich network of blood vessels) in the ventricles of the brain.

This CT scan shows a section through the brain of a child with hydrocephalus. The ventricles (red) are filled with an excessive amount of cerebrospinal fluid.

Hydrocephalus is an abnormal build-up of CSF in the cavities of the brain. This child, who has a shunt (drainage tube) in place, is undergoing physiotherapy.

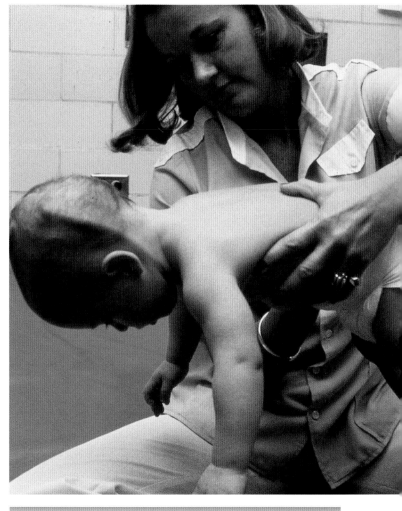

The role of cerebrospinal fluid (CSF)

CSF is a clear, watery fluid that bathes and cushions the brain and spinal cord. It is continuously produced by the choroid plexus, a dense network of blood vessels within each of the ventricles.

The fluid circulates between the ventricles, the subarachnoid space between two of the

three membranes that surround the brain and spinal cord (the meninges), and the narrow canal in the centre of the spinal cord.

CSF is produced by the choroid plexus, a network of ventricular blood vessels. The function of CSF is to cushion the brain and spinal cord.

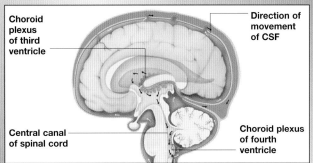

Choroid plexus of third ventricle

Direction of movement of CSF

Central canal of spinal cord

Choroid plexus of fourth ventricle

Neural tube defects and spina bifida

In early pregnancy, a fetal structure called the neural tube develops into the brain, spinal cord and meninges. If the tube does not close normally, a defect in the nervous system can result. The spinal cord is most often affected, causing the condition known as spina bifida. Spina bifida varies in severity between cases, but it is known to be associated with the development of hydrocephalus.

PREVENTION
It is now known that folic acid, taken around the time of conception and continued throughout early pregnancy, reduces the risk of spina bifida. Since folic acid supplementation was introduced, the incidence of the condition has declined by around 75 per cent.

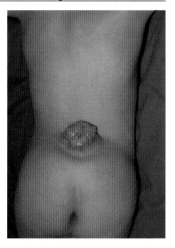

Hydrocephalus may be associated with spina bifida. Severe cases of spina bifida result in the exposure of part of the baby's spinal cord.

Signs and symptoms of hydrocephalus

The signs and symptoms are variable, their severity being largely determined by the age at which hydrocephalus begins and the speed at which the intracranial pressure rises.

ENLARGED SKULL
In infants, the bones of the skull have not yet fused and the skull can expand to accommodate the increasing amount of fluid. As a result, the head enlarges more rapidly than it should:
■ The sutures, or joins between the skull bones, widen
■ The fontanelles (the soft areas on an infant's head) become larger and may bulge due to the raised pressure
■ The veins on the scalp may also become dilated (widened).

SYMPTOMS
In older children and adults, the skull cannot expand and the symptoms of raised intracranial pressure develop. These include:
■ Headaches
■ Nausea and vomiting
■ Poor appetite
Raised pressure can also affect infants if the expansion of the skull fails to keep pace with the increasing amount of fluid.
In addition, compression of specific areas of the brain may cause other symptoms:
■ Unsteady walking
■ Visual problems
■ Hormonal disturbances, the most common manifestation of which is impaired growth.

SPEED OF ONSET
If the condition develops rapidly, headache and vomiting may soon be followed by drowsiness and, later, by coma. If hydrocephalus develops slowly, the symptoms tend to be subtle. Changes in an older child's behaviour and personality, and a gradual deterioration in schoolwork, may become evident.
Raised pressure in the skull eventually damages brain tissue, which may in turn result in disability.

One sign of hydrocephalus in children is an enlarged head. In most cases, however, the condition is treated before it reaches this stage.

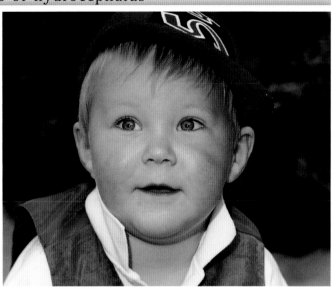

Prenatal diagnosis

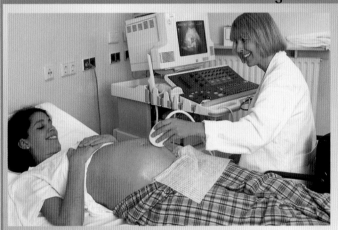

Hydrocephalus may be detected during pregnancy on a routine ultrasound scan.
Ultrasound and other scanning techniques, such as CT or MR imaging, may be performed on babies or children to confirm the diagnosis of hydrocephalus, look for an underlying cause and determine what treatment is required.

Hydrocephalus is sometimes noted during routine antenatal ultrasound scanning. The diagnosis is then confirmed with CT scanning or MRI.

Treating hydrocephalus

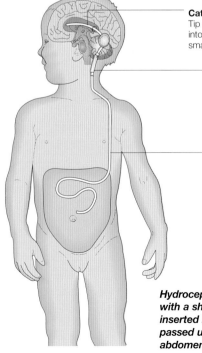

Catheter
Tip of the shunt inserted into ventricle through a small hole made in the skull

Valve
Releases excess CSF from ventricle

Tubing
Passes under the skin of the chest; lower end is coiled within the abdomen to allow for the child's growth

Hydrocephalus can be treated with a shunt. A narrow tube is inserted into the ventricle and passed under the skin to the abdomen or the heart.

The priority in treatment is to reduce the pressure in the ventricles, with the aim of minimizing damage to the surrounding brain tissue. Any underlying cause, such as a brain tumour, will be addressed.
In some cases, the obstruction to the flow or uptake of CSF is a temporary problem and the only treatment required may be drugs that slow the production of CSF.

INSERTING A SHUNT
Many children, however, require the insertion of a shunt – a narrow, flexible tube that diverts CSF from the ventricles to another part of the body, where it can be absorbed.
The tube is inserted into one of the ventricles through a small hole made in the skull and then directed under the skin to the abdominal cavity or, less commonly, the heart. Excess tubing can be coiled within the abdomen to allow for a child's growth.

Shunts may have two possible complications: blockages and infection. Parents need to be alerted to the signs of these and are advised to seek immediate medical help if they are apparent. Symptoms vary according to age, but include:
■ Headache
■ Lethargy
■ Reduced appetite
■ Changes in behaviour.

PROGNOSIS
The prognosis is very variable and depends on many factors, including the age of onset of the condition, the underlying cause and how soon the condition is effectively treated.
Children with hydrocephalus are at increased risk of developmental problems and learning disabilities. In some cases, however, if a shunt can be placed early enough, damage to the brain tissue may be averted and the child may develop normally.

Meningitis

Symptoms

Meningitis – inflammation of the meninges, membranes in the skull and spine – can affect people of any age but it is often a childhood disease. Inflammation is due to infection caused by a virus, a bacterium (the more serious form) or rarely a fungus. Meninigitis and associated septicaemia (blood infection) are medical emergencies and they should be treated in hospital urgently.

The common signs and symptoms of meningitis are different in adults and children. It is important to note that in the case of bacterial meningitis, the symptoms of septicaemia may also be present and symptoms are included here. Anyone with meningitis may have a high temperature, vomiting and drowsiness – a baby will be floppy and unresponsive or will be fretful.

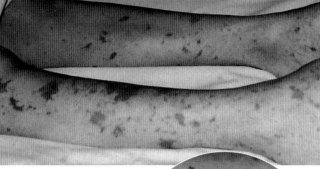

If a glass tumbler is pressed firmly against a septicaemia rash, the rash will not fade. You will be able to see the rash through the glass. If this happens get medical help immediately.

In addition babies and toddlers may have:
- A high-pitched whimpering cry
- A pale, blotchy complexion
- A tense bulging fontanelle

Children and adults will complain of a severe headache and may become drowsy and confused. They may also experience:
- A Dislike of bright lights
- Neck stiffness (unable to touch the chin to the chest)
- Joint or muscle pains
- Fits

If the infection spreads to the blood (septicemia) it will cause additional symptoms. The clearest sign of septicaemia is the appearance of bruise-like rashes, caused by bleeding from the small blood vessels (capillaries) in the skin. The rash may appear suddenly and spread rapidly to cover the limbs and whole body. This is a medical emergency.

Diagnosis

A lumbar puncture is performed to confirm the diagnosis of meningitis. In this procedure, a needle is inserted in the back into the spinal canal, and cerebrospinal fluid (CSF) is extracted. This fluid, which surrounds the spine and brain and contains the meningitis bacteria or viruses, is then sent for detailed examination. Microscopic examination, will enable doctors to make an initial diagnosis of whether the infection is bacterial or viral. Identification of the precise organism takes longer but treatment will start without delay. Blood samples and throat and nose swabs will also be taken to identify the infection.

In a lumbar puncture, spinal fluid (CSF) is taken from the spinal canal, using a hollow needle with an added tap. White blood cells and the presence of bacteria during microscopic examination indicate serious infection.

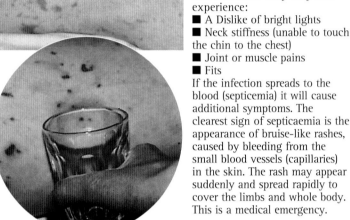

Iliac crests
A line between the hip bones that delineates the level of the puncture. The patient lies curled up on their side for maximum flexion of the spine

Lumbar vertebrae
The five bones of the lower backbone

Puncture needle
Normally inserted between the 4th and 5th lumbar vertebrae

Prognosis

Viral meningitis usually resolves with supportive treatment. In infections due to bacteria, early diagnosis and treatment with appropriate antibiotics are key to survival. Late diagnosis may lead to complications and the condition can be fatal. Following meningitis, a person may have complications due to nerve damage. These include hearing loss, cerebral palsy, epilepsy, learning difficulties and memory problems. If septicaemia was present, then toxins in the blood can cause tissue damage to limbs, leading to gangrene and occasionally limbs need amputation.

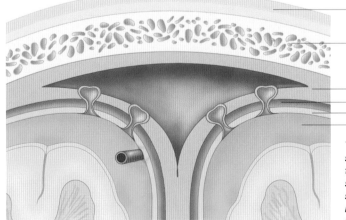

Scalp

Skull

MENINGES
Dura mater
Arachnoid
Pia mater

Brain

This skull cross-section shows the meninges, the three membranes that surround the brain and the spinal cord. Meningitis causes an inflammation of the layers, which, if not treated in time, can kill.

Causes

Meningitis can be caused by bacteria, viruses and rarely by a fungus or protozoa: these travel to the brain via the blood stream. Some of the organsims are naturally occurring in the nose and the back of the throat, and can be spread person-to-person by close physical contact. However, experts are unclear as to why some people develop serious infections and others do not, although people with suppressed immunity may be more susceptible.

The principle types of bacteria organism that cause meningitis are:
■ Newborns Group B *Streptococcus, Escherichia coli, Listeria monocytogenes*
■ Infants and Children *Streptococcus pneumoniae, Neisseria meningitidis, Haemophilus influenzae* type b
■ Adolescents and Young Adults *Neisseria meningitidis, Streptococcus pneumoniae*
■ Older Adults *Streptococcus pneumoniae, Neisseria meningitidis, Listeria monocytogenes*

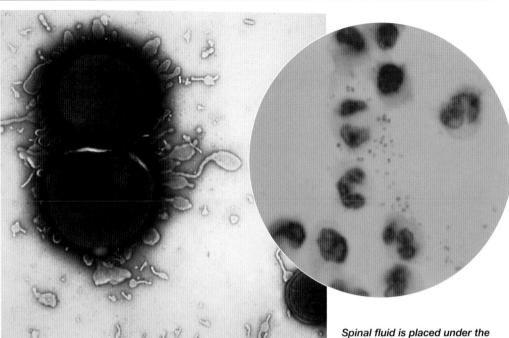

This micrograph shows a meningococcus *bacterium,* Neisseria meningitidis. *It is one of the micro-organisms that causes meningitis. The bacterial infection spreads quickly and can result in septicaemia, characterized by a distinctive rash that spreads rapidly over the body.*

Spinal fluid is placed under the microscope for initial analysis. Meningitis is suspected with the presence of bacteria (small dark-red spots) on the white blood cells that appear here as large red patches.

Incidence

Two-thirds of all meningitis cases occur in children under 15 years old. Of these, 80 per cent occur before the age of five. Neonates (babies up to three months) and children between six and nine months are the most at risk. In the neonatal period, infection is primarily due to the E. coli organism that lives in the gut and arises from umbilical infection.
■ Most cases of bacterial meningitis begin as septicaemia; the germ enters the bloodstream from the nose
■ Ear infections may be responsible for introducing meningitis
■ In rare cases, meningitis will result from infection from a compound (open) fracture of the skull.

Meningococcal septicaemia is characterized by the rapid spread of a bruise-like haemorrhagic rash over the patient's body.

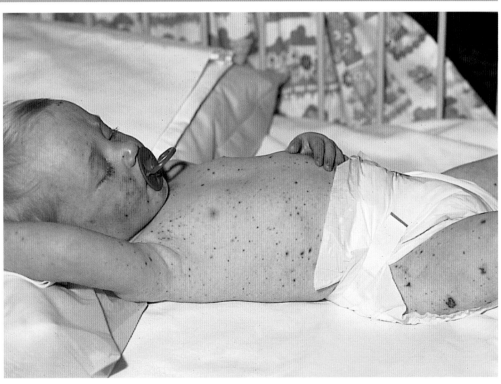

Treatment and Prevention

If bacterial meningitis or septicaemia is suspected, penicillin should be given as soon as possible, preferably by injection into muscle tissue. A single injection may be life-saving: fatality rates range from 7 to 20 per cent, depending on the type of infection. Intravenous antibiotics will be commenced based on clinical diagnosis.

Once the analysis has established the type of organism causing the meningitis, the antibiotic treatment will be reviewed and adapted if necessary. Treatment usually lasts for at least 10–14 days.

Viral meningitis will usually only require treatment with rest and painkillers; antibiotics are not effective against viruses. Vaccines against infections that cause meninigitis are routinely given as part of childhood immunization programmes; these include Hib and meningitis C. Close family contacts of a person with meningococcal meningitis may be given antibiotics or immunizations to protect them against the infection.

Causes of meningitis

Meningitis is an inflammation of the meninges – membranes that cover and line the brain. This occurs when microbes access the subarachnoid space beneath the outermost pair of these membranes and multiply.

MENINGITIS IN CHILDREN

The bacteria responsible for meningitis in children after the first few months of life are among the common colonists of the nose and throat in healthy individuals. Three species are responsible for the great majority of cases:

Neisseria meningitidis, also known as *meningococcus*, is currently the main cause of meningitis in the UK, as well as causing the even more serious life-threatening infection, meningococcal septicaemia. Group B and group C strains are responsible for nearly all of the infections. *Streptococcus pneumoniae* is currently the next commonest in the UK.

Haemophilus influenzae type b, otherwise known as Hib, used to be a common cause of meningitis in the UK. However, since 1992 all infants have been offered the very effective Hib vaccine, which has led to an enormous reduction in the number of cases.

MENINGITIS IN NEONATES

Around the time of birth, neonates (babies up to six weeks old) may be exposed to bacteria that colonize the maternal gastrointestinal and genital tracts, and some of these may cause meningitis. These include:
■ Enteric Gram-negative bacteria, particularly Escherichia coli; type K1 strains are

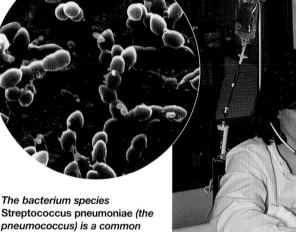

The bacterium species Streptococcus pneumoniae *(the pneumococcus) is a common cause of meningitis in the UK.*

particularly associated with invasive infection
■ Group B streptococcus
■ *Listeria monocytogenes* (a cause of bacterial food poisoning and septicaemia).

VIRAL MENINGITIS

Viral meningitis is generally a less serious condition than bacterial meningitis. However, as well as causing inflammation of the meninges, viruses can infect the brain itself, leading to encephalitis (inflammation of the brain), with fever, confusion and signs of brain dysfunction. Typically, viruses cause a mixed infection – meningoencephalitis – with

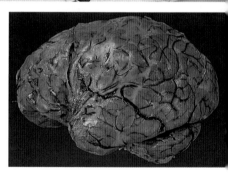

In paediatric intensive care, a nurse attends a young child who is suffering from a severe case of meningitis.

features of both meningitis and encephalitis.

Viruses that cause these conditions include:
■ Mumps virus. Mumps meningoencephalitis used to be very common, but wide use of mumps vaccine has greatly reduced its incidence.
■ Enteroviruses, among the common viruses causing diarrhoea and sore throats, can cause meningitis.

This brain was removed after a fatal case of pneumococcal meningitis. *The meninges are thickened and the brain is covered with pus.*

Signs and symptoms of meningitis

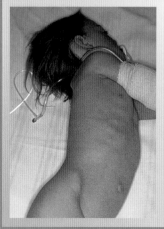

Spasm of the neck muscles causes the head to arch back, as seen in this severe case of meningitis.

General signs and symptoms of infection are seen from an early stage. At the beginning, the symptoms are similar to those of flu. These may include:
■ Fever
■ Nausea, and sometimes vomiting
■ Aches and pains
■ Shivering, and cold, pale or blotchy skin
■ In a baby, no interest in feeding.

Specific signs and symptoms of meningitis soon appear, relating to the fact that the meninges are inflamed. These include:
■ Very severe headache
■ Neck stiffness, arising from spasm of neck muscles as a result of irritation of nerves passing through the inflamed meninges
■ Severe discomfort from light (photophobia)
Other signs and symptoms, caused by a swelling of the brain as a result of inflammation, appear as the infection progresses:

■ Irritability, or, in a baby, moaning or high-pitched crying
■ Drowsiness or confusion
■ In a baby, floppiness or unusual stiffness
■ In a baby, bulging of the anterior fontanelle (soft spot between the skull bones) on the top of the head
n Convulsions, as a result of pressure on vital centres of the brain, or as the consequence of disturbance of brain metabolism from the infection.
Unless urgent steps are taken to reduce the inflammation, the infection may prove fatal.

Transmission of the meningitis infection

Some organisms can enter the brain through a brain injury or via the blood from a different area of the body. Bacteria that may cause meningitis beyond the neonatal period are generally spread from one person to the next in droplets of secretions from the respiratory tract. These can be spread through close physical contact such as kissing. Most people who are naturally colonized with the bacteria are perfectly healthy the organisms so it is important to understand that transmission, or the resulting colonization, is unlikely to lead to meningitis in an individual case.

Ten percent of adults and up to 40 per cent of older teenagers may be naturally colonized with the meningococcus, but at present in the UK less than 4 people per 100,000 per year develop meningococcal disease.

Close physical contact such as kissing can transmit the bacteria that causes meningitis.

Protection against infection

The bacteria that cause meningitis are common colonists of the nose and throat at all ages, and generally do no harm at these sites. Indeed, their presence may be useful in stimulating the immune system to generate subsequent protection. However, for reasons not yet understood, the bacteria occasionally invade the bloodstream and if they are not eliminated from the circulation, they may spread to the meninges and cause meningitis.

The chief protection against this lies in the immune system, and, in particular, the presence

Breast milk contains antibodies that can protect a child against meningitis. This is important in the early stages of life as a baby has an immature immune system.

of specific antibodies that bind bacteria and assist in their removal. Antibodies may be present as a result of prior exposure to the microbes, or through vaccination.

NATURAL ANTIBODIES
Another source of protection for newborn infants is passive acquisition of antibodies from the mother's blood, delivered through the placenta before birth. Babies are also protected by antibodies in their mother's milk. Antibodies that babies acquire via the placenta can last in the circulation for about the first three or four months of life at concentrations sufficient to protect against infection. After this period there are insufficient antibodies to clear bacteria adequately, and

infants become susceptible to invasive infection. Thereafter, young children remain at risk of bacterial meningitis until they have acquired natural immunity through exposure to colonizing bacteria, or have received protection – where available – through vaccination.

Natural immunity will develop with age, but the process may take many years. For example, before Hib vaccine was available, nearly all children nevertheless acquired natural immunity to Hib infection by the age of five years, but until that age, and particularly in younger children, many were susceptible. The vaccine has reduced the period of susceptibility to close to zero, as the course of vaccination should be completed by four months of age. Other bacteria that cause meningitis, such as meningococcus, also generate natural immunity, but this may not develop until adult life, and many individuals remain susceptible throughout their life.

Antibiotic treatment for bacterial meningitis

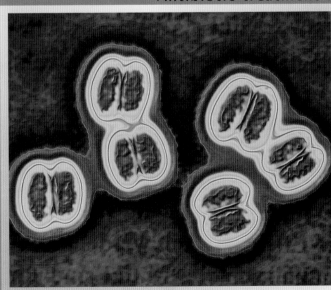

Bactericidal antibiotics must be administered without delay in cases of meningitis to minimize the risk of brain damage. As time is of the essence, treatment has to be started before the specific bacterial cause is identified. Therefore, broad spectrum antibiotics are used to ensure that all possibilities are covered.

A common choice to treat children beyond the neonatal period is a cephalosporin, such as ceftriaxone or cefotaxime.

Meningococci commonly colonize the nose and throat, but, rarely, they invade the blood-stream to cause septicaemia and meningitis. Urgent antibiotic treatment is then needed to reduce the risk of brain damage.

These are potent antibiotics that penetrate the meninges to kill bacteria in the cerebrospinal fluid. They are active against virtually all strains of the bacteria that commonly cause meningitis in this age group. Because very occasionally strains of pneumococcus may be resistant to these cephalosporins, an additional antibiotic such as vancomycin may be used in the initial stage of treatment.

In neonatal meningitis, it is necessary to prescribe a combination of antibiotics to cover the range of bacteria that may be responsible for the infection. Cefotaxime and ampicillin, or gentamicin and ampicillin, are widely used.

Reye's syndrome

Reye's syndrome is a rare condition that may be triggered by a viral infection. Treatment should be started as soon as possible to reduce the risk of brain damage occurring.

Reye's syndrome is a rare disorder, characterized by damage to the brain and the liver. Almost exclusively a childhood disease, Reye's syndrome is a serious condition, requiring urgent treatment to avoid the risk of complications.

COMPLICATIONS

The condition may be fatal, usually due to swelling of the brain tissue. In addition to the brain swelling, Reye's syndrome is associated with the build-up of fat in the liver. As a result, the function of the liver is impaired.

CAUSES

Reye's syndrome develops a few days after the onset of, or recovery from, a viral illness. A variety of viral illnesses may precede the syndrome, including chickenpox and influenza.

The cause is unknown, but there is thought to be an association with taking aspirin. Since 1986, therefore, it has been recommended that aspirin should not be given to children under 12 years. Paracetamol can be used as an alternative treatment.

DECLINE

The condition was only recognized about 30 years ago. Over the last 15 years, there has been a dramatic decline in the number of cases diagnosed in the UK and the USA.

Reye's syndrome may follow a viral infection such as chickenpox. The condition can cause swelling of the brain and requires urgent treatment.

The influenza virus is shown (left) under the microscope. Rarely, a child with flu may go on to develop Reye's syndrome.

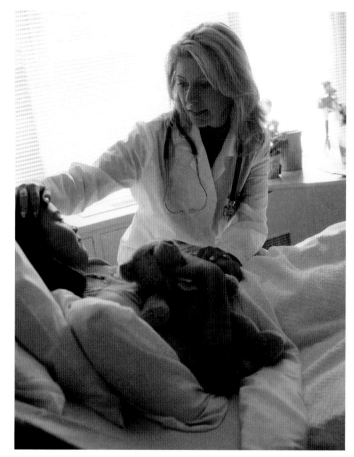

Pattern of symptoms

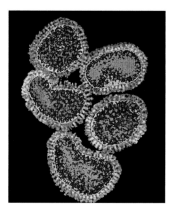

Reye's syndrome mainly affects children aged between six months and 15 years. However, small babies and young adults are occasionally affected. Boys and girls are affected equally.

RAPID DEVELOPMENT

The symptoms develop rapidly, in some cases over a few hours. Any of the following may occur:
■ Nausea and vomiting – the first symptom is usually profuse vomiting, followed or accompanied by lethargy
■ Disturbed consciousness – a characteristic feature; over a period of up to 24 hours an affected child may become disorientated and agitated
■ Visual hallucinations
■ Convulsions (fits) – these

The onset of symptoms of Reye's syndrome is often rapid. A child may develop breathing problems and require oxygen or assisted ventilation.

occur in about 30 per cent of affected children
■ Low blood sugar levels – particularly in children under the age of two years
■ Breathing difficulties
■ Jaundice – the yellowing of the skin associated with impaired liver function.

Without treatment, drowsiness is likely to follow, leading to loss of consciousness.

VARIABLE PATTERN

The pattern of the syndrome is different in infants, in whom vomiting is a less common feature. In affected infants, the first symptoms tend to be breathing problems and convulsions. A history of a viral illness before the onset of symptoms is common.

The rate at which the symptoms progress varies greatly in all those affected. The condition may stabilize at any stage.

Treating and diagnosing Reye's syndrome

Early diagnosis is essential to ensure the best treatment for Reye's syndrome. The outcome varies from child to child, but it largely depends on how quickly the symptoms develop and how soon medical attention is sought.

The outcome of Reye's syndrome depends on how early the condition is diagnosed and how effectively the swelling of the brain can be treated. Some children make a full recovery. For others, impairment of brain function persists, sometimes resulting in learning problems or movement difficulties.

For a number of children the condition is fatal; death occurs in up to 40 per cent of cases. The condition is more likely to be fatal if symptoms develop quickly and progress to coma.

MAKING THE DIAGNOSIS

Reye's syndrome is a medical emergency; the earlier the diagnosis can be made and treatment initiated, the better the prognosis. There are no specific tests for the condition. A careful examination will be

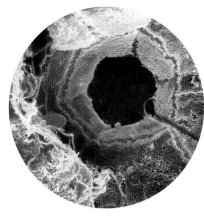

Liver cells are examined to confirm a diagnosis of Reye's syndrome. The microscopic appearance may reveal damage.

carried out, followed by tests to exclude other possible causes of the symptoms and to confirm the diagnosis. The examination may reveal signs of raised pressure in the skull caused by the brain swelling; the liver may be of normal size or enlarged.

Samples of blood may be taken and tested to check the levels of particular liver enzymes that, if raised, indicate impairment of liver function.

TESTING BRAIN AND LIVER FUNCTION

An EEG (electroencephalogram) may be performed to assess the electrical activity in the brain and look for signs of impairment of brain function.

The brain may be further examined by CT (computed tomography) scanning or MRI (magnetic resonance imaging).

CT involves X-rays being passed through the body at different angles. The information is then processed by a computer to form cross-sectional pictures of the part of the body to be examined, in this case the brain.

MRI also produces detailed images of the body, but instead

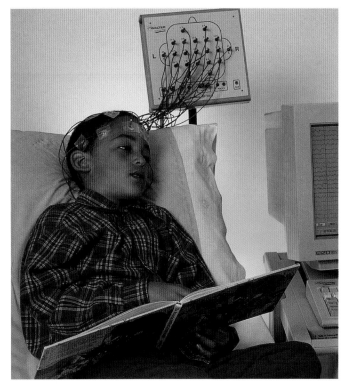

of using X-rays, the body is surrounded by a large magnet and is then exposed to short bursts of harmless radiowaves that cause hydrogen ions in the body to emit radio signals. Different types of tissue contain different amounts of hydrogen ions and produce strong or weak radio signals. These signals are analyzed by the computer and formulated into images.

Finally, a liver biopsy may be

If a child has Reye's syndrome, an EEG may be carried out. This records electrical activity in the brain, which is shown as brain wave patterns on a monitor.

performed to confirm diagnosis. A sample of liver tissue is removed by a hollow needle passed through the skin and between the right lower ribs. Additional tests may be required to rule out other conditions.

Intensive care treatment

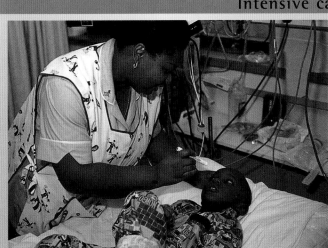

Children with Reye's syndrome are admitted to a paediatric intensive care unit. There they will be monitored closely and given medication.

Children with Reye's syndrome require admission to an intensive care unit, where they can be given constant specialist care.

Lowering pressure

There is no specific cure for Reye's syndrome, the treatment being particularly aimed at lowering the raised pressure within the skull, so reducing the risk of irreversible damage to

the brain. This usually involves treatment with intravenous drugs.

If breathing is affected, support with a mechanical ventilator may be necessary until the condition improves. Intravenous medication may also be required to control convulsions and this treatment may be continued in oral form for at least another six months. Throughout the illness, careful monitoring will be required.

Long-term follow-up will also be necessary to monitor the child's progress and to assess the need for any continued support, such as physiotherapy and special help with education.

Head injuries

Head injuries are the most common injury in children. The flexible nature of the child's skull normally protects the brain from permanent damage, but in a few cases, the consequences can be more serious.

Each year, around one in 200 children will stay the night in hospital with a head injury. The actual number of head injuries each year, however, is probably greater than this because not all injuries are reported to a hospital. Such injuries are the commonest cause of acquired disability in children, affecting approximately 3,000 children aged between 1 and 15 years each year in the UK.

CAUSES OF HEAD INJURY

The cause in each case is often related to the child's age and sex. Head injuries in infants under the age of one occur mainly as a result of non-accidental injury in other words, child abuse.

In children between one and five years old, domestic accidents, such as falling down flights of stairs or out of windows, are a common cause of head injury. Over the age of five, however, most head injuries result from pedestrian road-traffic accidents (RTAs).

Overall, boys suffer head injuries more frequently than girls by a ratio of about 2:1 throughout childhood (up to the age of 15). The largest group to suffer is boys in their teenage years – again, because of RTAs.

Other, less common, circumstances in which children suffer head injuries include car crashes involving the child as a passenger, riding accidents – falling off a bicycle or a horse – or, occasionally, sporting accidents, particuarly in contact sports.

INITIAL ASSESSMENT

Most children with head injuries are taken to their local A&E department, where they will be assessed and stabilized. If necessary, they will be referred to the neurosciences department for further care and assessment, but this depends on the severity of the injury. Doctors in A&E will consult with the relevant doctors in the neurosciences department as to whether the child should be transferred for specialist treatment.

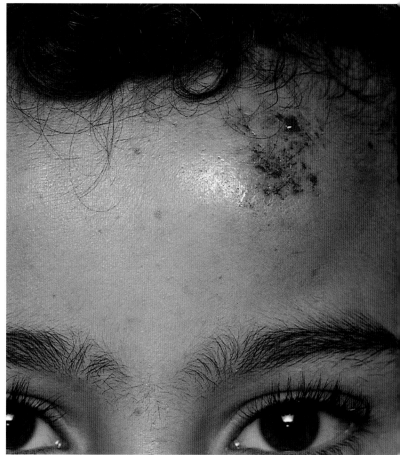

In the majority of head injuries – such as this bruising and swelling as a result of a playground fall – there are no long-term effects. However, if the child is knocked unconscious, they may be hospitalized for at least 24 hours.

Emergency transfer after serious injury

A child who has suffered a serious accident, for example after a road traffic accident, would be brought in by ambulance or, in extreme cases, helicopter air-ambulance to the nearest suitable hospital.

The immediate priority for the paramedic staff at the scene is to achieve a good airway, because hypoxia (deficiency of oxygen in the tissues) may result in serious brain damage. The child will be ventilated manually or intubated (have a tube inserted into their throat if normal breathing is difficult) by the paramedics.

During the journey to hospital, the main aim is to keep the child stable before further treatment.

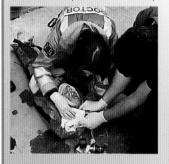

1. When a young boy falls from a window, it's obvious that urgent medical attention is required. The paramedic team is accompanied by a doctor, assessing the boy's injuries and stemming initial blood loss.

2. The emergency is serious enough to warrant an air-ambulance. Once the boy is strapped on to the stretcher, with his neck supported and a 'back-board' in place to stabilize his spine, he is transferred to the waiting helicopter.

3. To maintain respiration in his critical state, the boy is 'bagged' with a hand-held respirator that administers air directly through a face-mask. Blood is being given intravenously to replace that which he lost from the injuries to his head.

4. The hospital has been given advance warning of the incoming case, so the 'crash' team is ready as the paramedics arrive at the intensive therapy unit. Specialists in neurosciences and paediatric trauma will also be present.

Assessment and treatment

The extent of a child's head injury must be established quickly – especially if the patient is unconscious. In order to do this, doctors use a three-part scoring system.

If the child is unconscious, the head will have been injured significantly. If the child is conscious, the doctor will check over the scalp for bruising and swelling. In either case, the level of consciousness will be tested to assess what further action is required.

GLASGOW COMA SCALE

The child's level of consciousness following a head injury can be assessed using the Glasgow Coma Scale, a standardized scoring system that is modified for use with children.

The scale looks at the overall level of responsiveness to stimuli by the eyes, limbs (motor response) and by speech (verbal response). The scores are added to make an aggregate that gives an idea of the child's condition.

From a potential maximum of 15, a score of 13 or over indicates that the child has not suffered a significant head injury. However, the score is often good to begin with and then deteriorates because of internal bleeding.

SERIOUS CASES

A score of less than eight means that mechanical ventilation will be required if this has not already been administered during the transfer to hospital. These are very serious cases; the child is extremely ill and may not survive. Many such cases will not make it to the hospital alive, and others will die in the Intensive Care Unit. Those who do survive with such a low score on the scale are not likely to do well in the long-term.

Children with head injuries must be assessed rapidly. Initially, A&E doctors look for alertness and responsiveness to voice and pain. Thereafter, a full Glasgow Coma Score should be obtained, determining the course of action.

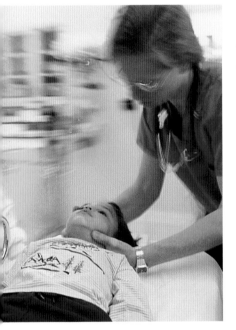

Paediatric Glasgow coma score

4–15 YEARS		0–4 YEARS	
Response	**Score**	**Response**	**Score**
Eyes		**Eyes**	
Open spontaneously	4	Open spontaneously	4
Open to verbal command	3	React to speech	3
Open in response to pain	2	React to pain	2
No response	1	No response	1
Motor response		**Motor response**	
Obeys verbal command	6	Spontaneous or obeys verbal command	6
Response to painful stimulus		*Response to painful stimulus*	
Localizes pain	5	Localizes pain	5
Flexes limb with pain	4	Withdraws in response	4
Flexes abnormally	3	Flexes abnormally	3
Extension	2	Extension	2
No response	1	No response	1
Verbal response		**Verbal response**	
Orientated, converses, interacts, appropriate words	5	Smiles, orientated to sounds, objects, interacts	5
Disorientated, converses	4	Cries, inappropriate words	4
Inappropriate words	3	Inappropriate crying	3
Incomprehensible sounds	2	Inconsolable crying, irritable	2
No response	1	No response	1

SPECIFIC INVESTIGATIONS

The early tests done in A&E look at general brain function. More detailed investigations will be undertaken in the neurosciences and intensive care units. These tests include measuring the intracranial pressure (ICP) – the pressure inside the brain – using a probe inserted through the skull. By subtracting the ICP reading from the mean (average) arterial blood pressure, the resulting figure is the 'mean cerebral perfusion pressure', the pressure at which oxygen is being supplied to the brain.

Doctors also look at the pattern of the brainwave using an electroencephalograph (EEG). Even when the child is unconscious, signals are still sent between the retina and the brain, via the 'visual pathway'. The activity of the pathway is detected by EEG, which therefore provides a good warning sign if the brain has been badly injured.

X-ray and CT scans

After the severity of a child's head injury has been established clinically, the patient may be further examined if the signs warrant it. Once the child is stable, they will undergo X-ray examination and a CT (computerized tomography) scan. An X-ray of the neck is usually taken with the first skull X-rays to confirm or discount cervical spine damage. If there is any doubt about the neck it is kept in a collar, because the chance of fracture and dislocation is high.

Scanning takes from 30 to 60 minutes to complete and cannot

In computerized axial tomography (CT or CAT scan), the X-ray emitter and detector rotate around the patient. Unlike normal X-rays, this technique can produce 3D images.

If the coma score is less than eight, a CT scan will usually be taken as soon as possible. This will highlight brain tissue damage or blood clots.

therefore be carried out on a patient who is still in need of resuscitation.

As well as the damage to the head, chest injuries must be assessed as the resulting hypoxia (low blood oxygen) will exacerbate any brain injury.

Head injuries in children

About 1 in 800 children with head injuries develop serious problems that can lead to death. An understanding of the three main types of head injury is therefore vital, as seemingly simple injuries can often hide internal complications.

Localized skull fracture

One of the most common types of head injury is a direct, localized blow to the head. This may cause a fracture of the skull and haemorrhage (bleeding) beneath – indicative of a bruise on the brain.

Children with such injuries usually wake up quite quickly, but often have a neurological deficit depending on which side of the head they are hit. This will usually be a weakness or loss of speech, which improves as the bruise recovers. For these children, the outlook is good because the rest of the brain is usually undisturbed.

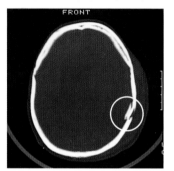

This CT scan shows a fracture (circled) in the right parietal bone of the skull.

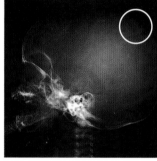

A simple, linear fracture in the skull such as this would probably not have affected the brain.

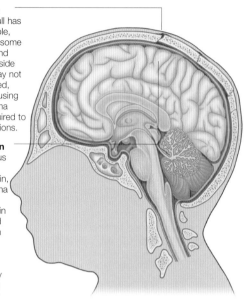

Simple fracture
A blow to the skull has resulted in a simple, linear fracture. In some cases, the skin and tissues on either side of the fracture may not have been affected, and observation using the Glasgow Coma Scale will be required to assess complications.

Unaffected brain
There is no serious damage to the tissues of the brain, confirmed by coma assessment and CT scan. In certain cases of localized fracture, the brain may bruise and haemorrhage, although the effects are usually short term. There may occasionally be more major bleeding around the brain.

Larger impact injury

Major trauma to skull
Multiple fractures and possible penetration by foreign objects. Skull is significantly deformed.

Haemorrhaging
Intracranial (within the skull) bleeding from the meninges (membranes surrounding the brain), and the brain. As the brain is compressed, extradural haematoma (blood clotting within the outer membrane) may occur.

If the blow to the head is more forceful or over a larger area, multiple fractures of the skull and penetration by the object are possible. Common causes of such potentially devastating injury include falling and hitting the head on concrete, or receiving a blow to the head. Such injuries cause distortion of the brain, micro-tears of the tissue and sometimes massive bleeding can result. Immediate surgery may be needed to rectify the damage when bleeding has stopped, and more long-term neurological problems are to be expected.

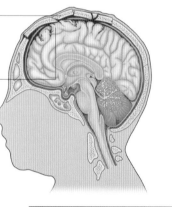

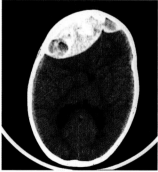

This scan of a large fracture shows an extradural haematoma (white) – an accumulation of blood from the membranes of the brain.

Diffuse axonal injury

The diffuse axonal injury is the typical injury suffered when a child is flung through the air at high velocity in a road traffic accident. It may produce no visible bleeding in the brain but it causes very severe swelling and long-term damage. The priority in this case is to reduce the pressure inside the head, such as by giving diuretic drugs.

These injuries are a matter for concern, because in diffuse injury, all parts of the brain are affected, and may also be accompanied by brainstem damage due to angulation and whipping of the head relative to the neck.

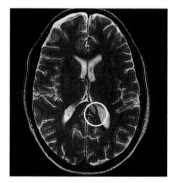

MR scans are needed to see the subtle lesions of diffuse axonal injury. This injury causes swellings in the brain (circled) and may result in long-term disability.

Skull
With diffuse axonal injury, the skull – and sometimes the brain – may show no visible signs of damage.

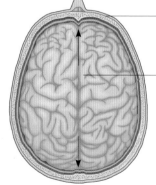

Brain movement
A rapid change in direction, such as when a child is hit by a car or falls out of a window, causes the brain to smash against the inside of the skull and rebound.

Widespread damage can result from microscopic shearing of delicate nerve tissue.

Long-term management

After initial assessment and treatment, the procedure involves waiting for the child to regain complete consciousness and managing the waking-up process.

When the child comes round after the injury, which may be a few minutes or several days later, further neurological examination (include additional scanning) may give an indication of any permanent damage.

The child will go through an initial state of confusion as they wake up, but many make quite a rapid recovery. However, the learning difficulties can take several months to assess fully; it is not until about six months after the accident that problems likely to persist in the long-term can be fully identified.

RECOVERY MANAGEMENT

During these crucial months, many different approaches will be needed for the patient's recovery. These include physiotherapy, occupational therapy, speech therapy and neuropsychology. Patients with severe injuries can also be very irritable and difficult to manage.

The age of the child can affect the severity of the possible resulting brain damage, being worse in younger children. Furthermore, the younger the child, the more likely they are to die from a severe head injury.

AFTER-EFFECTS

With any head injury, there are many possible sequelae (medical disorders resulting from the injury). A child with a minor head injury can have short-term

Post-traumatic stress is common after a head injury, so the careful management of the child is required to help them overcome the resulting phobias and insecurities.

problems – typically classified as post-traumatic stress disorder. These may be manifested as behavioural difficulties, nightmares, phobias and disturbances of their learning due to loss of concentration. However, this is not evidence of brain injury, but rather a response to a life-threatening occurence.

In more severe cases, brain damage may result in physical disabilities. A child who has a physical disability is also likely to have some learning difficulties. Many patients will have no physical disability, but still have problems with memory, concentration, behaviour and the ability to learn at speed. They may find it difficult to keep up with the rest of the class once they are back at school, so counselling may be offered.

FRONTAL LOBE TRAUMA

Frontal lobe injuries are very serious and can be devastating because they affect not only behaviour but also personality. Frontal lobe damage also affects the brain's 'executive function'. This is the ability to assimilate

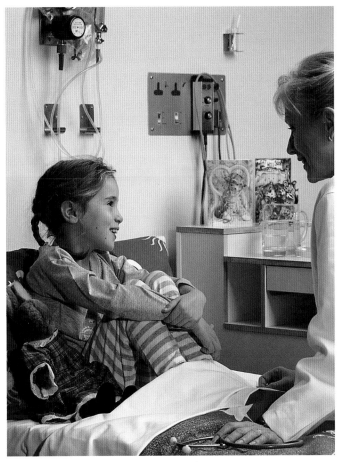

individual components of information into a whole and is the key to our understanding of and interaction with the world. Affected children therefore have difficulty planning, organizing and co-ordinating thoughts. The production of speech may also be difficult, and the child may have social disinhibition.

Fortunately, because most paedatric head injuries are not severe, the majority of affected children will make a complete recovery. Despite the relatively common occurrence of such injuries, long-term neurological effects such as epilepsy and cranial nerve damage following head trauma are very rare.

Shaken baby syndrome

The majority of head injuries in children under a year old result from non-accidental injury. A cause of bleeding around the brain and diffuse axonal injury in infants is so-called 'shaken baby syndrome', in which frustrated parents or child-minders shake a crying baby in order to silence it.

An infant's head control is not as effective as an adult's because of their undeveloped neck muscles. As a result, rapid back and forth motion during shaking causes the brain tissue to suffer rapid acceleration and deceleration stresses combined with rotational movement and whiplash. This trauma affects the entire brain, and the resulting disability is severe. In most cases, there will be no external evidence of injury.

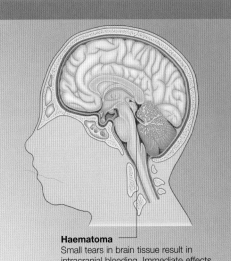

Rotational
The widespread movement of the brain causes lobar tearing. Areas particularly affected are the frontal lobe, brainstem and cerebellum.

Whiplash
Rapid movements of the head relative to the neck. Causes acceleration and deceleration injuries.

Haematoma
Small tears in brain tissue result in intracranial bleeding. Immediate effects range from confusion to coma or death.

DAMAGING MOVEMENT:
Shaking causes two main types of damaging movement: rotational and whiplash.

AXONAL DAMAGE:
Potentially fatal results are diffuse axonal injury and haematoma (bleeding and clotting).

Emergency craniotomy

A severe head injury can cause a blood clot to form inside the skull.
This life-threatening condition will rapidly cause a patient's
breathing to stop and heart to fail if neurosurgery is not performed.

Head injury is a common cause of death and disability throughout the world. When complications develop, an emergency neurosurgery procedure known as a craniotomy may be needed to relieve the pressure on the brain caused by cerebral haematoma (blood clot). A craniotomy involves the removal of a portion of the skull to expose the brain and its meninges – tissue membranes that enclose the brain. The blood clot can then be removed and the bleeding controlled.

BRAIN COMPRESSION

The skull is a fixed-volume box, and the presence of a significant blood clot within it will lead to brain compression or displacement. With a clot expanding beneath the vault of the skull, the inner part of the temporal lobe may protrude downwards. Without urgent treatment, the brain begins to be pushed downwards towards the foramen magnum, the large hole at the base of the skull through which the spinal cord runs.

The inner part of the temporal lobe (uncus) may herniate

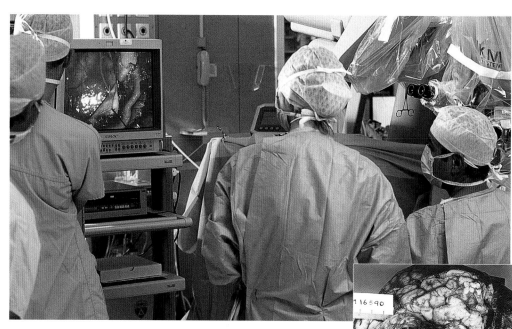

downwards through the space between the tentorium cerebelli (the layer of dura that separates the cerebral cortex from the cerebellum) and the midbrain. This is tentorial or uncal herniation, also known as 'coning'. It is a life-threatening condition, as it will rapidly pressurize vital centres in the

The neurosurgeon (seated) performs surgery utilizing a video light microscope. His view is displayed on the monitor.

brainstem that control the heart and breathing. Unchecked, this will lead to fatal respiratory arrest. Craniotomy is therefore performed to remove the clot.

This removed brain shows contusion (bruising) on the right-hand side.

Head injury complications requiring craniotomy

Linear skull fracture
This simple crack in the skull may not be a problem in its own right. However, the presence of a linear skull fracture warns of an increased risk of developing a blood clot inside the skull (intracranial haematoma). This is particularly likely if the fracture runs across a major blood vessel, such as the middle meningeal artery.

Intracranial haematoma
A collection of blood between the inside of the skull and the dura, producing a white lens-shaped appearance on this computed tomography (often called CT scanning) image. In a patient who has regained consciousness after a head injury, a skull fracture increases the risk of developing an intracranial haematoma requiring surgery.

Subdural haematoma
A collection of blood lying over the surface of the brain underneath the dura. It is commonly due to bleeding from small superficial veins, often torn by shearing forces, or from a laceration of the brain. A CT scan will reveal the extent of bleeding; if small and localized, surgery may not be required. Careful observation of the patient is essential.

Herniation, or 'coning'
As coning begins to occur, the oculomotor (eye movement) nerve will be compressed. This will result in the pupil on the same side dilating and failing to constrict in the normal way when a bright light is shone into it. Evaluation of the size of the pupils and their ability to react to light is critical for monitoring patients with head injuries.

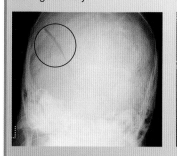

A skull X-ray will usually be performed before a CT scan. A fracture is seen at the top left.

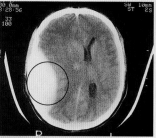

The white indent (circled) on this CT scan is an accumulation of blood inside the skull.

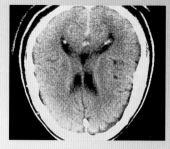

The CT scan shows that a layer of blood (white) has collected around the surface of the brain.

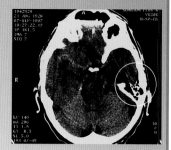

On this CT scan, an expanding clot has caused the temporal lobe to herniate downwards.

Head injuries

Most head injuries result from an accident involving a blow to the head. Even if there is no obvious fracture of the skull, there is often underlying damage.

INCIDENCE

Head injuries account for about 10 per cent of the workload of A&E departments in the UK. Most of these will be relatively minor (classified as loss of consciousness for up to 15 minutes). However, more than 11,000 people suffer a severe head injury (with coma lasting more than six hours) each year. Head injury accounts for 25 per cent of all accidental deaths and 40 per cent of deaths in road accidents.

Males are two to three times more likely to have a head injury than females, with 15–30 year olds the highest risk group. Head injury accounts for 15 per cent of all deaths in people aged 15–25 years. About half occur in road accidents, and 20–30 per cent in injuries at home or work.

Sporting accidents cause another 10–15 per cent, while 10 per cent result from assaults; alcohol is involved in many of these cases. Bike riding can be hazardous for children, with almost 20 per cent of paediatric head injuries the result of cycling accidents.

OUTCOME

The mortality after head injury is about nine per 1,000 cases. This means that a large number of people survive a head injury, but many of these will be left with disabilities.

Many head injuries could be avoided by simple safety measures. Crash helmets for cyclists and motorcyclists can dramatically reduce injuries to the skull and brain if an accident does occur.

The skull may be depressed with broken pieces of bone being pushed inwards, like a cracked egg. Sharp edges of bone may tear the tough membrane covering the brain (the dura matter) and may lacerate the cerebral cortex. Bleeding may then occur and there is a serious risk of infection.

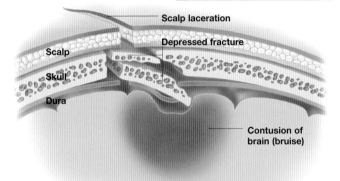

Scalp laceration

Depressed fracture

Scalp

Skull

Dura

Contusion of brain (bruise)

Primary and secondary injury to the brain

PRIMARY INJURY

The brain has a soft, jelly-like consistency. When the head is suddenly accelerated (by the impact of a moving object, for example) or decelerated (when the moving head hits the ground or a car windscreen) the brain moves inside the skull with a circular motion.

This produces shearing forces that can tear nerve fibres in the brain, resulting in a condition called a diffuse axonal injury. Additionally, the brain may be bruised (contusion) or lacerated, especially where the undersurfaces of the frontal and temporal lobes move across the irregular surface of the base of the skull.

The bleeding may be within the substance of the brain (intracerebral haematoma) or over its surface (traumatic subarachnoid haemorrhage).

BRAIN DAMAGE

The above are all types of primary injury, occurring at the time of the impact to the head. The degree of primary brain damage corresponds to the length of the period of loss of consciousness after the injury and to the duration of post-traumatic amnesia (PTA).

PTA is the time from the moment of injury until normal continuous 'running memory' for ongoing events is restored. It includes the period of coma and subsequent confused behaviour and is a useful indicator of the severity of a head injury. Some consequences of a diffuse axonal injury may take longer to appear.

SECONDARY INJURY

In the hours after head injury, other factors can add to the initial brain damage.
■ Hypotension: other injuries may accompany the injury to the head, causing bleeding and shock, and leading to a fall in blood pressure (hypotension). This may impair the blood

supply to the brain (cerebral perfusion), producing further damage.
■ Hypoxia: if the airway is not clear or if breathing is not normal, whether because of the head injury itself or associated chest or face injuries, then there may be reduced levels of oxygen in the blood. This may lead to further brain damage due to an inadequate supply of oxygen (hypoxia).
■ Cerebral swelling: brain swelling (cerebral oedema) may develop after trauma, making it harder for blood to flow normally into and around the brain as the pressure inside the skull (intracranial pressure) rises relative to the blood pressure.
■ Infection: penetrating injuries that breach the skin, skull bone and dura increase the risk of intracranial infection through the direct inoculation of micro-organisms. Fractures of the skull base may allow infection to spread from the nasal sinuses or the ear. Meningitis (inflammation of the membranes) or a brain abscess may result.

The duration of coma and post-traumatic amnesia (PTA) are useful predictors of long-term outcome after head injury. Age is an important factor, with older people having a lower chance of a good recovery after a severe head injury.

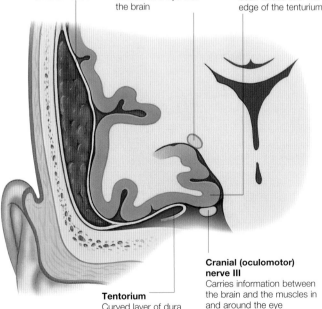

Blood clot
Exerts pressure on brain lobes

Cranial (optic) nerve II
Carries information between the eye and the brain

Area of herniation
Temporal lobe has been forced over the edge of the tenturium

Cranial (oculomotor) nerve III
Carries information between the brain and the muscles in and around the eye

Tentorium
Curved layer of dura

The temporal lobe has been pushed across by the blood clot and is beginning to herniate over the edge of the dura of the tentorium. It is pressing on the oculomotor nerve, causing the pupil on that side to dilate.

Alzheimer's disease

Symptoms

Alzheimer's disease is a form of dementia, a chronic disorder of the mental processes due to progressive brain disease. It is most common in older people, particularly over the age of 80, but occasionally occurs in younger people.

People with Alzheimer's disease become increasingly forgetful and eventually develop severe memory loss, particularly of recent events. Their ability to concentrate, cope with numbers and verbally communicate declines, and they often become anxious and depressed. Sudden mood swings and personality changes are common, as is socially unacceptable behaviour.

With advanced disease, patients are often disorientated, especially at night, and may neglect personal hygiene and become incontinent. Some people become docile and helpless; others are aggressive and difficult to care for.

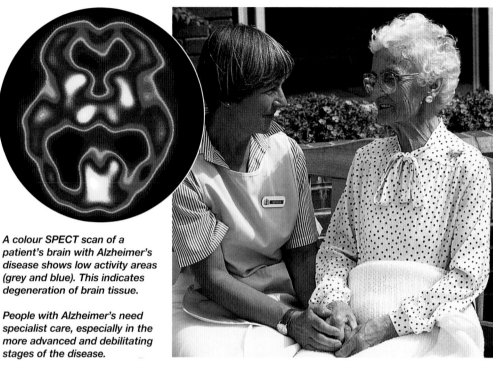

A colour SPECT scan of a patient's brain with Alzheimer's disease shows low activity areas (grey and blue). This indicates degeneration of brain tissue.

People with Alzheimer's need specialist care, especially in the more advanced and debilitating stages of the disease.

Causes

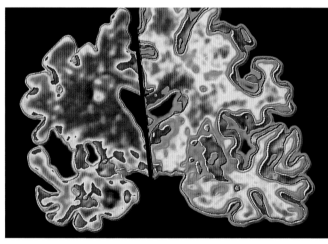

Many people have a genetic predisposition to Alzheimer's disease, but most are unlikely to develop the disease unless other factors come into play. Only 15 per cent of people with Alzheimer's disease have a family history of the condition, so the disease is not usually directly inherited.

CHROMOSOME MUTATIONS
The first gene to be linked to Alzheimer's disease was found on chromosome 21. This chromosome is abnormal in people with Down's syndrome who, as a group, are at high risk of developing Alzheimer's disease. Genes increasing the

A computer-enhanced image contrasts the brain of an Alzheimer's patient (left) with a normal brain (right). The Alzheimer's brain has lost volume due to cell death.

risk for developing Alzheimer's disease have been identified on other chromosomes. The mutation of a single gene causes about five per cent of cases of Alzheimer's disease and three genes have been identified that, if mutated, can cause severe disease under the age of 65.

Attempts are being made to identify the factors that lead to Alzheimer's disease in genetically predisposed people.

Diagnosis

There is no single diagnostic test for Alzheimer's disease, and the diagnosis is usually made by eliminating other potential causes of dementia. Tests include blood and urine checks, electrocardiography and electro-encephalography. Scans may provide a clue to the diagnosis by showing cerebral atrophy (shrinking of the brain). Mental status tests may be important.

A definite diagnosis can only be made by examining brain tissue at post-mortem. Brain cells are destroyed by a build-up of disordered protein

A CT scan may help confirm a diagnosis of Alzheimer's disease. Changes in brain structure may be visible.

strands (neurofibrillary tangles), particularly in the areas of the brain that deal with memory. Clusters of degenerating nerve cells containing a protein core (amyloid plaques) are also characteristic.

A striking change is the loss of acetylcholine, a chemical neurotransmitter in the brain. Patients with the most severe dementia have the lowest levels of acetylcholine.

This coloured CT scan shows the atrophy of the brain that occurs in Alzheimer's disease. The arrows highlight areas of reduced brain volume.

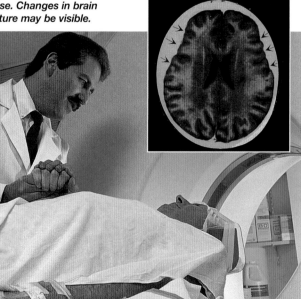

Treatment

No currently available drug can reverse memory loss that has already occurred, and patients often need an immense amount of supportive care as their mental and physical state declines. With severe dementia, drugs may be needed to control anxiety, restlessness, paranoia and hallucinations.

DRUG THERAPIES
Two drugs, donepezil (Aricept) and rivastigmine (Exelon) are now available in the UK. These drugs can slow the rate of deterioration in some patients, but not all, and they do have side effects. They act by increasing the level of acetylcholine in the brain.

Drugs that mimic the action of acetylcholine stimulate the regrowth of nerves, or inhibit the formation of amyloid or neurofibrillary tangles may become available. Trials are under way to see whether vitamin E or selegiline, a drug used in Parkinson's disease, or anti-inflammatory drugs have a place in Alzheimer's treatment.

This coloured TEM shows beta protein filaments, which occur in Alzheimer's brain tissue. Senile plaques are produced that consist of tangled masses of filaments, as shown here.

The mini-mental stated examination (MMSE) is used by doctors to assess a person's memory and to judge levels of cognitive impairment.

Prognosis and prevention

Currently, there is no cure for Alzheimer's disease. Affected people inevitably deteriorate with time, but the rate of decline is variable.

There is no known way of preventing the disease, but a healthy lifestyle, education and a stimulating environment may help. Trials are underway to see whether supplementing the diet with folic acid and vitamin B_{12}, or taking low-dose aspirin or cholesterol-lowering drugs reduces the risk of being affected.

Specialists are looking at the possibility of transplanting nerve cells into the brain to help restore normal function in people with Alzheimer's disease.

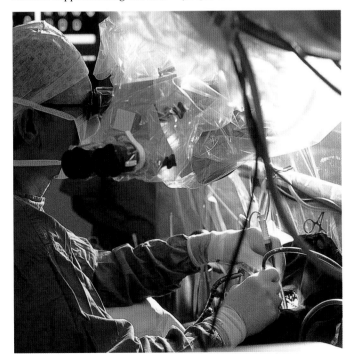

Incidence

Alzheimer's disease was first described in 1906 by Alois Alzheimer, a German psychiatrist and pathologist. He reported, following pathological examination, that the brain of a 56-year-old woman who had died after suffering from progressive dementia for many years contained neurofibrillary tangles and amyloid plaques in the cerebral cortex – the area of the brain responsible for memory and reasoning. Alzheimer deduced that these changes were the cause of her illness.

Dementia currently affects about 36 million people worldwide, and this number may double by the year 2025 if the expected increase in the world's population of people over 65 takes place. In the UK, about 850,000 people suffer from dementia and about 60–70 per cent of these people have Alzheimer's disease.

Alzheimer's disease affects 5–10 per cent of people aged 65–74 and 20–50 per cent of those aged 75 and over. Men and women are equally likely to be affected.

The financial cost of caring for these patients is immense and the disease also has a physical and emotional toll on carers.

Although much research into the treatment of Alzheimer's disease is being done, as yet, the deterioration of the cerebral cortex (a section of which is shown here) is irreversible.

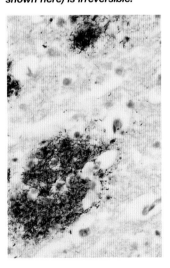

Diagnosing Alzheimer's

Alzheimer's disease is gradual in progression and is initially difficult to differentiate from the normal effects of ageing. Memory loss is the predominant symptom, and this is often the first complaint.

Older people often suffer from benign senile forgetfulness, which 'takes the edge off' their memory. This condition is probably not associated with the later onset of AD, although medical opinion is still divided on this.

Memory loss is always associated with AD and is often, but not always, an early symptom. In the early stages of the disease, the sufferer is aware that memory and thinking processes are being eroded and that they are being slowly 'robbed' of their mental powers. This can cause anxiety and depression, which can make the diagnosis even more difficult.

This diagnostic complexity often slows the process whereby doctors confirm their own suspicions and inform the patient and their family or carer.

DIAGNOSTIC FACTORS

Diagnosis depends upon the identification of the following factors:
■ The presence of two or more deficits in cognition –

the mental process by which knowledge is attained and maintained, including perception, reasoning and intuition
■ Progressive loss of memory
■ Absence of any other medical disorder
■ Onset after at least 40, and usually 60, years of age
■ Decline in thinking function and intellectual capacity.

A firm diagnosis is made by excluding other conditions with similar symptoms. Early investigation has not been common in the past; however, the advent of new memory-enhancing drugs is changing attitudes towards making early diagnosis of this disease.

With AD, about one diagnosis in 10 is incorrect; in such cases, another condition is found to be the cause of the symptoms.

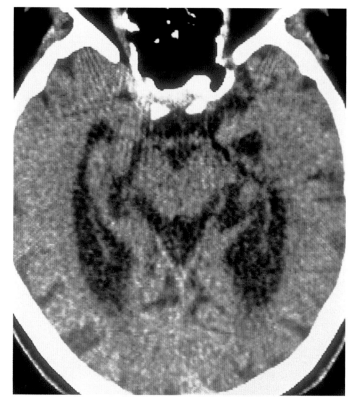

This CT scan of the brain of an Alzheimer's patient reveals enlarged ventricles (central dark areas). This indicates shrinking of the brain tissue.

Investigating AD

A doctor will organize a psychological, functional and social appraisal of the patient, including a variety of memory tests.

Investigations such as MR scanning (right) may be helpful in confirming a diagnosis. This enables damaged areas to be seen.

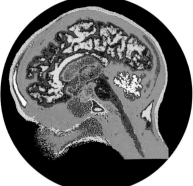

Differential diagnoses that can mimic dementia in the elderly include the following:
■ Depression
■ Acute confusion (due to infection or medication)
■ Thyroid over- and underactivity
■ Brain tumour
■ Vitamin B_{12} deficiency.
These conditions can be treated

and once resolved, symptoms of dementia may disappear.

To identify true dementia and exclude other conditions, the GP should arrange for some simple investigations and procedures:
■ Blood tests
■ Memory tests
■ Depression tests
■ X-ray to exclude tumour
■ CT scan or MR scan if memory

enhancement medication is being considered. Management of a dementia patient should involve the extended primary care team and the social and community psychiatric nurse. They are usually delegated the task of checking for ability with functions of everyday living and social support using standardized assessment scales.

Diagnosis of Alzheimer's disease relies on being able to exclude other causes of dementia and brain damage. Magnetic resonance scanning is therefore a useful investigation.

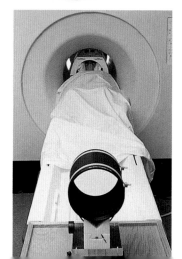

Managing Alzheimer's disease

Managing Alzheimer's disease has concentrated on alleviating symptoms associated with dementia and providing quality care for those patients incapacitated by the disease. Some drugs are helpful but much treatment involves non-drug based therapies.

No current drug treatment can stop or slow the progression of Alzheimer's disease. Some drugs may, however, alleviate certain symptoms.

'MEMORY ENHANCERS'
One or two drugs – for example Exelon and Donepezil, which are acetylcholinesterase inhibitors – are now available on restricted NHS release. These drugs stop the neurotransmitter acetylcholine being destroyed in the brain and have been called memory enhancers. They appear to improve memory in the short-term for some patients who are in the earliest stages of AD.

OTHER PROBLEMS
Behavioural problems may occur in AD, and these include:
■ Aggression and shouting
■ Wandering
■ Sleep disturbance.
   Antisocial responses can be treated with sedatives and antipsychotic medications. However, these drugs can cause the dementia and the behaviour to worsen and should be used in small doses in cases of very disturbed behaviour and subjected to frequent review.

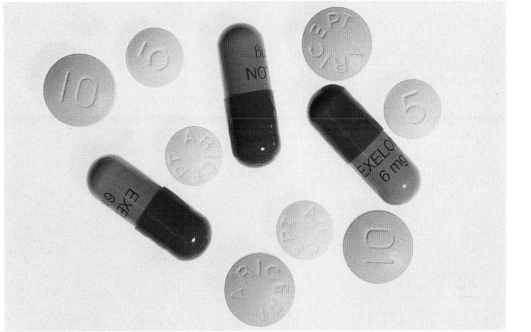

Antidepressants can be effective in improving the depression that some people with dementia also suffer. Treatment of depression will often improve other unpleasant symptoms of dementia and may encourage better sleep patterns.

Drug treatment should be used to treat the illnesses of old age that people with dementia suffer just as others in their age group. Treatment of pain, inflammation and infection may improve behavioural problems caused by the dementia.

No medications have yet been developed that can slow or halt the progression of Alzheimer's disease. However, some drugs may help to alleviate symptoms associated with dementia, such as antidepressants and acetylcholinesterase inhibitors.

Non-drug treatments for AD

In the absence of appropriate curative therapy, non-drug interventions should be considered by the care team. These are often instituted by nurses and occupational therapists, but can also be carried out by the family carer.
   These psychosocial or behavioural treatment strategies may involve:

■ Reality orientation – a technique that encourages verbal orientation and functioning and seeks to improve cognition
■ Reminiscence therapy – encourages patients to recall events from their past
■ Validation therapy – an empathetic approach that affirms the patient's personal reality.

Treatment plans for managing Alzheimer's disease should involve all members of the care team. This includes nurses and family carers.

PLANNING TREATMENT
Therapy will help some but not all patients, and may also be beneficial only at certain stages in the progression of dementia.
   Irrespective of the treatment models adopted, every person with dementia should have a healthcare management plan developed by the primary care team involved. This should be agreed with the family carer –

It is important to provide the highest quality care for patients with AD. Care plans need to be adapted for patients at regular intervals as AD progresses.

usually a spouse who will be caring at home.
   A patient with AD requires highly organized support services to maintain them in the community and ensure that they have good healthcare and the best quality of life that a devastating terminal illness such as AD will allow.

Non-Alzheimer's dementias

Disease of the blood vessels of the brain is a major cause of dementia in the elderly. The symptoms are similar to those of Alzheimer's disease, but the treatment and management plans differ.

Over 70 different causes of dementia have been recognized. Alzheimer's disease is responsible for about half to two thirds of all cases of dementia, with the majority of the rest caused by blood circulation-related problems. These are called the vascular dementias and can be preventable, as high blood pressure is often related to the condition.

Several types of vascular changes are involved, resulting in variations in the presenting symptoms of the dementia. It is now recognized that some people will have both Alzheimer's disease and vascular disease affecting the brain.

PATHOLOGY
Vascular dementia has been divided into three categories:
- Acute onset
- Multi-infarct
- Subcortical.

The changes in the brain can be due to:
- Multiple infarcts – death of brain tissue caused by an obstruction to blood flow
- White matter ischaemia – when the white matter of the brain is starved of sufficient oxygen and nutrition

- Strategically placed infarcts – their position crucially affects brain function

CAUSES
Vascular dementia is related to the cause of the underlying circulatory problem, often atherosclerosis (hardening and thickening of the arteries). Restrictions of blood flow may result in high blood pressure.

When the condition affects the vessels of the brain, it is known as cerebrovascular thrombosis or ischaemia. Brain function can be affected by alteration of blood flow in or to brain arteries.

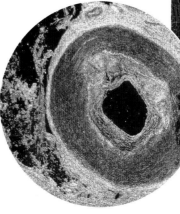

Vascular diseases such as atherosclerosis are associated with dementias. Narrowing of an artery may also cause high blood pressure.

Alzheimer's disease is not the only cause of dementia in the elderly. Vascular disease is a common cause and can be prevented in some cases.

Patterns of cerebrovascular disease

Patterns of cerebrovascular disease that can result in dementia include:
- Ischaemic cerebrovascular disease – a diffuse small vessel disease affecting the brain matter below the outer cortex. It is common in people with high blood pressure. There is a varying degree of brain cell death with loss of white matter of the brain. The person has difficulty walking and a progressive dementia. This is sometimes called Binswanger's encephalopathy.

- Multiple brain cortex infarcts (death of outer tissue of the brain due to obstructed blood supply) – a major cause of dementia. This often occurs due to blood clots in the heart passing into the large blood vessels that supply the brain's circulation.

Multiple small infarcts are typically due to high blood pressure related to small vessel disease. Clinicians categorize vascular dementia into two groups: multi-infarct dementia and Lewy body dementia.

Blood pressure must be monitored in the elderly, as high blood pressure can damage small blood vessels in the brain, causing death of brain tissue.

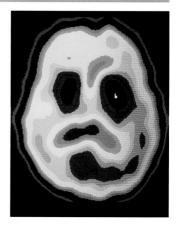

The symptoms of dementia occur due to the loss of brain cells. This PET scan shows areas of atrophy in the cerebrum as darker patches.

Multi-infarct dementia

Multi-infarct dementia describes many, often tiny infarcts in the cerebral cortex and the deeper areas of the brain. These cause brain damage that is patchy although extensive, and the total of all the tiny sites of damage correlates with the degree of intellectual impairment.

CLINICAL FINDINGS
People with the condition usually have generalized atherosclerosis throughout the body, but it is not the narrowing of vessels with reduced blood flow that damages the brain's nerve cells. In the cerebral cortex and deeper areas of the brain, many tiny areas of damage (infarcts) occur due to obstruction of the local blood supply by blockages such as thrombi (blood clots), otherwise termed strokes. The combination of many of these small strokes produces the dementia, as more and more brain areas lose their function in an irregular progression in symptoms.

Extensive areas of the brain will continue to work normally and the cause of death with this form of dementia is often a feature of generalized atherosclerosis, such as coronary artery thrombosis (a clot blocking blood flow to the heart).

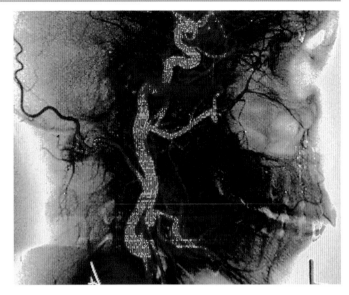

An angiogram will determine if there are any blockages or narrowing of the blood vessels. The carotid artery is seen as the large orange vessel in the neck.

Lewy body dementia

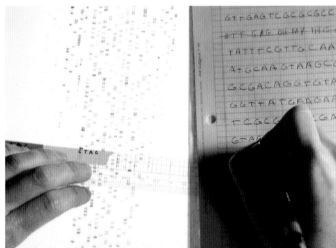

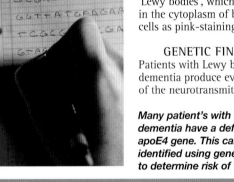

Diffuse Lewy body dementia has recently been recognized as a separate condition. The patients have senile plaques (lesions associated with brain cell loss) in their cerebral cortex, and 'Lewy bodies', which are seen in the cytoplasm of brain nerve cells as pink-staining structures.

GENETIC FINDINGS
Patients with Lewy body dementia produce even less of the neurotransmitter

Many patient's with Lewy body dementia have a defective apoE4 gene. This can be identified using genetic testing to determine risk of the disease.

acetylcholine than those with Alzheimer's disease.

Genetically, the gene apoE4 is over-represented in people with Lewy body dementia, and is associated with Parkinson's disease.

TREATMENT
It is important for doctors to differentiate the diagnosis of Alzheimer's disease from vascular disease and multi-infarct dementia from Lewy body dementia where possible, as drug management varies for the conditions. At present, there is no cure or preventative therapy for Alzheimer's disease or vascular dementias.

Symptoms of dementia

As a patient's dementia progresses, they will require more support in their daily lives from carers. Eventually, this care may need to be given on a 24-hour basis.

The clinical features of dementia relate to the progressive damage to the brain that occurs as the condition progresses. The symptoms do not differ from those of Alzheimer's disease, although the loss is often gradual with Alzheimer's disease and a step-by-step progression with vascular dementia. Deficits occur in:
- Information processing
- Memory
- Expression of speech
- Mobility and coordination
- Continence

Behavioural changes
There is disturbance in thinking, emotion and behaviour, and disinhibition means normal social constraints are lost. An affected person's behaviour may be distressing for family and carers, in particular when faced with:
- Repetitive actions or questions
- Restlessness and wandering
- Anxiety and shouting
- Lack of inhibition
- Suspicion and sometimes, aggression

Early symptoms of dementia may be noticeable as changes in personality and behaviour. Some patients may become socially withdrawn.

Diagnosing vascular dementia

The first signs of vascular dementia may be a change in a person's behaviour, loss of memory or decline in intellectual function. It is important that other causes of these symptoms are ruled out.

Vascular dementias may become apparent earlier than Alzheimer's disease, with an onset from age 55. There is often marked variation in the presentation of symptoms and fluctuation in the thinking process initially and over time. There may be a plateau when there is little change in symptoms and then a sudden worsening, followed by a period of stability before further deterioration.

COURSE OF THE DISEASE

The disease course relates to the occurrence of the brain infarcts. It can be abrupt, with an initial fall at the onset with intermittent confusion, speech difficulties and transient ischaemic attacks. Then there may be a step-by-step deterioration in brain function, skills and personality.

Ultimately there will be:
■ Deficits in cognition, the mental process by which knowledge is acquired, including perception, reasoning and intuition
■ Progressive memory loss
■ An inevitable decline in intellectual capacity.

Often there is high blood pressure and there may be evidence of vascular disease.

A doctor will conduct an overview of the person's physical, medical and psychological status. Drugs which may cause dementia-like symptoms will be noted.

Tests can be used to determine the loss of cognitive functions and intellectual abilities. This is helpful in the diagnosis of all types of dementia.

Investigations

Blood testing can rule out many other causes of dementia-like symptoms. These may include thyroid disorders, anaemia and diabetes.

Initial investigation is directed towards exclusion of other causes of dementia and conditions that can mimic dementia. Depression, vitamin deficiency, thyroid disorder, tumour, infection, repetitive head injury and confusional states have all to be considered and discarded or treated.

DIAGNOSTIC TESTS

Routine tests should include:
■ A memory test – the abbreviated mental test or the mini-mental state examination

Imaging techniques such as MR imaging are useful in assessing areas of brain damage. This MR scan shows a region of the brain affected by a stroke (red).

assessment tests are often used in primary care health checks
■ Blood tests for anaemia, thyroid function, glucose levels
■ Blood pressure monitoring
■ Liver function tests
■ Imaging techniques – X-rays

are required to exclude a tumour; if blockage of the carotid arteries is suspected, ultrasonography of the vessels will be indicated. CT and MRI brain scans are used to differentiate between Alzheimer's disease and vascular dementias.

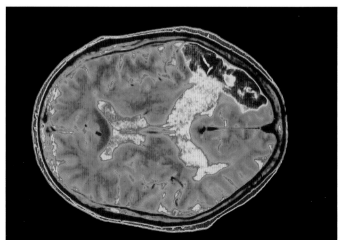

Managing dementia

As yet, there are no drugs that can halt or cure dementia. Management aims to slow the progression of the disease and improve quality of life.

Good management of people with vascular dementia depends upon effective liaison between members of the primary care team. Continuing care is dependent upon the GP, community and practice nurses, health visitor, community psychiatric nurse, community social worker, occupational therapist, dietitian and the support of secondary health care facilities, such as respite care.

GOALS OF CARE
All or a few specialists may be involved at any given time. Effort is directed at maintaining the patient in their own home for as long as possible and helping them to use their remaining skills and competence to best advantage.

As vascular dementia progresses, physical functions such as balance and movement may be affected. These patients will need help with mobility.

Community nursing and care in the home is necessary for patients who have lost the ability to carry out daily living tasks, such as preparing meals.

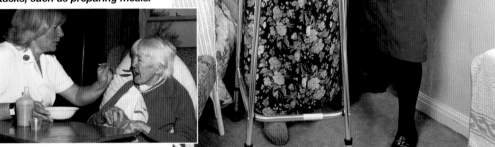

Drug therapies

Drugs can be taken to control or lower blood pressure; this may slow progression of the disease. Lipid-lowering agents – which reduce levels of lipids in the blood – may also be worthwhile in the early stages of decline. These are of particular value in people who have already had transient ischaemic attacks.

Antiplatelet drugs – for example, aspirin – which prevent blood clots may reduce the incidence of small strokes affecting the brain. Patients with narrowing of the carotid artery may benefit from surgery.

Some patients who are able to live at home may still need community nurses to supervise them while taking drugs. This prevents accidental overdose.

ASSOCIATED PROBLEMS
People with dementia often suffer from depression; antidepressant drugs may lift the depression and help some of the behavioural problems that occur with dementia.

Neuroleptic drugs, such as thioridazine and haloperidol, are often used to treat the behavioural disturbance associated with dementia, but their side effects can be serious and are a cause of agitation in people with dementia. When used, the dose should be small and under constant review. This type of drug should not be used in patients who have Lewy body dementia, as these people are very sensitive to them and can become seriously ill from side effects.

Aspirin is used in low doses in patients who have had, or are at risk of having, blood clots. Aspirin is an anticlotting agent and so inhibits coagulation.

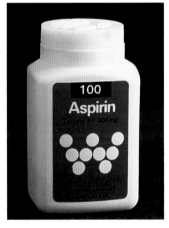

Non-drug treatments

Non-drug treatments are often used in patients who react badly to drug therapy. Treatments include:
- Reminiscence work
- Reality orientation
- Music therapy.

Their value has been poorly researched but they can be carried out by family carers and appear to improve quality of life.

Carers can help with a number of non-drug therapies in the home. These are believed to provide a higher quality of life.

Promoting healthy lifestyles

Vascular dementia is theoretically preventable. National health-promotion campaigns targeting hypertension, coronary thrombosis and cardiovascular disease should mean fewer people in future will suffer from this debilitating disease.

Changes in lifestyle may diminish its incidence. A low-fat diet, non-smoking habits and daily exercise decrease the possible occurrence of vascular dementia.

Preventative measures, such as giving up smoking, may reduce the incidence of vascular dementia in the future.

Parkinson's disease

Symptoms and signs

Parkinson's disease is a degenerative brain disorder leading to a reduction of a nerutransmitter (chemical I the brain) known as dopamine. The condition can affect people of any age, but is usually diagnosed in those over the age of 50. A distinction is made between Parkinson's disease and 'parkinsonism', in which the same symptoms are produced by different causes, for example drugs. The three common signs of Parkinson's disease are a tremor (shake) often initially in the hands or arms, slowness of movement and stiff muscles (rigidity). These combined symptoms can lead to a stooping posture, 'shuffling' gait and a noticeable loss of arm swing on walking. An affected person can develop a a masklike expressionless face and may have difficulty in swallowing

and communication. Muscle aches and cramps are common, and fatigue is often present. A person's writing may become small, tremulous and untidy and this may be one of the first signs that friends or family notice.

As the disease progresses a person may need a walking stick, a frame and eventually a wheelchair. Although not everyone with Parkinson's disease loses their intellectual function, some will develop dementia. Depression often develops as a person's symptoms worsen and they lose independence. In the later stages, a person usually needs fulltime care and support.

The most common initial sign of Parkinson's disease is a coarse, rhythmic slow tremor of the hands. It diminishes during conscious movement.

Diagnosis

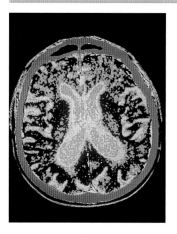

There are no clinical tests for Parkinson's disease so diagnosis is made entirely on the clinical picture, which is usually characteristic. Careful history and examination are required to exclude causes of parkinsonism. These include:

■ Drugs – phenothiazines, reserpine, methyldopa

This coloured CT scan is from a Parkinson's patient. Loss of density in the brain tissue has caused the ventricles (blue) to increase in size.

■ Infections – following brain swelling (encephalitis)
■ Toxins – including carbon monoxide and manganese
■ Hypothyroidism
■ Vascular – cerebrovascular disease
■ Trauma to the head – particularly in boxers
■ In combination with other conditions, for example Alzheimer's disease or Huntington's chorea, CT and MR scans and biochemical tests may be necessary to exclude other causes of the symptoms.

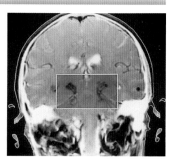

The boxed area in this MR scan is the basal ganglia of the brain. This area contains dopamine-producing cells, which are lacking in Parkinson's disease.

Causes and prognosis

The main cause of symptoms is damage to, and death of, cells in a particular area of the brain leading to loss of a chemical called dopamine. Dopamine is a 'neurotransmitter' and plays an important role in co-ordinating the body's movement. It is unclear why the brain cells die: there is some suggestion that the condition may run in families but this is uncommon. Researchers are also considering environmental causes, such as pesticides, but there is no strong evidence for this.

Parkinson's disease tends to be progressive and people with the condition gradually become more restricted. However, the rate of progression varies a

great deal between individuals and many people with Parkinson's disease remain reasonably active.

Since the introduction of L-dopa therapy, life expectancy in people with Parkinson's disease has increased. Studies have shown that with present day treatment, a person is likely to live as long as an unaffected person of the same age.

A person with Parkinson's disease undergoes a medical examination. The doctor is assessing the flexibility of the hands; rigidity of the muscles in the limbs is a common symptom of Parkinson's.

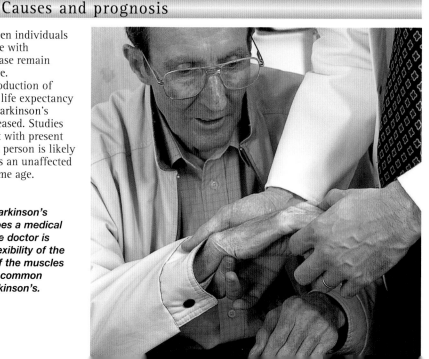

Treatment

DRUG TREATMENT

The mainstay of treatment is medication but treatment usually starts only when the symptoms become severe enough to interfere with the activities of daily living. There are a number of drugs used to treat the condition. As research into Parkinson's disease continues medication changes as the effects are observed over time.

There are three main groups of drugs used to treat Parkinson's disease. These are:

■ Levodopa is the most important drug in treating Parkinson's disease and is prescribed for all individuals with symptoms. Levodopa is a drug that is converted into dopamine once it is inside the body; the dose of levodopa is gradually increased until symptoms start to improve.

■ Dopamine agonists act in a similar way to dopamine but have a milder effect so are usually better in the early stages of the disease when symptoms are not severe. Apomorphone is a dopamine agonist given by subcutaneous injection that is given to particular people who experience 'on-off syndrome'. This term is used to describe episodes of suddenly worsening symptoms.

■ MAO-B inhibitors, such as selegiline, act on the brain chemical that destroys dopamine and prevent it working.

Dopa
The chemical that begins the pathway (the substrate); L-dopa boosts the level of substrate

Dopamine
Dopa is converted into neurotransmitter dopamine; facilitates communication between cells

Dopamine re-uptake
Dopamine binds to dopamine receptors and is then recovered; amantadine blocks re-uptake

Dopamine receptor
Binding of dopamine to the receptor results in signal transmission along the adjoining cell; induced by dopamine agonists (pergolide, apomorphine)

Breakdown of signal
An enzyme called monoamine oxidase breaks down the nerve signal; inhibited by the drug selegiline

Nerve cell
The synaptic bulb at the end of the nerve cell releases neurotransmitter into the synapse

Synapse
Physical gap between two nerve cells

Nerve cell
Neurotransmitter binds to specific receptors

Parkinson's disease affects groups of nerve cells involved in movement, where the neurotransmitter dopamine facilitates signals across nerve junctions (synapses). Various drugs can partially restore this system.

Other treatment

Supportive treatment
Occupational therapists and physiotherapists are important in helping to maintain independence in everyday activities for as long as possible.

In the later stages of the disease, when mobility is limited, family support and day care are very important.

Symptomatic treatment
Treatment may be required for constipation, depression or musculo-skeletal pain.

Surgery to the thalamus of the brain was popular in the 1950s and 1960s. Surgery is now considered only for patients resistant to drug therapy and whose tremor is severe.

Incidence and prevention

Parkinson's disease affects about 6 million people worldwide. After the age of 50, the prevalence is about 1 in 500. It is slightly more common in men than in women and does not seem to run in families. Interestingly, patients with Parkinson's disease are less likely to die from lung cancer than the rest of the population.

As the cause of Parkinson's disease is currently unknown, prevention is not possible. The use of embryonic brain cell implants has been mentioned, but their use raises serious ethical issues, as their source would be aborted fetuses.

Parkinsonism occurring following the administration of antipsychotic drugs will usually resolve following cessation of the drug treatment.

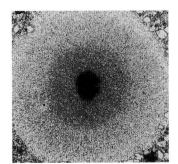

A sufferer of Parkinson's disease is helped to walk by a nurse. The shuffling, unbalanced walk and slow trembling are typical of the disease. This false-colour electron micrograph shows a structure found in brain cells called a Lewy body. This is a pathological feature of Parkinson's disease.

Stroke

A stroke is a disturbance in brain function due to either a blockage in a blood vessel supplying the brain or a haemorrhage. It is a major cause of disability and death among elderly people.

A stroke is a sudden, acute disturbance in brain function that can develop over a period of minutes or hours, and which lasts for more than 24 hours. It is a serious consequence of cerebrovascular disorders (disorders of the blood vessels of the brain and meninges), and is the third most common cause of death in the UK after heart disease and cancer.

WHO IS AFFECTED?
Stroke is the single greatest cause of physical disability, with an incidence of 5 per 1,000 of the general population, and a higher incidence in elderly people. About half of those affected die, often within 24 hours of the event. A third are left with some functional disability and the remainder make a good recovery.

Doctors often refer to a stroke as a 'cerebrovascular accident' (CVA), the term indicating a problem affecting the blood vessels running from the heart to the brain.

Cerebrovascular events that last less than 24 hours are known as transient ischaemic attacks (TIAs); they are not usually associated with any obvious structural damage or lasting disability.

WHAT CAUSES A STROKE?
In older people, a stroke is the result of an interruption of the blood supply to the brain, or of a ruptured blood vessel bleeding deep within the brain.

An obstruction to the brain's blood supply (ischaemia) deprives nerve cells of vital oxygen and nutrition. Brain cell and nerve pathway damage occur, disturbing brain function and central control over the peripheral nerves and muscles.

In elderly people, stroke is often associated with high blood pressure and atherosclerosis. Blood from ruptured vessels (haemorrhage) within the cranium compresses brain tissue, with effects that can include paralysis and speech loss.

Risk factors

The likelihood of suffering from a stroke increases with advancing age. Other factors can also predispose to a stroke, such as:
- Previous TIA
- Previous stroke
- High blood pressure
- Heart failure
- Recent coronary thrombosis
- Atrial fibrillation (abnormal heart rhythm)
- Diabetes
- Family history of stroke
- High alcohol intake
- Smoking.

Blood supply to the brain

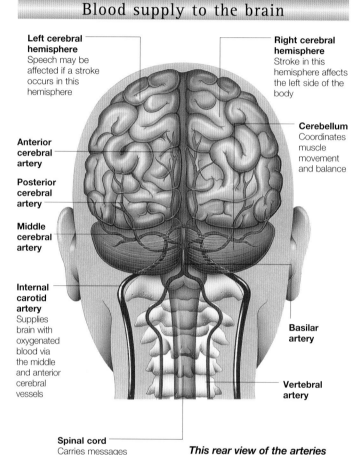

Left cerebral hemisphere
Speech may be affected if a stroke occurs in this hemisphere

Right cerebral hemisphere
Stroke in this hemisphere affects the left side of the body

Anterior cerebral artery

Posterior cerebral artery

Middle cerebral artery

Internal carotid artery
Supplies brain with oxygenated blood via the middle and anterior cerebral vessels

Cerebellum
Coordinates muscle movement and balance

Basilar artery

Vertebral artery

Spinal cord
Carries messages to and from the brain and body

This rear view of the arteries of the head shows the major arteries supplying the brain. A blockage of any of these major vessels can result in stroke.

Disruption of the brain's blood supply

The left and right carotid arteries are the main arteries to the cerebral hemispheres. About 20 per cent of blood output from the heart goes to the brain.

The brainstem and cerebellum (the parts of the brain that govern movement) are supplied by the vertebral arteries, which fuse to become the basilar artery.

80 per cent of vascular events in the skull are due to cerebral infarction and 20 per cent are due to bleeding. Cerebral infarction occurs when the brain is damaged due to a lack of blood, such as when a vessel becomes blocked. If the blood supply is not restored quickly, that part of the brain will die.

Blood vessel blockage may be due to thrombus or embolus. A thrombus (blood clot) may be formed by atherosclerosis (hardening and thickening of arteries with fatty deposits), which narrows and obstructs the vessel, starving the brain of blood, oxygen and nourishment. An embolus may be a tiny piece of clot that breaks away from an atherosclerotic neck artery, or even from the heart itself.

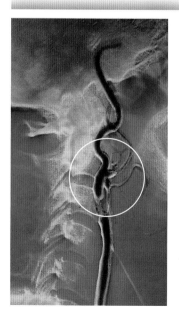

A false-colour angiogram reveals an obstruction (circled) in the carotid artery. This may be caused by atherosclerosis, a build-up of plaque in the vessels.

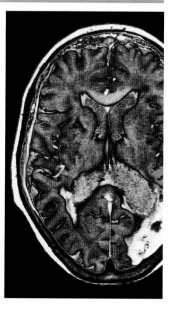

This false-colour MR scan shows a haemorrhage in the left hemisphere of the brain (the white area on the right of this image). Affected tissue often dies.

Symptoms and stroke diagnosis

The symptoms of a stroke directly reflect the area of the brain affected; a stroke in one cerebral hemisphere will show symptoms in the opposite side of the body. The clinical diagnosis of a stroke may be confirmed by examination and scanning.

The symptoms of a stroke are determined by the site of the brain infarct (tissue death) or the bleeding artery. Strokes that affect one of the two halves of the brain (the cerebral hemispheres) are five times more common than those affecting the brainstem.

SITE OF DAMAGE

Different parts of the body are affected, depending on the areas of damaged brain. If the front of the brain is affected, there may be personality changes and mood disturbance with poor emotional control, such as laughing or crying at inappropriate moments. The speech centre may be affected if there is damage in the left cerebral hemisphere.

PARALYSIS AND SENSATION

When the motor areas of the hemispheres (areas responsible for voluntary muscle movement) are damaged, the control of limb movements on the opposite side to the damage will be affected. This results in loss of power or paralysis of the arm, leg or both – this is known as hemiparesis or hemiplegia.

If the brain area responsible for governing sensation is disturbed, there may be interference with sensation of pain, touch and joint position. The latter causes imbalance, leading to falls.

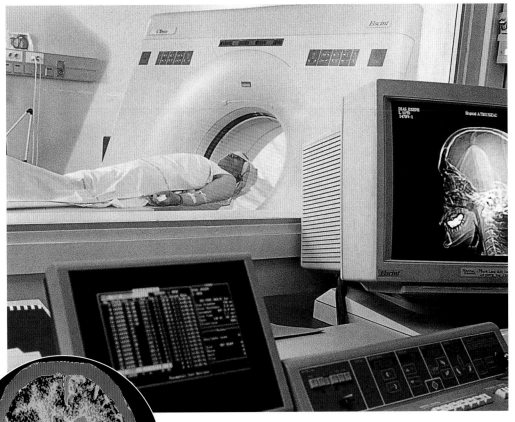

This false-colour CT scan shows an area of brain (yellow) affected by ischaemia or reduced blood flow. If left untreated, the brain tissue will eventually die.

CT scanning is an important tool in diagnosing stroke and determining the extent of brain damage. The images are seen as 'slices' through the head.

Diagnosis

A stroke is usually diagnosed from the signs and symptoms present, especially if the person has a pre-existing disease associated with risk of stroke. Such diseases include diabetes, hypertension (high blood pressure) and atherosclerosis. The condition can also be diagnosed if the person is known to have a source of emboli – in the heart, for example.

DIAGNOSTIC AIDS

To exclude the possibility of a rapidly growing tumour being the cause of symptoms, a skull X-ray may be required. To determine whether the cause is a haemorrhage or an infarct, CT scanning is a useful technique.

A further neurological examination of the motor and sensory systems and the eyes, and assessment of the mental state and physical function usually confirm the diagnosis.

Guidelines for good medical practice recommend that all stroke patients have blood investigations, blood pressure checks, an ECG (electrocardiogram to measure the electrical activity of the heart) or CT or MR scanning.

Echocardiography (ultrasound of the heart) may be undertaken when there is a suspected heart cause of emboli, such as after recent coronary thrombosis or where there is atrial fibrillation or known heart valve disease.

Onset of stroke

The onset of a stroke has several characteristics:
■ Cerebral infarction may take one or two hours to develop; embolic occurrences are often abrupt in onset. Intracerebral bleeding may occur suddenly, with headache, vomiting and impaired or lost consciousness.
■ There may be an associated paralysis with loss of muscle power on one side of the body. Disturbance in vision and impairment in speech, with slurring of words or even loss of speech can also occur. Urinary incontinence is common.
■ Reduced mental alertness and lost muscle power or limb

paralysis can vary in the first few days after a stroke, or worsen due to swelling of brain tissue and, in some cases, the extension of the infarct.
■ If death does not occur, there is usually an improvement in function over days and weeks as the swelling in the brain subsides.

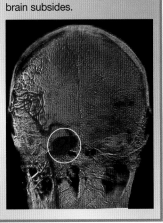

An aneurysm can be seen as a bulge (circled) in the carotid artery. If it ruptures, blood will haemorrhage into the surrounding brain tissue, causing a stroke.

Treatment after a stroke

Treatment for stroke victims is based on rehabilitation to regain mobility and a level of independence in everyday tasks. For severely disabled patients, treatment aims to manage the symptoms.

The faster a stroke is suspected and the person is taken to a specialist stroke unit or hospital, the better the chance of recovery. In these cases, immediate treatment with potentially life saving drugs, such as anticoagulants, can be administered promptly.

The majority of patients are admitted to hospital after a stroke and need the services of a multidisciplinary team. Many people also need help from a community rehabilitation team after discharge.

A person with previously good health suffering their first stroke has a good potential for survival and rehabilitation. However, no treatment can reverse or reduce local brain tissue damage.

DRUG TREATMENTS
Drug treatment depends on the cause of the stroke. In the case of a thrombus (clot), anticoagulants are used to prevent further clots and in some cases to 'dissolve' the existing thrombus. If high

Physiotherapy to strengthen the muscles and improve coordination is a vital part of rehabilitation. Many ordinary tasks need to be relearned.

blood pressure is the cause, then hypotensive drugs are used for control. The possibility of a further stroke can be reduced by long-term anticoagulant drugs including aspirin, which thins the blood.

MANAGEMENT
The general management of stroke is aimed at maintaining the airway and breathing. Swallowing may be affected and a nasogastric tube may be passed into the stomach for feeding to avoid the inhalation of food and the development of pneumonia.

A physiotherapist works with an elderly stroke patient. Paralyzed limbs must be exercised 'passively' from the onset of the stroke to avoid later spasticity.

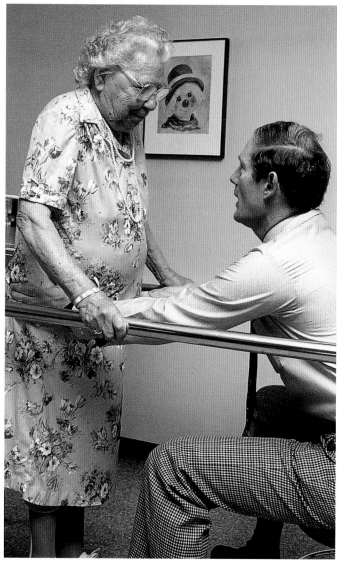

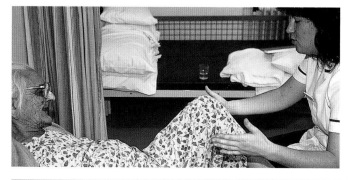

Rehabilitation

The objectives of rehabilitation are aimed at avoiding further physical and mental deterioration and achieving the best possible recovery of function for the activities of daily living. This involves a multi-professional team including physiotherapists, occupational therapists, speech therapists, prosthesis technicians and nurses.

Orthoses (surgical appliances, such as back splints and leg

Active exercises, where patients try to build strength and flexibility, are important in regaining independence.

braces) are often required to support unstable joints. Following a stroke, active interventions may be required over a period of six months. After this time, major improvement is unlikely.

Physiotherapy should begin soon after the stroke. The limbs are put through a full range of passive movements repeatedly each day. Of patients surviving the first two weeks after the stroke, two-thirds regain independence, despite some disability. The remainder will die in the next two months or become long-term disabled.

After a stroke, a patient may receive electrical stimulation of the affected muscles. This helps build up wasted muscles.

Prognosis

The prognosis immediately after a stroke is difficult to determine. Drugs can reduce the chance of another stroke, but functional recovery can be limited.

The presence of coma, complete hemiplegia (paralysis of one side of the body) and eye palsy suggest a poor prognosis for a stroke victim. Incontinence is also a poor prognostic feature and is associated with recurrent urinary tract infection. The onset of pneumonia can be a fatal complication.

PREDICTING RECOVERY
Neither the progression of symptoms nor the ultimate functional outcome of the stroke

An intracerebral haemorrhage caused by a major burst artery. Brain tissue has been pushed out of shape by the blood leaking from the vessel.

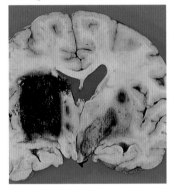

can be predicted in early post-stroke days. Recovery, and its extent, depends upon the site of the damage, the age of the person and the general state of their health.

Any functional disability existing after six months is likely to be permanent. About half of those affected with moderate or severe hemiplegia recover sufficiently to be able to walk and attend to basic activities of daily living. In general, the sooner an improvement in mobility occurs, the better the prognosis.

INCIDENCE
Mortality rates for stroke victims have been falling over the last 40 years, but the incidence remains the same, with more patients admitted to hospital as the number of elderly people in the population increases. In the absence of a cure for stroke and the damage that it causes, prevention is important.

Occupational therapy is another important treatment for patients recovering from a stroke. This patient is using an 'elevation board' to improve hand–eye coordination and grip.

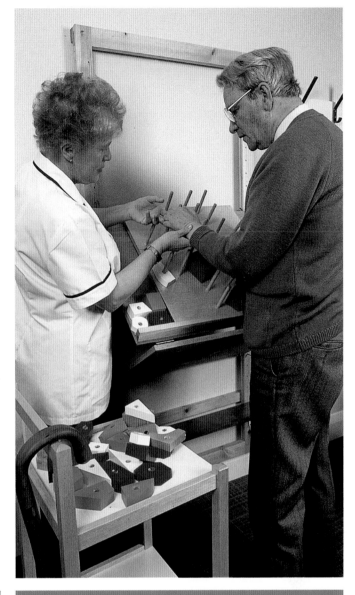

Preventing strokes

High blood pressure is the single most important risk factor for stroke in the elderly. Therefore, early treatment of high blood pressure, irrespective of age, is important, as is a reduction in smoking and alcohol habits. Reducing blood cholesterol and fats should also reduce the occurrence of stroke disease.

BLOOD PRESSURE
Comparative trials have shown a reduction of stroke by one third in people who have had high blood pressure significantly reduced. Blood pressure refers to the pressure of blood in a major artery and is read as two figures: systolic pressure is the first and highest figure, taken when the ventricles of the heart are contracting; diastolic is the lower figure, taken when the ventricles are relaxed. Blood pressure above normal (140mm Hg systolic and 90mm Hg diastolic) at whatever age should be treated to lower the risk of

stroke occurrence. Both fatal and non-fatal strokes are less likely to occur after blood pressure is lowered.

About a third of all people with transient ischaemic attacks (TIAs) suffer from a later stroke. TIAs should be investigated and any high blood pressure or carotid artery stenosis treated.

OTHER FACTORS
Heart irregularities increase the risk of stroke disease and irregular rhythms, such as atrial fibrillation (a type of heart arrhythmia with rapid, irregular beats), should be treated.

Environmental extremes can also affect the circulation, making the blood more viscous and the cells stickier. This means blood vessel blockage by means of a blood clot is more likely. For this reason, the elderly should avoid long exposure to direct summer sun and should use heating in living accommodation in the winter.

Complications

A stroke may have additional, longer-term effects, depending on the severity of the initial attack and the rate of recovery:

Neurological effects
- Brain swelling, leading to confusion
- Epilepsy
- Depression
- Mental impairment.

Other effects
- Heart irregularity
- Pneumonia
- Contractures of the joints
- Spasticity of the limbs
- Deep vein thrombosis
- Kidney failure
- Urinary incontinence
- Urinary infection
- Pressure sores due to extended bed rest.

Deep vein thrombosis is caused by a blood clot in the leg. Symptoms include swelling and pain.

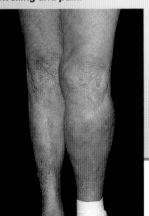

Pressure sores are a risk for any bedridden patient. Moving the patient regularly and good hygiene help to control sores.

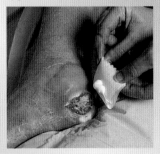

Cerebral palsy

Symptoms

Cerebral palsy (CP) is a leading cause of physical disability, and around one child in 400 is affected. It is defined as 'a disorder of posture and movement caused by a discrete non-progressive lesion of the developing motor pathways of the brain'. The main associated disabilities include:

■ Hypotonia – loss of normal muscle tone
■ Spasticity – limbs resistant to passive movement
■ Ataxia – shaky movements
■ Athetosis – involuntary movement.

Although the extent of the brain damage does not progress with time, the manifestations of CP develop as the brain matures.

Newborns may show a variety of symptoms, including:

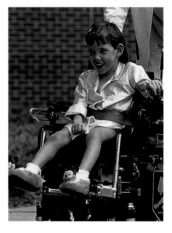

Children with CP may also have defective sight and hearing. The nature of CP means that the brain damage does not worsen.

■ Poor sucking ability
■ Abnormal muscle tone
■ Abnormal reflexes
■ Convulsions or drowsiness.
  CP may not be suspected for several months until motor development is abnormal or delayed. Signs of this include:
■ Normal head control not showing by three months
■ Unable to sit unsupported at 10 months
■ Baby stiff on handling
■ Persistence of primitive reflexes
■ Characteristic involuntary movements at one year
■ Ataxic CP children are hypotonic (have diminished muscle tone) and may later show intention tremor.
  The distribution of neurological involvement leads to the classification of the spasticity of CP: quadriplegia – all limbs involved; diplegia – arms or legs involved; hemiplegia – arm and leg on one side only involved; atonic or ataxic CP – depending on the area of the brain involved.

The main symptoms associated with CP are concerned with movement. The severity of the disability varies a great deal.

Other features

CP may be complicated by other neurological and mental problems. Intellectual impairment varies, so speech development is important in predicting a prognosis.

■ Visio-spatial and auditory perceptual disabilities can lead to learning difficulties. Speech and feeding difficulties affect up to 50 per cent of the patients, such as difficulty swallowing and dysarthria (speech disturbance).

■ Orthopaedic complications associated with CP can include contractions of muscles due to spasticity, leading to contractures within the joints. Discrepancies in growth can occur, with conditions such as pelvic tilt and curvature of the spine resulting. Convulsions affect 25–30 per cent of people with CP.

■ Behavioural and emotional problems can occur. Parental over-protection and community attitudes often prevent children with CP attaining their full physical potential.

Diagnosis

CP may be diagnosed at birth but this is frequently delayed, particularly in mildly affected children. In these cases, CP is generally recognized during the second year of life due to abnormalities in the child's gait (posture and walking).

As there are several different causes of CP, diagnosis may not be straightforward. If CP is suspected in the early weeks of life, monitoring developmental milestones at regular intervals may make diagnosis possible before two years of age. Careful attention to the mother's concerns often reveal the diagnosis at the earliest possible time.

This baby is displaying the abnormal muscle tone and posture that is a typical presentation of CP in newborns.

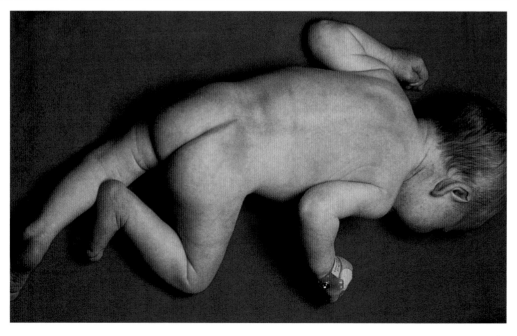

Causes

Prenatally, CP can be caused by cerebral malformations due to disturbances of brain development, intra-uterine vascular accidents (interrupted placental blood flow,

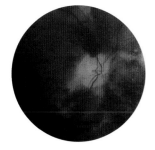

Infection with cytomegalovirus, shown here, has been identified as a possible cause of cerebral palsy in the antenatal period.

haemorrhage), trauma, infection – including inflammation of the brain, for example, due to toxoplasmosis, cytomegalovirus or hypoxia (lack of oxygen reaching the tissues).

Prematurity and low birth weight, prolonged labour, traumatic delivery, asphyxia and intra-uterine growth retardation are all important factors in spastic CP. Complications of jaundice in the newborn may also cause CP, although this has diminished in frequency because of improved postnatal care of neonates.

Another cause of CP is cerebral malformation. This may result from haemorrhaging (circled) within the brain before birth.

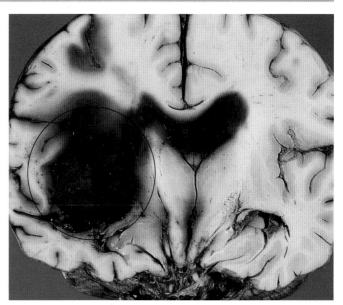

Treatment and management

Physicians, therapists and educators all play an important part in the multi-disciplinary team involved in the frequent assessment of people with CP and the structured treatment programmes designed for them.

Physiotherapy helps normal motor development and prevents contractures. Intellectual disability is managed by specially trained doctors and personnel. Visual impairment, squints, deafness and orthopaedic deformities are treated by specialists in each particular field, and epilepsy is controlled with

Using a special control, this boy can operate a computer. Such equipment can play an important role in the lives of people with CP.

appropriate medication.

Specialist schools and units for physically disabled people provide speech therapy, physiotherapy and hydrotherapy. Facilities for the children's physical needs are provided, including special furniture and mobility aids, physiotherapy equipment and hydrotherapy pools, together with provision for their educational needs.

More and more children are now being cared for in the community. As many children with CP as possible are encouraged to attend normal schools to help avoid the social stigma of physical handicap. Employment is also a special consideration, and support is available for people with CP when seeking employment.

Prognosis and Prevention

The degree of disability will determine the seriousness of the prognosis. Many children with less severe forms of CP lead normal lives. Remedial physiotherapy is helpful for

many children with CP and some will attend special units.

Speech disorders are common, as are behavioural disorders, mainly due to frustration. Contractures of the limbs may need future surgery to improve mobility as neglect of these deformities can lead to osteoarthritis. 60 per cent of people with CP will have some degree of intellectual handicap; 20 per cent are affected by visual impairment and hearing loss; and about 30 per cent will have epilepsy.

Specialist equipment is often needed to help with every day life. Children with cerebral palsy may need adapted pushchairs or wheelchairs to aid mobility.

Increased testing during pregnancy to diagnose congenital disorders and better obstetric care has reduced the incidence of CP caused by trauma. Early and adequate treatment of haemolytic diseases of the newborn – where the mother develops antibodies that destroy the baby's red blood cells – by exchange transfusion reduce the incidence of brain damage.

The early treatment of intra-cerebral infections with antibiotics also reduces the incidence of CP. Infections occurring in the first three months of pregnancy – for example, pertussis and rubella – are now preventable by immunization.

Difficulties associated with cerebral palsy

In addition to disorders of posture and movement, children with cerebral palsy often have learning difficulties. Although many benefit from mainstream schooling, special schools are available.

Many children with severe cerebral palsy have normal to above-average intelligence. However, learning difficulties are present in about 60 per cent of affected children.

LEARNING DIFFICULTIES
In particular, children with quadriparetic cerebral palsy often have moderate to severe learning difficulty. This reflects the degree of damage to an individual's brain.

In early childhood, the extent of individual learning difficulties may not be immediately apparent. It is only when a child begins to talk that significant delays in development of speech or communication become obvious

OTHER PROBLEMS
There are several other disorders that are associated with cerebral palsy, including:
■ Constipation
■ Epilepsy – found in 40 per cent of cases
■ Squints, visual impairment and hearing loss – these are all common, each occurring in about 20 per cent of cases
■ Problems with language development and speech – again the degree of impairment of these skills varies with the degree of overall disability
■ Behavioural disorders – these are common. Children with cerebral palsy are likely to suffer from frustration and, possibly, depression because of their day-to-day difficulties.

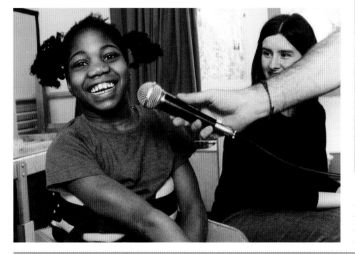

Many children with cerebral palsy have difficulties with language and speech. Music therapy can help to inspire confidence and improve communication skills.

Children with cerebral palsy often have learning difficulties. Education and play therapy are therefore a vital part of care for an affected child.

Education and intelligence

Education is a very important part of overall care for children with cerebral palsy. Some affected children are educated in a mainstream school and integrate well with other students.

SPECIAL SCHOOLING
Those children with cerebral palsy who have more severe learning difficulties and physical disability usually need special schooling in order to maximize their educational potential.

In these schools, affected children are cared for by a multidisciplinary team consisting of teachers, physiotherapists, educational psychologists and occupational therapists.

Using individualized teaching programmes, each child is encouraged to reach his or her maximum potential.

Children with severe learning difficulties may need teaching on a one-to-one basis. However, many children with cerebral palsy are able to integrate into mainstream education.

Caring for children with cerebral palsy

Although cerebral palsy cannot be cured, drug therapy, surgery or physiotherapy
help to alleviate symptoms. The child's physical and psychological needs are assessed
by a team of medical experts, who provide support for patients and their carers.

Cerebral palsy is diagnosed on the basis of a child's symptoms – often a failure to develop normally and reach milestones. In general the earlier cerebral palsy is diagnosed, the better the outcome of treatment.

As there is no cure for cerebral palsy, this treatment revolves around keeping a child's muscles supple and helping him or her reach maximum potential, both physically and psychologically.

MEDICAL SUPPORT

A wide range of input and support is usually available from a multidisciplinary team including paediatricians, GPs, nurses, psychologists, social workers, physiotherapists, speech therapists and occupational therapists.

To some extent, the amount of help needed depends upon the degree of disability, the social circumstances and how the children themselves and the carers are able to cope.

Each child is assessed and individual capabilities and difficulties are taken into account. Care is then planned according to each individual's needs.

DRUG THERAPY

Drug treatment can be of help in some cases. Anti-epileptic drug therapy may be needed, for example to control fits associated with epilepsy.

Muscle relaxants can also be of help in reducing muscle spasm. Diazepam and baclofen are commonly used muscle relaxants.

SURGERY

Surgery can sometimes be used to deal with muscular contractures. These are permanently contracted stiff muscles, which develop after prolonged periods of paralysis or significant muscular weakness. These contractures can make walking a very difficult task; surgical correction of contractures may therefore help to improve mobility.

Despite restricted movement, many children are able to lead an active life. Therapists and parents will work together to encourage regular exercise.

The earlier treatment starts in childhood, the more successful the outcome is likely to be. Younger children with cerebral palsy are encouraged to learn through play.

The role of physiotherapy

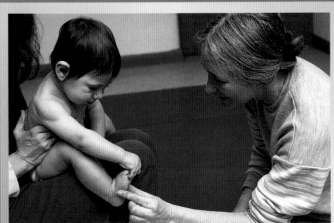

Physiotherapy for cerebral palsy is vital in preventing severe joint deformities and contractures. There are three main techniques used by physiotherapists:
■ Bobath technique – inhibits the existing 'inborn' reflexes and increased muscle tone and teaches correct patterns of movement. The baby is placed in particular positions and

Physiotherapy plays an important role in managing cerebral palsy. It aims to improve muscle tone and teach correct movements.

specific exercises are used
■ Proprioceptive technique – through guiding certain activities with a child, the physiotherapist inhibits spasticity in some muscle groups and enables contraction of others. The proprioceptive senses, stretch, pressure, touch and visual and auditory stimulation are used
■ Peto technique – a single movement is broken down into its smallest components. These individual components are practised over and over again, and then combined to produce the single action.

Multiple sclerosis

Symptoms

Multiple sclerosis (usually referred to as MS) is a chronic disease of the central nervous system (CNS), primarily affecting young and middle-aged adults. The illness causes damage to the myelin sheaths that surround and insulate the nerve cells in the brain and spinal column. The patches of inflammation are called lesions or plaques, and they affect the function of the nerves involved. This means that symptoms are variable, depending on which part or parts of the CNS are affected.

Typical symptoms that might be displayed are as follows.

White matter of the brain:
■ Memory and concentration difficulty
■ Dementia
■ Depression
■ Confusion

Optic nerve:
■ Retrobulbar (optic) neuritis: inflammation of the optic nerve resulting in blurred vision and pain on moving the eyeball, sometimes loss of vision in one eye

Brain stem:
■ Lack of hand co-ordination
■ facial weakness
■ Difficulty in swallowing
■ Dysarthria (slurred speech)
■ Double vision
■ Nystagmus (rapid involuntary eye movements)
■ Unsteady gait

Spinal cord:
■ Weakness
■ Heaviness in the limbs
■ Loss of sphincter control (incontinence of urine or faeces)
■ Urinary problems, such as increased frequency, bladder irritability
■ Paraesthesiae (pins and needles) in limbs, face or trunk

Paroxysmal symptoms:
■ Trigeminal neuralgia, brief spasms of searing pain in the trigeminal nerve of the face
■ 'Useless hands' – loss of joint and position sense
■ Lhermitte's sign – 'electric shock' sensation down the trunk or arms on flexing the neck.

Axon
Carries nerve impulses from the cell body

Myelin sheath
The insulating layer surrounding the axon, allowing more efficient electrical conduction

Cell body
The major portion of the nerve cell, from which the nerve fibres extend

Above is a normal nerve sheath, and right is a demyelinated nerve sheath. Local damage to the myelin sheath interferes with the conduction of nerve impulses. Symptoms of MS depend on the type of nerve cells affected.

Demyelination
In MS, the myelin sheath is damaged and may eventually develop scar tissue. This reduces the insulating properties and may damage the axon itself

Lesions
Local areas of damage to the nerve cell, also known as plaques

Macrophages
Scavenging cells from the immune system remove damaged sections of myelin

Diagnosis

Diagnosis of MS by a doctor is difficult at the outset, because of the very nature of the illness: symptoms are often short-lived and may disappear in a few weeks. The diagnosis must therefore be clinical, confirming the presence of plaques in at least two areas of the CNS at two or more separate times.

The episodes must last for a minimum of 24 hours and be at least a month apart. Furthermore, other conditions that show similar symptoms must be excluded, such as AIDS, lymphoma (tumour of the lymph nodes), Friedreich's ataxia (an inherited disorder of the nervous system) or spinal damage.

A lumbar puncture needle is inserted into the lower back under local anaesthetic, and a small sample of cerebrospinal fluid is collected. This sample can then be tested for particular antibodies.

A specific diagnosis of MS has to be supported by results from several investigations, which may include:
■ **Lumbar puncture** – the cerebrospinal fluid (the fluid enveloping the brain and the spinal cord) can demonstrate abnormalities of the immune system not seen in blood serum.

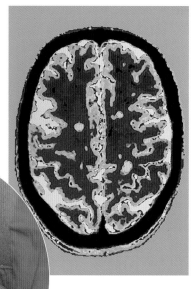

In this computer-digitized and colour-enhanced MR scan of an affected brain, MS plaques can clearly be seen as the palest areas.

■ **Electrophysiological tests** – visual and brain stem responses will typically be slowed in MS.
■ **MRI** (magnetic resonance imaging) of the spinal cord or brain will reveal affected areas. The location of the first symptom will dictate the area to be scanned.
■ **Cystoscopy** (looking into the bladder), **urodynamics** (recording of bladder pressures) and **renal and bladder ultrasound**, for assessing patients with urinary symptoms.

Because no test can be 100 per cent conclusive it may take months or even years for a diagnosis to be confirmed. A doctor will often not make a diagnosis known to the patient until there is reliable confirmation of the disease.

Prognosis

MS is an unpredictable illness. The typical pattern is of relapses lasting a few weeks, followed by remissions that may last for months or even years. Less often, the illness takes a progressively worsening course from the start. The physical disability that may occur during the course of the illness is unpredictable, and may result from incomplete recovery, slow progression or a combination of the two.

Early age of onset, occurrence of optic neuritis or sensory disturbance (pins and needles) often indicate a better prognosis. A poor prognosis is associated with paralysis and bladder or cerebral dysfunction.

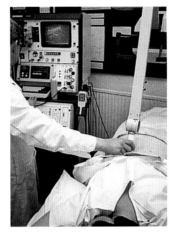

A doctor performs a renal and bladder ultrasound on a patient who has shown some of the characteristic signs of MS. The results of the scan will contribute towards the diagnostic picture for confirming the condition.

A high degree of remission from the first attack and a long-lasting first remission may indicate a better outcome. Frequent relapses may be associated with increased disability. The more lesions that are apparent in a scan, the higher the chance of increased disability.

Types of multiple sclerosis

There are four main types of multiple sclerosis:

Benign MS (around 20 per cent of cases) starts with a number of mild attacks followed by a complete recovery, with no worsening over time and no permanent disability.

Relapsing-remitting MS (25 per cent) involves attacks that can last from hours to months, during which symptoms may recur or new ones appear, followed by periods of recovery of any length of time, even some years.

Secondary progressive MS (about 40 per cent develop this form) starts in the same way as relapsing-remitting MS, but remissions stop and the MS moves into the progressive stage.

Primary progressive MS (15 per cent), also known as chronic progressive, involves steadily worsening symptoms, and progressive disability. There is no clear cycle of attack and remission. The illness may continue to worsen, or may stabilize at any time.

Incidence

In the UK, about five new cases per 100,000 people are diagnosed every year. The typical age is 20-40 years and 67 per cent of cases are female. The disease primarily affects Caucasians in northern Europe and North America, as it is more common in temperate zones and rarer in the tropics. Some 15 per cent of cases in the UK have an affected first-degree relative, although it is not an inherited condition. If a parent has MS, the child has a 20 to 40 times greater chance of becoming affected. It should be remembered, however, that the overall likelihood even in these instances is still lower than that of suffering from cancer or heart problems.

Causes

So far, no definite cause for MS has been identified. It has been suggested that an immunological response to an outside infection is a factor behind MS. Recent research has shown that injections of beta-interferon (a substance that interferes with the growth of certain viruses) produce a favourable response, slowing the progress of the disease by reducing the severity of relapses.

Some researchers believe that MS is an autoimmune disorder, where tissue is destroyed by the body's own immune system. In either case, certain cells of the immune system are associated with the MS lesions. There is as yet no known means of preventing MS.

Treatment and management

Physiotherapy, occupational therapy, goal-orientated rehabilitation and psycho-social counselling can all help a patient cope with MS. Making the most of a patient's own potential will allow them to live as independently as possible. A doctor should assess mobility, such as whether or not the toilet and the bath can be used independently, and should regularly review these functions to ensure maximum benefit. Although there is no cure for MS, medical treatment with steroids can speed recovery from an acute relapse and can lengthen the interval between relapses.

Specific drug treatment to alleviate certain symptoms is of benefit as follows:

The symptoms of MS are often individual to the sufferer and vary in their severity. Drug treatment, lifestyle and dietary modifications, and counselling can all make the disease more manageable and extend periods of remission.

- Carbamazepine tablets for trigeminal neuralgia
- Baclofen, tizanidine for spasticity (baclofen may be injected into the cerebrospinal fluid through a lumbar puncture)
- Anticholinergenic drugs for bladder instability
- Laxatives for constipation
- Beta-blockers, clonazepam or isoniazid for tremor
- Methyl prednisolone in short courses and oral steroids suppress disease activity
- Amantadine (also used in Parkinsonism) for fatigue
- A diet rich in linoleic acid (a chemical found in corn and soyabean oil) is believed by some to be beneficial.

Motor neurone disease

Symptoms

Motor neurone disease (MND) is a rare, incurable condition that results from the degeneration of neurones (nerve cells) that carry information from the brain and spinal cord to the muscles. The condition usually affects people in their 60s and 70s.

CLASSIFYING MND

There are four main types of motor neurone disease. These classifications are based on the anatomical position of the motor neurones that are affected. Broadly speaking, there are two types of motor neurone. Upper motor neurones have their cell body in the brain and an axon that projects into the spinal cord. Lower motor neurones have their cell body in the brainstem or spinal cord and an axon that projects into a muscle.

The four main types of motor neurone disease are:
■ Amyotrophic lateral sclerosis (ALS). This is the most common type of MND and results from the degeneration of both upper and lower motor neurones. It is characterized by symptoms of muscle weakness, muscle twitching (fasciculations) and stiffness
■ Progressive bulbar palsy (PBP). This is also the result of degeneration of upper and lower motor neurones, although in this disorder only the muscles involved in speech and swallowing are affected

■ Primary lateral sclerosis (PLS). A less common form of MND in which only the upper motor neurones degenerate
■ Progressive muscular atrophy (PMA). This occurs when lower motor neurones degenerate.

SIGNS

Symptoms are initially mild but gradually progress. Loss of muscle tone and power in the limbs is often the first symptom, with difficulties swallowing and slurred speech also common. If the muscles to the lungs are affected, then a person will have difficulty breathing, although this tends to be a later sign. Many people with MND have changes in their behavior although intellect is generally not affected.

With progressive muscular atrophy, the tendons of the hands become more prominent as the muscles waste. Eventually, the hands become flexed.

The symptoms of MND vary significantly, depending on which motor nerves are affected. However, even when movement is restricted, people with MND can lead a full life.

Diagnosis

The diagnosis of MND is usually based on progressive, typical symptoms and referral to a neurology specialist is vital. Most investigations are carried out in order to exclude other disorders that may have the same signs and symptoms as MND. These may include blood tests to rule out diabetes or thyroid disease, for example.

Nerve conduction studies will exclude motor neuropathy, and will test how well the nerves are functioning. An electromyogram (EMG) can also measure the nerves' ability to transmit electrical signals. In some patients, a biopsy of muscle tissue may be necessary to exclude polymyositis (an autoimmune muscular disease).

IMAGING

In some patients, a biopsy of muscle tissue may be necessary to exclude polymyositis (an autoimmune muscular disease). Nerve conduction studies will exclude motor neuropathy, and an electromyogram (EMG) will show widespread denervation. CT and MR scanning may be used to exclude brain tumours. MR imaging or myelogram (specialized X-ray of the spinal cord) may also be taken of the cervical and thoracic spine to rule out spine abnormalities that could be causing symptoms, for example a tumour.

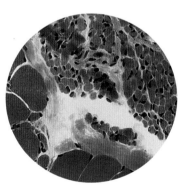

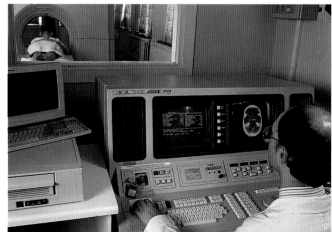

CT scanning may be used to rule out other possible causes of the patient's symptoms, such as a brain tumour.

This micrograph shows muscular atrophy. The muscle fibres supplied by damaged neurones become small and atrophic (wasted), appearing in distinct groups (right of image), compared to normal fibres.

Treatment

The treatment of MND is aimed at relieving the symptoms:
■ When there is a difficulty with swallowing (dysphagia), the patient's diet may be modified and, in extreme cases, liquid food may be given via a nasogastric tube or by gastrostomy (an opening made directly into the stomach)
■ Excessive salivation is managed using portable suction and anticholinergic drugs
■ Muscle cramps can be treated using quinine, which acts as a muscle relaxant
■ Patients with speech disorders affecting pronunciation (dysarthria) require speech therapy and, in some cases, communication aids
■ Spasticity is treated with drugs that relieve muscle spasms and rigidity. This also enables physiotherapy to take place
■ Respiratory failure may be helped with physiotherapy and with non-invasive ventilation (a respirator)

This woman is using a communication device that she can 'speak' through. The keyboard is activated by a pointer attached to her head.

■ Depression is treated with psychological support and medication
■ Difficulties with the activities of daily living can be addressed by occupational therapy, as well as aids such as wheelchairs and stair lifts
■ Limb weakness may require splints and collars or more advanced control systems.

Simple, practical measures – such as the provision of a lifting chair – help to make life easier for people with MND.

Managing MND

■ Social and psychological support are vital as MND is progressive and terminal
■ A multi-disciplinary team is required to meet the changing physical and psycho-social needs of affected people and their carers
■ A palliative (end-of-life) care plan should be drawn up in conjunction with the patient and his/her family
■ Drug therapies are limited. Riluzole is the only drug that may extend survival (though only for about three months).

The tongue may appear wasted in patients with progressive bulbar palsy. This is because the nerves in the motor cranial nuclei are affected.

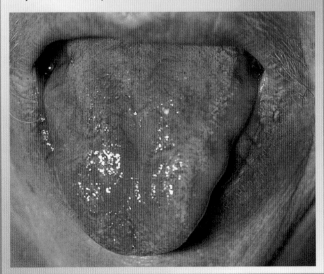

Causes

About 90 per cent of MND patients have no family history of the disease. This form of the disease, known as sporadic MND, has no known cause. In the remaining 10 per cent, the disease is thought to have an inherited component (familial MND).

In 1993, researchers located a mutated gene, called SOD1, responsible for around one fifth of the cases of familial MND. As a result of this mutation, a defective protein is produced. In healthy people, this protein protects motor neurones by clearing away toxic waste products called free radicals.

Incidence

Six in 100,000 people are affected by motor neurone disease. Incidence (the number of new cases a year) is two cases per 100,000 of the population per year.

The incidence rises with age and MND is rare in patients under 50; the peak incidence is between 60 and 70 years of age. The condition is familial (inherited) in about 10 per cent of all cases. Men are affected more often than women.

Prognosis

Prevention of MND is not yet possible. Degeneration of the motor neurones leads to progressive signs of upper and lower motor neurone dysfunction. The average expected survival for patients with motor neurone disease is between three and five years from first symptoms. A small proportion of patients – about 10 per cent – live for more than 10 years.

Early involvement of the medulla oblongata (one of the brain centres responsible for respiration) worsens the prognosis.

Brain tumours

Brain tumours are abnormal growths that develop in the brain
or the meninges. These tumours are either benign (non-cancerous)
or malignant (cancerous), and can be equally serious.

A brain tumour is an abnormal growth of tissue within the skull, and may be benign (non-cancerous) or malignant (cancerous). Brain tumours are primary or secondary, depending on whether they develop from brain tissue or spread from malignant tumours elsewhere within the body.

Although benign tumours are not cancerous, they can have equally devastating effects.

INCIDENCE
Primary brain tumours are rare, accounting for two per cent of newly diagnosed tumours. Between six and nine new cases are diagnosed per 100,000 of the population each year. They can occur at any age, but are most common between the ages of 55 and 65 years and in children between the ages of 3 and 12.

CAUSES
In many cases, doctors are unable to ascertain the cause of a primary brain tumour.

Exposure of the brain to radioactivity, however, increases the risk. There also appears to be a genetic link with certain types of brain tumours. In addition, several genetically transmitted diseases, such as neurofibromatosis, are associated with primary brain tumours.

Secondary tumours in the brain have usually spread from cancers of the lung, breast or kidney.

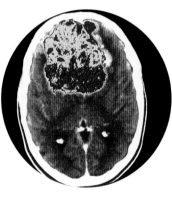

A benign brain tumour (yellow mass, upper left) is shown on this MRI scan. It has arisen from the protective coverings of the brain.

Brain tumours, whether benign or malignant, are relatively rare. They are, however, more likely to develop in adults between the ages of 55 to 65.

Types of brain tumour

Primary tumours, both benign and malignant, are classified according to the type of brain tissue in which they originate, for example the nerve cells or meninges.

Malignant tumours are graded between 1 and IV depending on their degree of malignancy; grade 1 tumours are effectively benign and grade IV tumours are highly malignant.

COMMON TUMOURS
There are several types of primary brain tumour:
- Gliomas – these are the most common malignant tumours and account for approximately 20 per cent of tumours. They include astrocytomas (which arise from astrocyte cells) and oligodendrogliomas (formed from oligodendroglia cells)
- Meningiomas – these benign tumours develop from the meninges (the membranes covering the brain and spinal cord), and account for about 20 per cent of tumours. They grow slowly over many years to compress the underlying brain and can reach the size of a grapefruit
- Pituitary adenomas – these benign growths of the pituitary gland account for about five per cent of tumours
- Neurofibromas – these are

slow growing, usually benign tumours. They develop from Schwann cells.

RARE TUMOURS
Other, less common brain tumours include:
- Craniopharyngiomas – these are benign but can be difficult to remove completely as they are close to crucial structures in the brain and may recur
- Cerebral lymphomas – these are similar to lymphomas elsewhere in the body
- Posterior fossa and cerebellar tumours of childhood. Most childhood brain tumours are infratentorial, posterior fossa tumours, within the cerebellum or adjacent brainstem. Medulloblastomas are the most frequent childhood tumours, followed by cerebellar astrocytomas and brainstem gliomas (very rare).

There are many other very rare tumours, which include haemangioblastomas, epidermoid cysts, pineal gland tumours, gangliogliomas and germ cell tumours.

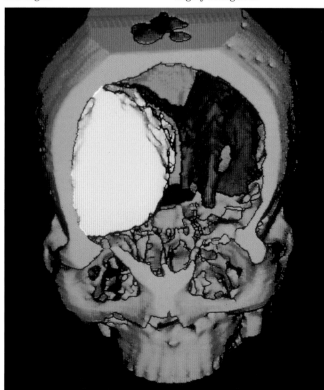

This 3-D CT scan shows a large meningioma (yellow) in the coronal section of the brain. A meningioma is a benign tumour developing from the meninges.

Symptoms of brain tumours

Symptoms of brain tumours are dependent upon the area of the brain
affected. Raised pressure within the skull is one consequence of brain tumours, which
causes a number of symptoms including headaches, drowsiness or even coma.

Raised pressure within the skull

Even a small increase in the amount of tissue or fluid within the skull rapidly raises the pressure inside the skull (raised intracranial pressure).

PRESSURE ON THE BRAIN
Brain tumours cause raised intracranial pressure in three ways:
■ By increasing the amount of tissue within the skull
■ By causing adjacent brain tissue to swell
■ By blocking the flow of cerebrospinal fluid within the brain, causing hydrocephalus and a rapid rise in pressure.

Slow-growing tumours such as meningiomas may reach enormous size. They gradually compress the surrounding brain, which accommodates without increasing intracranial pressure. As a result symptoms develop very gradually.

INITIAL SYMPTOMS
Raised intracranial pressure causes a headache that tends to be worse in the morning and on coughing, straining and bending forwards (activities that normally raise the intracranial pressure). It is a severe pain, not helped by ordinary painkillers.

There may be vomiting, with or without nausea. As the pressure continues to rise, consciousness deteriorates. This may begin with sleepiness, progressing to lethargy, drowsiness and eventually to coma.

EXAMINATION
Clinical examination may initially be normal, although abnormalities are usually noticed during an eye examination. The optic discs at the back of the eye swell, reflecting intracranial pressure, a condition known as papilloedema. Papilloedema is rapidly followed by optic atrophy in which the discs appear pale. In addition, there may be a third-nerve palsy causing double vision.

COMA
As intracranial pressure continues to rise, a person may lose consciousness. The heart rate slows down and the blood pressure rises. This is caused by increasing pressure on the cardiovascular centre in the brainstem. At this stage urgent treatment is needed to lower the intracranial pressure before brain death occurs due to critical pressure on the brainstem.

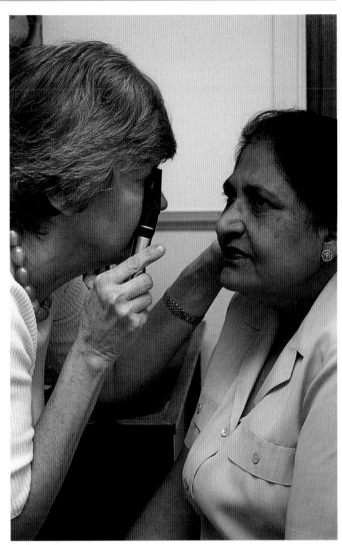

Neurological signs

Neurological signs are due to the local compression, destruction and irritation of different areas of the brain. Depending upon the position of the tumour, it will affect physical or mental functions, such as movement, sensation, balance or speech.

EFFECTS OF TUMOURS
Pituitary fossa tumours affect the visual fields by damaging the optic chiasma and causing loss of lateral vision.

Very rarely, patients may present with psychiatric symptoms; a person with a frontal lobe tumour may experience depression, whereas someone with a temporal lobe tumour may hear voices. These patients almost always have other symptoms.

Symptoms are often present before the clinical examination shows signs of neurological abnormalities. A full neurological examination, however, will usually show asymmetrical function.

People with brain tumours may experience symptoms such as headaches. These symptoms often occur before neurological signs become obvious.

Epilepsy and hormonal changes

Areas of abnormal electrical activity in the brain (epileptic focuses) can develop wherever the brain tissue is damaged or compressed. Epilepsy is most commonly associated with meningiomas, although any type of tumour or vascular malformation can cause epilepsy. Any adult who has a seizure for the first time should have a CT scan.

Hormonal abnormalities
Pituitary tumours may secrete prolactin, leading to menstrual irregularities and occasionally abnormal production of breast milk. In addition, the pressure of the tumour on the rest of the gland may gradually lead to pituitary failure. Typically thyroid and reproductive hormones are affected first.

Craniopharyngiomas can also cause pituitary failure.

Cerebral and cerebellar tumours

Symptoms

The brain is protected by the bony skull, and brain tumours therefore have little room to expand without pressing on other parts of the brain, damaging the nervous system and threatening life.

Possible symptoms include:
- Headache – particularly in the forehead (frontal) region
- Nausea
- Intellectual impairment with loss of memory, impaired judgement, confusion, drowsiness or dementia
- Difficulty formulating or understanding speech (aphasia)
- Personality and behaviour changes
- Eye problems (double vision, visual impairment or blindness)
- Hearing loss
- Fits (seizures)
- Disturbances of balance and limb movements.

Persistent frontal headaches made worse by bending over may alert a doctor to look for signs of brain disease.

Causes

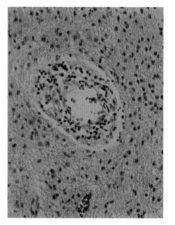

Eighty per cent of brain tumours arise from the substance of the brain (primary tumours), while 20 per cent result from the spread of cancer elsewhere in the body (secondary tumours). Cancers of the lung, breast, kidney, colon, stomach and thyroid are particularly liable to cause secondary tumours, and 40 per cent of melanomas (skin cancers) will reach the brain.

The microvascular cell proliferation seen surrounding this blood vessel is a hallmark of malignancy in astrocytomas.

The cause of most primary brain tumours is unknown. They almost always arise from cells in the supporting tissues or membranes of the brain or lining of the ventricles, and almost never from neurones. They may be benign or malignant, but they do not metastasize (spread) to other sites. The outcome of a tumour is determined by the affected region.

Cancer of the breast (circled) is associated with a risk of metastatic (secondary) spread to the brain.

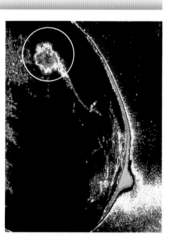

Structure of the brain

The brain consists of right and left cerebral hemispheres. Each hemisphere consists of:
- An outer layer of 'grey matter', the cerebral cortex; these cells almost never form tumours
- A core of 'white matter' composed of nerve fibres, which connect the neurones to the rest of the body
- Support cells for the neurones, a common source of brain tumours; they include oligodendrocytes, which produce insulating myelin sheaths for nerve fibres, and astrocytes, which nourish the neurones and may help store information.

The brain is covered by membranes – the meninges – from which benign tumours called meningiomas may arise. Other possible sites are the cerebellum, which controls balance, and the brainstem, which regulates respiration and the heartbeat.

The three membranes that line the brain – the meninges – are sites for tumours. These are called meningiomas.

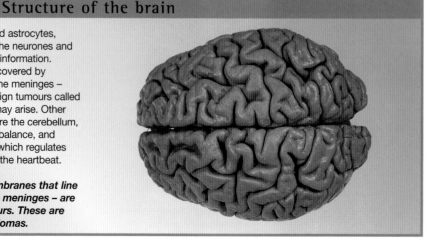

Diagnosis

Diagnosing a brain tumour is difficult as the symptoms are often insidious and the signs can be difficult to detect. It is important to search for signs of raised intracranial pressure: headache, vomiting and papilloedema (fluid accumulation in the optic nerve, causing it to swell).

Other signs of damage to the nervous system may be evident, but their absence does not exclude the presence of a tumour.

IMAGING TECHNIQUES
■ Magnetic resonance imaging (MRI) is the most effective tool for diagnosing brain tumours
■ Conventional X-rays are no longer used, having been replaced by CT scanning
■ Angiography (X-ray examination of the blood vessels) may reveal a tumour.

Since many tumours are secondary to other cancers, a general medical examination and routine tests, such as a chest X-ray, are very important.

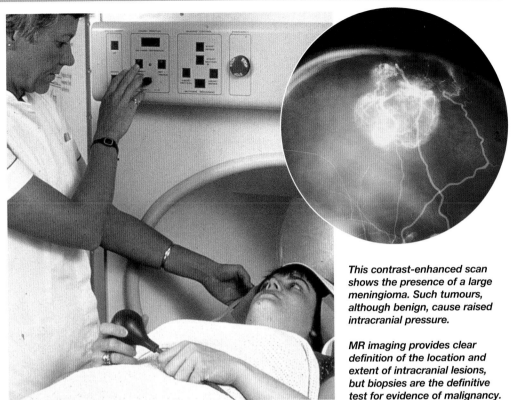

This contrast-enhanced scan shows the presence of a large meningioma. Such tumours, although benign, cause raised intracranial pressure.

MR imaging provides clear definition of the location and extent of intracranial lesions, but biopsies are the definitive test for evidence of malignancy.

Treatment

Surgery plays a major part in the treatment of many brain tumours. Surgeons often remove a small portion of the tumour for microscopic examination (biopsy) to identify its type and plan future treatment.

Some benign tumours can be completely removed, curing the patient. If a cure is not possible, surgery may still be used to reduce the bulk of the tumour, reducing the pressure on the brain and relieving symptoms. Some benign tumours that cannot be removed completely re-grow only very slowly, so surgery may well be an option.

Brain tumours are often treated using surgery. The tumour may be removed whole or in part. If there is no cure, surgery will alleviate symptoms.

Patients with incurable malignant tumours may benefit if the bulk of the tumour is reduced. Stereotactic surgery, using a CT-guided scan, helps surgeons operate on deep tumours.

OTHER TREATMENTS
■ Radiotherapy – sometimes effective, but can cause unpleasant side effects
■ Chemotherapy – not often effective, although much research is being done
■ Analgesics – may be needed to control pain
■ Corticosteroids – patients with raised intracranial pressure and cerebral oedema may gain rapid relief from corticosteroids; this may be injected in an emergency
■ Anticonvulsants
■ Anti-emetics.

Prognosis

Prognosis varies according to the type of tumour. The outlook is good for some benign tumours, but very poor for malignant tumours – less than 50 per cent of patients survive for one year after diagnosis.

Gliomas (primary tumours originating from the supporting tissues of the brain) almost never spread outside the central nervous system. This type of tumour is common in children.

Types of glioma include astrocytomas and oligodendrocytomas:
■ Astrocytomas are the commonest primary malignant brain tumours; some grow slowly over many years while others cause death within a few months – they are usually relatively benign in childhood
■ Oligodendrogliomas grow slowly over many years; they usually occur in adults and have a relatively good prognosis.

Other tumours include medulloblastomas and ependymomas, which arise from cells lining the ventricles (fluid-filled cavities) in the brain:
■ Medulloblastomas are the most common brain tumours in children; 60 per cent respond well to chemotherapy or radiotherapy
■ Ependymomas often occur in childhood and adolescence and grow at a variable rate; less than 30 per cent of affected children survive long-term.

Diagnosing and treating brain tumours

Imaging techniques, such as CT and MR scans, can be used to diagnose brain tumours. Depending on the type and location of the tumour, treatment may involve neurosurgical procedures.

MRI scans and contrast enhanced CT scans of the brain have revolutionized the diagnosis of brain tumours.

The appearance of an abnormal mass in the brain is usually diagnostic of a tumour, although occasionally it may be difficult to differentiate between a stroke – a large area of dead brain tissue – and a malignant glioma. For this reason it is always necessary to confirm the diagnosis with a histological sample taken at the time of surgery.

HEADACHES

Brain tumours are the least common cause of headache. A careful history will usually distinguish between migraine, tension headaches and other causes. In those people who develop severe headaches or a change in their usual pattern of headaches, a CT scan may help with diagnosis.

A CT scan may also be necessary to exclude a pituitary tumour in people whose pituitary function is abnormal.

DIFFERENTIAL DIAGNOSIS

In terms of physical symptoms, it may be difficult to differentiate a stroke from a brain tumour, especially where the paralysis has developed gradually over a few days, or where there were neurological symptoms prior to the stroke.

Other causes of neurological signs include conditions such as multiple sclerosis or abnormalities in the blood vessels of the brain. MRI or CT scans are usually helpful in these cases to make a definitive diagnosis.

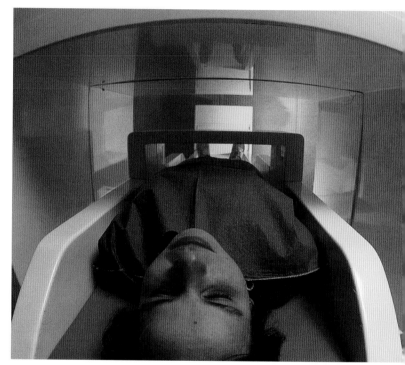

Tumours can be diagnosed using magnetic resonance imaging (MRI). This technique uses a strong magnetic field to produce images.

Treatment of benign tumours

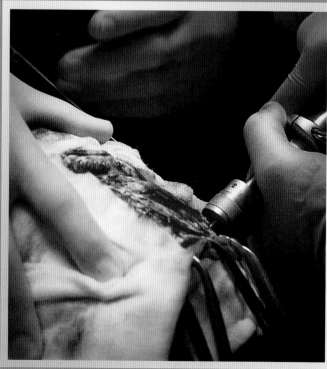

Most benign brain tumours are surgically removed once the patient has been stabilized. Any brain tissue swelling is reduced with steroids, and epileptic seizures are treated with anti-convulsants.

Craniotomy

Most benign brain tumours are removed under general anaesthesia using a craniotomy procedure, in which a portion of the skull is removed to gain access to the brain tissue.

Although, ideally, the tumour should be removed in its entirety, practically this is a very difficult objective to achieve. However, in cases where the whole tumour is completely excised, it is unlikely to recur.

Surgical removal of a brain tumour requires opening the skull. Once inside the brain, pinpoint accuracy is vital to avoid damaging healthy tissue.

Meningiomas

Occasionally, meningiomas develop from the meningeal covering on the base of the skull. In these cases neurosurgery is limited by the difficulty of reaching that area surgically.

Therefore these tumours cannot be removed completely and frequently recur. Repeated operations are often necessary to prevent the tumour pressing on vital structures within the brain. Radiotherapy can occasionally reduce the size of the tumour.

Pituitary tumours

These days, pituitary tumours are removed using a transnasal approach, avoiding the need to cut through brain tissue. This has reduced the complications from approaching the tumours through a craniotomy.

Pituitary adenomas can be removed completely but patients are usually given radiotherapy to prevent further problems.

Treating malignant tumours

The majority of brain tumours cause swelling in the surrounding tissue. In the short term, this can be dramatically relieved by high-dose steroids, such as dexamethasone, which is often used prior to surgery to protect the brain from post-operative swelling.

SURGERY

The initial aim of neurosurgery is to confirm the diagnosis and to determine the grade of malignancy of the tumour. This may be done during a major neurosurgical operation or as a biopsy. Tumours deep in the brain can be biopsied using stereotactic techniques, which accurately locate the tumour with minimal complications.

Neurosurgery often allows the bulk of a malignant tumour to be removed and consequently lowers the intracranial pressure. However, malignant tumours readily infiltrate the surrounding

brain tissue and it is therefore almost impossible to completely remove them. Nevertheless, radical surgery is important for medulloblastomas and may be curative for tumours such as astrocytoma. In cases where the tumour extends into parts of the brain that, for example, control speech, a decision may be made not to risk damaging healthy tissue.

RADIOTHERAPY

A course of conventional radiotherapy for highly malignant gliomas will increase survival by approximately six months following surgery, although there is no evidence that radiotherapy benefits the lower grade, less malignant tumours.

Once the diagnosis has been made, cerebral lymphomas are treated with radiotherapy and chemotherapy. Following surgery for medulloblastomas, whole head radiation prevents the tumour spreading through the rest of the brain. Stereotactic radiotherapy techniques direct the radiation more accurately to the site of the tumour. As the surrounding brain receives less radiation, larger doses can be given. Unfortunately stereotactic radiotherapy has not so far improved the prognosis.

Robot-aided surgery may be used to remove a tumour. This technique allows visualization of the tumour, and helps surgeons avoid damaging healthy tissue.

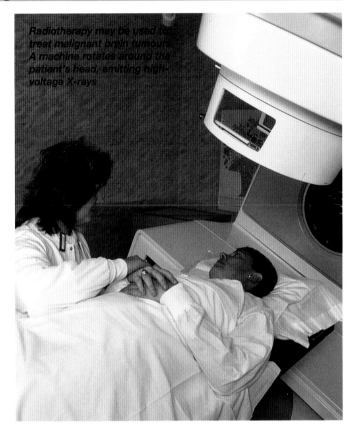

Radiotherapy may be used to treat malignant brain tumours. A machine rotates around the patient's head, emitting high-voltage X-rays

CHEMOTHERAPY

Malignant gliomas are not generally helped by chemotherapy, although some groups of tumours, such as anaplastic oligodendrogliomas, are highly chemosensitive. Some drugs may be used following tumour recurrence and they may have some benefit. Primary cerebral lymphomas are treated with high-dose methotrexate,

followed by radiotherapy. Chemotherapy is an important part of the treatment of childhood medulloblastomas.

OTHER THERAPIES

Experimental treatments including gene therapy, thalidomide infusion and growth-factor inhibition have been tried in some patients, so far without success.

Prognosis

The majority of brain tumours have a poor prognosis. The treatment of brain tumours is therefore based as much on the management of symptoms as on prolonging life.

Prognostic factors

The prognosis depends on the age of the person, the location and type of tumour, its relative malignancy and response to radiotherapy and chemotherapy. Generally the younger the person, the better the prognosis. Malignant gliomas are usually fatal within 12 months.

Prognosis for children

More children with posterior fossa tumours are surviving due to the improved chemotherapeutic regimes that have been introduced. The older the child is when the tumour develops, the better the chance of survival.

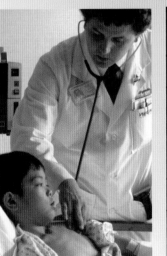

With improvements in chemotherapy, children tend to have a better prognosis. The outcome does, however, depend on the type of tumour.

Prognosis for different tumour types		
Tumour	**Usual (median) survival**	**5 yr survival**
Astrocytic tumours		
Astrocytoma Grade II	5 – 12 years	50 – 70%
Astrocytoma Grade III	18 – 30 months	<10%
Astrocytoma Grade IV	9 – 12 months	<2%
Glioblastoma multiforme	6 – 9 months	<1%
Oligodendroglioma Grade II-III	4 – 10 years	30 – 50%
Oligodendroglioma Grade IV	3 – 5 years	20 – 40%
Primary cerebral lymphoma	12 – 24 months	30 – 40%
Medulloblastoma	5 – 10 years	50 – 70%

Malignant brain tumour removal

Brain tumours can originate in the brain itself or spread there from cancer in other parts of the body. When malignant, they are potentially fatal and need to be removed surgically.

Brain tumours can be classed as either primary or secondary. Primary brain tumours originate from the substance of the brain. They occur in approximately 6 per 100,000 of the population per year, and about one in 12 of these tumours occurs in children under the age of 15.

Secondary brain tumours are metastatic (spreading) deposits of cancer that travel through the bloodstream from a tumour to elsewhere in the body or spread from adjacent tissue such as the skull or nasal cavity. The incidence of secondary brain tumours is higher than that of primary tumours.

TUMOUR SUBDIVISION

Primary brain tumours can be further subdivided, depending upon the cell of origin. There are two main cell types in the brain:

■ Neurones (nerve conducting cells), which perform brain function
■ Glial cells, which provide a supportive role for the neurones.

Neurones rarely form tumours, but glial cells have much more capacity for cell division, and multiply as a reaction to inflammation or to repair damage after a haemorrhage or head injury. However, if cell division becomes uncontrolled,

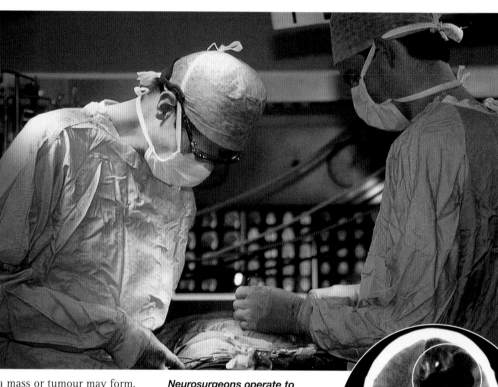

a mass or tumour may form.

The most common type of glial cells are known as astrocytes, and a tumour of astrocyte origin is therefore called an astrocytoma. This is the most common type of primary brain tumour, most often occurring in the cerebral hemispheres. It is this type of malignant tumour that is removed in surgery.

Neurosurgeons operate to remove an astrocytoma. This form of primary brain tumour is most common in patients of 40–60 years of age.

Before surgery, a CT scan of the patient's brain (an astrocytoma is circled here) will be used to create a computer-generated model of the patient's head. This model will aid the surgeons during the operation.

Presentation of brain tumours

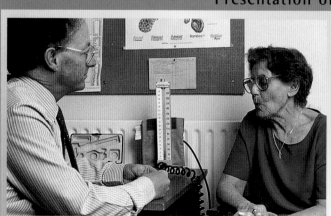

A patient is examined after complaining of blurred vision, severe headaches and weakness affecting one side of the body. She will undergo a series of tests before being referred to a neurosurgeon.

Brain tumours tend to become apparent in one of three ways:

■ Epileptic seizures – disturbance of the biochemical environment of the brain can lead to epileptic seizures
■ Neurological deficit – the infiltration of a vital brain area by

a growing tumour may result in a disturbance of brain function. This may lead to disability such as muscle weakness, visual deficit, loss of sensation or impaired co-ordination. Dysphasia (impaired speech) may also be evident
■ Raised intracranial pressure – the expansion of a mass within the head leads to signs and symptoms of raised pressure within the skull. This may result in headache, vomiting, blurring of vision and, ultimately, a deterioration in conscious level.

Identifying brain tumours

Before surgery to remove an intracranial tumour, a number of investigations need
to be performed in order to establish its location within the skull. These investigations
may also help determine the type of growth and how best to deal with it.

Tumours in any part of the body are often described as benign or malignant, but these terms are less easily applied to intracranial pathology:

■ Benign brain tumours may have life-threatening or disabling consequences if they expand unchecked within the confines of the rigid skull. Benign primary brain tumours may infiltrate vital areas of the brain and cause paralysis or other disability

■ Malignant brain tumours tend to follow a more rapid growth pattern. Unlike cancers arising in other organs, malignant brain tumours almost never spread to affect other parts of the body.

INVESTIGATION

Various techniques can be employed in the imaging and investigation of brain tumours:

■ Computerized tomography (CT) produces a 'sliced' image of the skull and brain. This can reveal if the tumour is intrinsic (originating within the brain, such as an astrocytoma) or extrinsic (outside the brain)

■ Magnetic resonance (MR) imaging provides a more detailed picture of brain anatomy. The brain can be examined in multiple planes, which may assist surgical planning. MR is also more sensitive to smaller tumours

■ Cerebrospinal fluid can be tapped (via a lumbar puncture) for cytological (cellular) examination.

Sites of intracranial tumours

Cerebral hemispheres
Tumours here may be intrinsic (originating within the brain) or extrinsic (originating outside the brain); with intrinsic tumours, brain tissue can be destroyed from within, while extrinsic tumours grow and place pressure on the brain

Ventricular system
The ventricles, where cerebro-spinal fluid (CSF) is produced can assist the spread of tumour cells by CSF circulating around the central nervous system

Hypothalamus
Astrocyte tumours may grow in the area of the brain concerned with temperature and hormone regulation

Skull and sinuses
Tumours may spread from the paranasal sinuses and skull

Posterior fossa
The cerebellum and brainstem are also affected by intrinsic and extrinsic tumours; tumours of the posterior fossa are relatively more common in children

There are many different types of intracranial tumour, each affecting the brain in a different way. This allows tumours to be classified by their location.

Removing a brain tumour

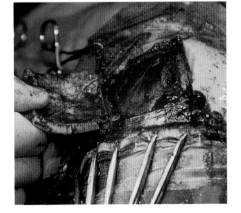

With the bone flap lifted away, the dura is clearly visible. This needs to be incised in order to access the tumour beneath.

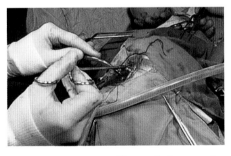

The tumour is removed in small pieces and sent to the hospital's neuropathologist for a preliminary examination, known as a 'frozen section'. The findings assist the surgeon in deciding intra-operatively (during surgery) whether to attempt a radical excision of the tumour or to complete a less aggressive debulking.

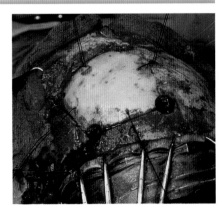

Once the dura has been closed, the bone flap is stitched into place and secured with surgical clips. The skin of the scalp is closed over the bone.

Drainage of a brain abscess

An abscess may arise in the brain as a result of infection that has spread from a nearby structure, such as the ear. Treatment involves drilling a burr hole in the skull and draining the abscess.

A brain abscess is a rare but extremely serious condition that, if not promptly treated, carries a high risk of disability or death. It occurs when a localized infection develops within the substance of the brain, leading to the formation of pus within a cavity. While infection is usually caused by bacteria, in rare cases it can be due to fungi.

BACTERIAL CAUSES

Different bacterial species may be responsible for an abscess but most infections are caused by streptococci and staphylococci. Bacteria may reach the brain by a variety of routes:
- They may spread from nearby sources of infection such as sinusitis or an ear infection
- They may be carried in the blood, from an infection in another part of the body such as the lungs or heart. The risk of blood-borne spread is increased in patients with a hole in the heart (septal defect), as this allows blood to bypass the lungs on its way to the brain
- They may enter the brain following trauma if there is a penetrating injury such as a severe, open-skull fracture in which fragments of bone are driven into the brain.

SYMPTOMS

In the early stages of an abscess, symptoms may be confined to local effects within the brain. If the abscess is situated near the parts of the brain that control movement or speech, the first problems may be weakness or speech disturbance. In addition the presence of an abscess may trigger epileptic seizures.

If the abscess becomes large it can cause a rise in pressure within the brain, which may result in headaches, vomiting and eventually coma.

An abscess in most parts of the body will cause symptoms of infection such as fever and sweating, but in the brain these may be mild or even absent.

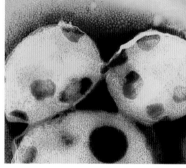

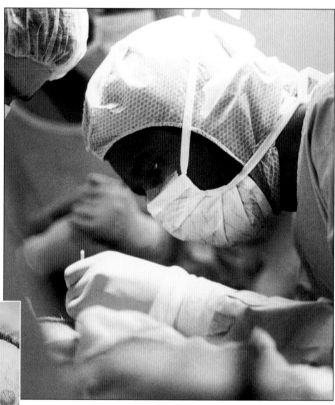

Abscesses are usually caused by bacterial infection. Several bacteria species have been found within brain abscesses.

When a brain abscess is diagnosed, urgent treatment is required. Surgical intervention is necessary to avoid permanent disability or death.

Investigations

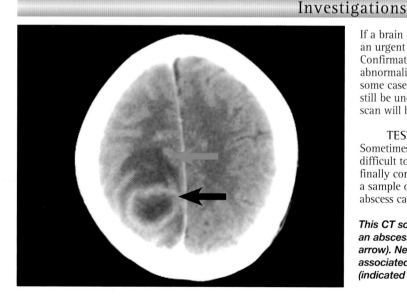

This CT scan of the brain shows an abscess (indicated by black arrow). Nearby, there is an associated patch of swelling (indicated by blue arrow).

If a brain abscess is suspected, an urgent CT scan is carried out. Confirmation reveals a ring-like abnormality within the brain. In some cases the diagnosis may still be uncertain and an MRI scan will be performed.

TESTING SAMPLES

Sometimes the diagnosis is difficult to make and can only be finally confirmed by obtaining a sample of pus from within the abscess cavity. Blood tests are also performed to determine:
- Whether there are bacteria in the circulation (septicaemia)
- The white blood cell count, which may give an indication of the response to treatment.

FURTHER TESTS

Once a diagnosis of brain abscess has been made, further tests may be required to ascertain the origin of the abscess, such as:
- Scanning the skull sinuses for signs of infection, using computed tomography (CT) scanning or X-rays
- Looking for signs of infection in the rest of the body using chest X-rays or echocardiography (heart ultrasound).

Treating a brain abscess

Large abscesses close to the skull may be drained using a hand-held needle.
Deeper, smaller abscesses require such precision aspiration that the needle must be
guided along an exact path, dictated by computer-generated measurements.

The first stage in treatment usually involves an operation to aspirate (drain) the abscess. Removing pus from the abscess will confirm the diagnosis; samples can be analyzed in the laboratory to define the precise strain of bacterium and dictate the best antibiotic. Where the abscess is large, pus removal will also reduce the pressure effects.

ASPIRATING THE ABSCESS
A variety of surgical approaches may be used, but in most cases a hole about the size of a penny is

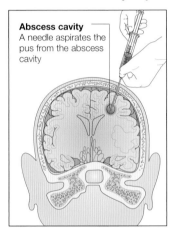

Abscess cavity
A needle aspirates the pus from the abscess cavity

Drainage of a brain abscess is performed by making a burr hole in the skull and inserting a needle into the abscess cavity. This may be done several times.

drilled through the skull so that a needle can be passed into the abscess and the pus removed.

If the abscess is large, near the skull surface and accessible, this can be performed with a hand-held needle. However, if the abscess is in a deep location, a stereotactic (computer-guided) operation may be needed.

STEREOTACTIC SURGERY
Stereotactic surgery involves clamping a specialized frame to the head. The frame is marked with exact measurements corresponding to markers given by CT scanning and allows a precise calculation of the position of the abscess. It means the surgeon is able to work extremely accurately – to within 2–3 mm – whereas free-hand surgery has an accuracy of around 2–3 cm.

In many cases the aspiration needs to be repeated. Under certain circumstances a larger opening in the skull may be required to allow a more radical removal of the abscess.

MEDICAL MEASURES
Once the diagnosis has been established, the mainstay of treatment is antibiotics, which act to clear the bacterial infection. Steroids may also be used if the abscess has caused a large amount of swelling in the

surrounding brain, contributing to increased cerebral pressure. Drugs for epilepsy are often prescribed, particularly if a fit has already occurred.

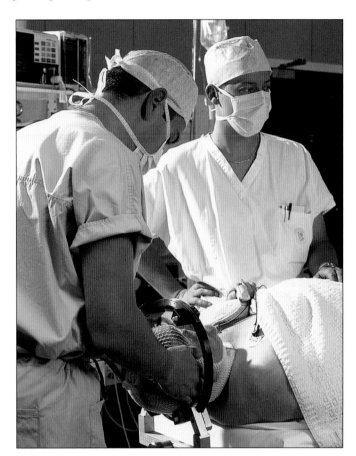

Stereotactic surgery involves clamping a calibrated frame to the head. This allows the needle to be exactly aligned with the abscess as shown on CT scans.

Case history

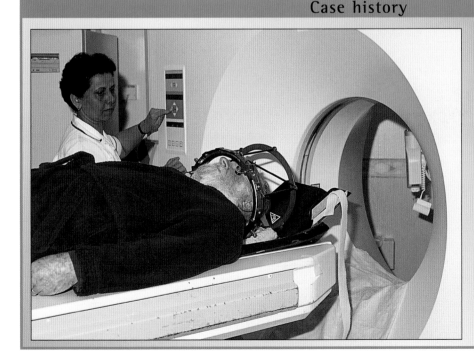

Mr Duns, aged 60, was admitted to hospital with a suspected heart murmur. After undergoing blood tests and echocardiography he was diagnosed with bacterial endocarditis (inflammation of the heart lining due to an infection). During a physical examination, the doctor noticed some weakness within Mr Duns' hand and realized that his patient was becoming increasingly confused and sleepy. These symptoms led the doctor to suspect that the bacterial infection had spread to the brain.

Mr Duns was referred to a neurological unit and an emergency CT scan was performed. A diagnosis of a cerebral abscess was made and it was decided that he should undergo urgent surgery. The deep location of the abscess led to a decision to drain it using the stereotactic system.

An emergency CT scan of Mr Dun's brain was carried out and this confirmed the presence of an abscess. Further scanning using a stereotactic frame was necessary to accurately locate the abscess.

Creutzfeldt–Jakob disease

Symptoms

Creutzfeldt-Jakob disease (CJD) is a type of spongiform encephalopathy, a degenerative disorder of the brain. It is a rare disease, occurring in only one person in one million worldwide each year.

Typically, symptoms appeared in people around the age of 60; the disease was rarely seen in younger people. However, in 1995 a new form of the disease, known as variant Creutzfeldt-

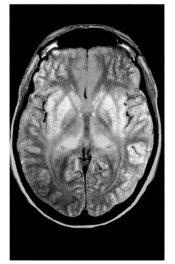

Jakob disease (vCJD), was diagnosed in several young people and, by December 2000, 23 cases of vCJD had been confirmed in the UK.

INITIAL SYMPTOMS
The outward symptoms of the disease vary but may include:
■ Subtle lapses of memory of day-to-day events
■ Mood changes and loss of interest in social activities
■ Inability to carry out previously simple tasks
■ In cases of vCJD the first symptoms are often irritability and insomnia.

LATER SYMPTOMS
Within a few weeks, more obvious symptoms appear:
■ Unsteadiness and hesitancy when walking
■ Deterioration of vision
■ Hallucinations
■ Slowing and slurring of speech and difficulty in finding the right words.

CJD is extremely difficult to diagnose. In some people, MR scanning of the brain can show areas of degeneration (yellow).

The disease then follows a rapid downhill course, with:
■ Incontinence
■ Jerky movements
■ Stiffness of limbs
■ Loss of ability to speak, feed or even move.

As the disease progresses, patients lose awareness of their surroundings; the agitation that is observed is a reflex

CJD is thought to be due to cross-infection with a similar bovine disease. Strict guidelines now exist to prevent infection.

action rather than real distress. Death occurs often within six months, frequently as the result of pneumonia. In about 10 per cent of cases the symptoms can continue for two–five years.

Causes

The infective agent involved in sporadic CJD, the form of the disease that accounts for 90 to 95 per cent of cases, was thought to be a virus. No virus, however, has been identified.

PRIONS
The current theory is that CJD is due to an infective agent known as a prion. It is thought that, in sporadic CJD, the prion is formed when, in

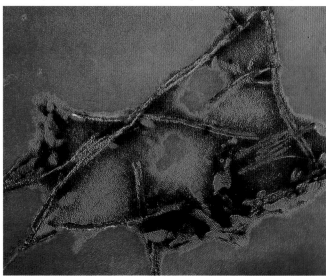

These prion protein strands are located in the brain tissue of a cow with BSE. Infection of the human brain with these proteins possibly causes CJD.

a very rare event, a protein molecule present in a normal cell membrane undergoes a spontaneous change, and that it then induces other molecules of the same type to do the same, thus setting up a chain reaction.

The prion has not yet been identified and the mechanism by which it causes spongiform encephalopathy remains unclear.

In other forms of CJD, the infective agent is transmitted in the following ways:
■ In the familial form of CJD – the disease is passed on genetically from one generation to the next
■ Contaminated neurosurgical instruments, dural grafts, corneal grafts and brain depth electrodes have been identified

CJD has been transmitted during surgical procedures. One such procedure is a corneal graft in which damaged tissue is replaced with a donor cornea.

as transmitting CJD. Over 100 UK cases have been associated with the use of injections of human growth hormone
■ It now appears that spongiform encephalopathies can be transmitted between species. Variant CJD in humans is thought to be the result of people eating beef infected with bovine spongiform encephalopathy (BSE).

Incidence

CJD is rare, affecting only one in a million people worldwide annually. Up until 2012 there have been 176 confirmed cases of CJD in the UK.

In the UK, the human population was probably exposed to the infective agent causing variant CJD (vCJD) in the early1980s through beef products affected by bovine spongiform encephalitis (BSE). However, the first case of vCJD was not diagnosed until 1995.

BSE EPIDEMIC

BSE was officially reported in 1985 in the UK, although the first cattle were infected years before in the 1970s.

The BSE epidemic may have developed because of the use of animal protein in cattle feed.

In the 1980s people in the UK were exposed to beef infected with BSE. This has probably resulted in the human form of the bovine disease, vCJD.

Diagnosis

CJD is not easy to diagnose, particularly as the early symptoms are often attributed to depression. As the disease progresses, certain investigations become possible, but they often serve only to exclude other neurological disorders.

INVESTIGATIONS

Investigations include:
- Computed tomography (CT) or MR scanning – occasionally shows areas of degeneration
- A lumbar puncture to remove spinal fluid – may be done to help eliminate other disorders
- An electroencephalogram (EEG) – sometimes detects characteristic disturbances in the brain's electrical activity
- Post-mortem examination of the brain – the only accurate diagnostic tool. This shows the characteristic loss of brain cells, which have been replaced by a network of fibres. The brain has many microscopic holes giving it a sponge-like appearance; hence the term spongiform encephalopathy. In vCJD, the cerebrum and cerebellum contain a large number of deposits of an abnormal protein.

A definitive diagnosis of CJD can be made only by studying the brain after death. The brain tissue is examined for the classic sponge-like appearance.

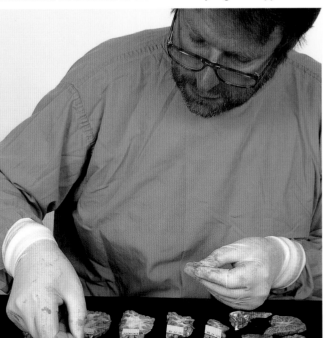

Prevention

CJD is not an infectious disease and is not caught by contact with someone who has the condition. Nevertheless, it is wise to take precautions, particularly when coming into contact with blood or brain tissue. There is no known way of preventing sporadic CJD, as the reason for the appearance of the infectious agent is unknown.

STERILIZATION RESISTANCE

Normal sterilization procedures do not appear to destroy the infective agent and neurosurgical instruments used in CJD cases are now destroyed.

The link between vCJD and BSE is as yet only a statistical one; a direct link has not been established by a laboratory test.

LEGISLATION

The statistical evidence of a link with BSE, however, appears very strong. As a result the UK government has taken steps to try to ensure that beef that may be infected with BSE is not consumed by humans and has imposed strict guidelines on the content of animal feed.

Treatment

As yet, there is no known treatment for CJD.

The identification of the molecular structure of the infective protein, or prion, may lead to development of new treatments. All that can be done is to care for an affected person as symptoms arise:
- Prescription of drugs to treat tremor (shakiness)
- Nursing care once a person becomes immobile
- Assistance with nutrition.

ADVANCES

Identification of the nature and structure of the infective agent may eventually lead to effective treatment of the disease.

Prognosis

Creutzfeldt-Jakob disease is invariably fatal. Over 176 people in the United Kingdom have died from variant CJD since 1995.

Ataxia

Ataxia is a neurological disorder that results in a loss of control over posture and limb movements. As the disease progresses, movement and speech can become severely limited.

Ataxia is a neurological movement disorder characterized by poor co-ordination and shaky movements, unsteady gait and a degree of clumsiness.

ROLE OF THE CEREBELLUM

Moving, or even just keeping still, involves the opposing actions of many different sets of muscles. These muscles must be co-ordinated so that each contracts or extends just enough, but not too much, to achieve the desired result. This is a highly complex process that is learned in infancy and normally requires no conscious effort thereafter.

The nervous impulses that control this process of muscle movement are produced and co-ordinated by the cerebellum: a highly crenellated (wavy-edged) area of the brain that is attached to the back of the brainstem. Ataxia is usually the result of damage to the cerebellum, which results in a significant disruption to the co-ordination processes.

CHARACTERISTICS

People suffering from ataxia have difficulty controlling body position, posture and movement of the arms and legs. They have trouble walking, and often adopt a characteristic stagger with legs splayed, known as gait ataxia. Rapid or fine movements are difficult, and sufferers may use broad zig-zag movements of the arms.

Severe ataxia leads to problems with control of fine motor co-ordination, making it difficult, or even impossible, to carry out daily tasks such as writing or using eating utensils.

Associated motor problems include tremor, muscle weakness and stiffness with spasticity. It also causes speech problems, such as unclear pronunciation (dysarthria).

Among the many forms of ataxia there are several that affect children from birth. Life expectancy is severely reduced by the condition.

Causes of ataxia

The most common causes of ataxia are stroke, head injury and cerebral palsy.

Brain injury
Insult or injury to the cerebellum sustained from a head injury or a stroke is a common cause of ataxia. The severity of the resulting ataxia depends on the extent of the damage to the cerebellum.

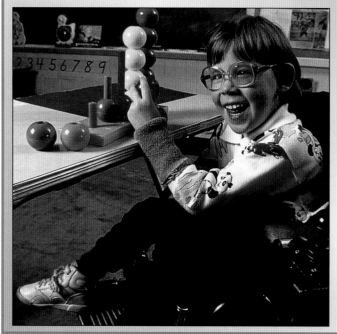

Cerebral palsy
Ataxia occurs in 10 per cent of children with cerebral palsy, which is often associated with other motor problems such as tremors, muscle stiffness or weakness, spasticity and dysarthria.

In most cases of cerebral palsy the cause is unknown, but it can result from oxygen starvation of the brain during pregnancy or birth, and is 10 times more common in premature infants. Cerebral palsy can also be caused by meningitis or fever during infancy. It is thought that the parts of the brain that control muscle movements, including the cerebellum, are particularly vulnerable during late pregnancy and very early infancy.

Other causes of ataxia
A number of other diseases or problems can damage the

Around 10 per cent of children with cerebral palsy also suffer ataxia. The damage to the cerebellum may be sustained during pregnancy or birth.

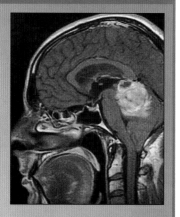

A brain tumour in the cerebellum can cause the symptoms of ataxia. This magnetic resonance scan shows a large tumour (circled).

cerebellum, leading to ataxia and related motor problems:
- Parkinson's disease
- Prolonged alcohol abuse
- Thyroid disease (very rare)
- Tumours of the brainstem or cerebellum
- Multiple sclerosis
- Poisoning
- Malnutrition.

Hereditary degenerative ataxia

There are several different types of degenerative ataxia, few of which are understood in any detail. Most of them involve progressive degeneration of the cerebellum, with associated, progressively worsening ataxia.

They are assumed to be caused by genetic disorders because they appear to run in families.

FRIEDREICH'S ATAXIA

This is the most common type of hereditary ataxia, affecting about one in 50,000 people. Age at onset is usually 5-15 years, although it can start as early as 18 months.

Symptoms include:
■ Progressively worsening ataxia – balance problems and falls are usually the first symptom
■ Impaired vision, hearing and speech
■ Scoliosis (spinal deformity)

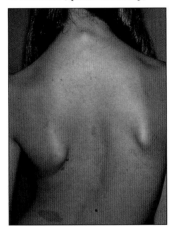

The initial symptoms of Friedreich's ataxia are balance problems and the development of scoliosis. The spine grows in an abnormal sideways curvature.

■ Diabetes
■ Severe heart problems.
Friedreich's ataxia is an autosomal recessive disorder, meaning that an affected person has inherited a recessive allele (part of a gene) from each parent.

ATAXIA-TELANGIECTASIA

Children affected by ataxia-telangiectasia (A-T or Louis-Bar syndrome) usually appear healthy at birth, before developing ataxia in the second year of life. The condition occurs in around one in 40,000 live births, although the true incidence may be higher because many infants may die before the disease is diagnosed.

The disorder is characterized by the following conditions:
■ Ataxia with associated spidery red veins on the face and ears (telangiectases)
■ Slurred speech and difficulty in reading and writing
■ Motor problems – eventually, the affected child is confined to a wheelchair
■ Problems within many of the systems of the body, leading to severe immunodeficiency and associated lung infections
■ Blood cancers – these are particularly difficult to treat as A-T sufferers do not tolerate exposure to radiation well.

VARIED ONSET

Many ataxias develop at different stages of life and have varying causes:
■ Early onset ataxias – there are at least 10 types of these, which affect much of the body, including the optic and reproductive systems. Most are thought to be hereditary, showing an autosomal recessive pattern of inheritance
■ Late onset ataxias – these can be inherited or idiopathic (arising spontaneously), appearing in adulthood and leading to progressive loss of

A-T is usually diagnosed before the age of two. Children affected by the disease have to work intensively with physiotherapists to retain their mobility.

motor abilities. Inherited forms generally follow an autosomal dominant pattern of inheritance (where there is a 50 per cent chance that the child of an ataxia sufferer will be affected)
■ Episodic ataxias – these are brought on by exercise, stress or being startled. The ataxia may be temporary, or permanent and progressive.

Diagnosis and treatment

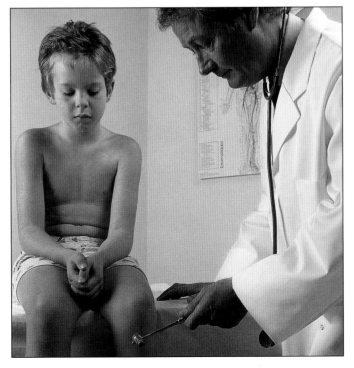

Ataxia following stroke or head injury will be diagnosed in hospital. In cases of progressive ataxia, worsening clumsiness or balance problems may result in a visit to a GP, who would reach a diagnosis by making a physical examination, focusing especially on reflexes. Ataxia in infants may be recognized through their failure to reach developmental milestones.

Confirmatory tests include:
■ Nerve conduction studies – electrodes are attached to the arms and legs to measure the speed of nervous impulses
■ Genetic tests for ataxias where the genetic defect is known
■ MR/CT scans of the cerebellum for signs of damage or wasting
■ Tests specific to the ataxia

Problems of balance or an increasing tendency to clumsiness are often the initial signs of ataxia. Reflex response is tested in making a diagnosis.

type – such as heart monitoring to check for the characteristic heart problems of Friedreich's.

TREATMENT

In general, ataxia is incurable and untreatable. It is important to keep slim and supple, and physiotherapy can help to retain mobility and lessen pain and stiffness. Some drugs, such as baclofen or diazepam, can help to ease the spasticity and stiffness associated with ataxia.

PROGNOSIS

Early onset ataxia has a very poor prognosis, largely because of the associated problems with the heart and other systems within the body. Few affected people survive to adulthood. Late onset ataxia may progress to a variable degree, with many sufferers becoming confined to a wheelchair and eventually having trouble communicating or performing daily tasks.

Rabies

Causes

Rabies is a zoonosis (a disease transferred from animals to humans) caused by a bullet-shaped virus known as Lyssavirus genotype 1.

The disease is passed on through contact with saliva from an infected animal and is usually transmitted by a bite. Once within a new host, the virus attacks the central nervous system of its victim. If the disease is not treated before symptoms develop, coma and death are almost inevitable.

TRANSMISSION
The natural carriers of rabies in the wild are animals such as foxes and bats, but these rarely pass on the disease to humans. Transmission most often occurs through domestic pets, usually dogs that have been bitten by an infected animal.

The disease is transmitted when infected saliva penetrates either broken skin or mucous membranes. If a person has been exposed to rabies, the risk of them developing the disease depends on the size, severity and site of the wound. The most dangerous bites are those to the head and neck and multiple bites carry a greater risk than single ones.

Although human-to-human transmission of rabies is virtually unknown, the saliva, urine, cerebrospinal fluid, tears and lung secretions of people with rabies do contain the virus.

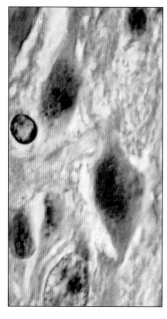

The bullet-shaped rabies virus (shown here magnified) belongs to the Rhabdovirus family. It is usually transmitted through the saliva of infected animals.

Rabies is passed on from animals to humans through a bite. Domestic animals, particularly dogs, are the most common route of transmission.

Symptoms

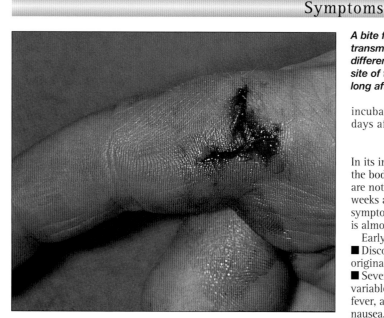

Once the virus has penetrated the body's surface, there are several stages to its behaviour:
■ It multiplies locally, penetrates into peripheral nerves and migrates though the axons to the spinal cord and brain
■ It then replicates at a quickly causing major disruption of central nervous function

It spreads down multiple peripheral nerve pathways until it reaches much of the body's tissues. Reproduction of the virus also occurs in the salivary and lacrimal glands.

The disease has an incubation period ranging from four days to several years. In 75 per cent of cases,

A bite from an animal can transmit infections of many different kinds. In rabies, the site of the bite is often painful long after it has healed.

incubation is complete 20–90 days after the bite.

SYMPTOMS
In its initial stages rabies evades the body's defences. Antibodies are not detectable until two weeks after the onset of symptoms, by which time death is almost inevitable.

Early symptoms include:
■ Discomfort at the site of the original bite, even if long healed
■ Several unspecific and variable symptoms including fever, anxiety, agitation, malaise, nausea, headache and diarrhoea.

The disease then develops into one of two types: furious rabies (the most common form) and paralytic rabies.

FURIOUS RABIES
In cases of furious rabies:
■ Initial agitation increases and may incorporate hydrophobia: a morbid fear of water. The mere sight of water can lead to hydrophobic spasms, involving violent contractions of the diaphragm, larynx and pharynx. Violent retching is common, occasionally causing the oesophagus and stomach to rupture
■ There may be convulsions, sufficiently powerful to cause cardiac or respiratory arrest
■ Confusion, agitation and hallucinations are interspersed with periods of lucidity
■ Over-stimulation of the autonomic nervous system can lead to cardiac arrhythmias (irregular heartbeat), hyper-salivation and fluctuating temperature and blood pressure
■ Death usually occurs within days of the onset of hydrophobia.

PARALYTIC RABIES
In cases of paralytic rabies:
■ Fever and headache are followed by flaccid paralysis that ascends, causing pain and involuntary twitching
■ Death usually occurs when the respiratory muscles succumb to paralysis. This can take up to one month.

Diagnosis

Before a diagnosis of rabies is made, tetanus must be excluded, as some of the symptoms are similar. However, tetanus has a shorter incubation period and there is no hydrophobia.

If possible, rabies should be confirmed in the animal that delivered the bite. This is done by performing a brain biopsy once the animal has been killed.
■ Infection with rabies is confirmed by looking for the virus itself, or for the antibodies to the virus. Tests will include taking samples of blood, cerebrospinal fluid (CSF) and a saliva swab.

Diagnosis can be confirmed through tests on the brain tissue of the animal that delivered the bite. Treatment normally precedes diagnosis.

IMMUNOFLUORESCENCE TEST
The rabies antigen can be identified by a technique called immunofluorescence, which allows the pathologist to observe the amount and distribution of antigen in a tissue section. The tissue for testing may be taken from:
■ The nape of the neck (a full thickness skin biopsy)
■ A brain biopsy.

TREATMENT BEFORE DIAGNOSIS
It is vital to begin treatment for rabies before any symptoms appear. This is because the risk of death increases rapidly with the onset of symptoms, becoming inevitable once symptoms are established. Confirmation of diagnosis, therefore, often comes after treatment has started.

Incidence

Rabies is found in most parts of the world, although most of Western Europe, e.g. Britain and France are rabies-free. Worldwide, there are around 50,000 deaths from rabies every year. Some regions, primarily India and Africa bear the burden of rabies infections, mainly due to bites from stray dogs.

Rabies in Britain
Britain's wildlife has been free of rabies since 1922. The last person to acquire indigenous rabies within Britain died in 1902. Although there have been around 12 deaths from rabies since that date, all were infections acquired while travelling abroad.

Treatment

Any injury inflicted by an animal in an area where rabies is endemic should be thoroughly cleaned. Tetanus boosters and antibiotics (against secondary infection) should be given.

VACCINATION
The only effective treatment is vaccination. The vital factor in managing rabies is to predict infection before symptoms appear and commence post-exposure prophylaxis (PEP). This is indicated if there is a bite injury from an unprovoked animal attack, in an area where rabies is endemic.

In the case of an unvaccinated person, PEP consists of:
■ An immediate infiltration of 20 IU per kg body weight of human rabies immunoglobulin

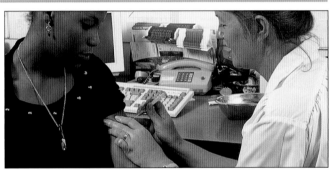

around the wounds
■ Injections of rabies vaccine 0, 3, 7, 14 and 28 days after being bitten, preferably into the deltoid muscle in the arm. The vaccine should not be administered via the same syringe or in the same body area as the immunoglobulin.

If the person has previously been vaccinated against

When travelling to areas where rabies is endemic, it is sensible to consider vaccination. Even after vaccination, boosters are necessary in the case of a bite.

rabies, booster dosages of vaccine are given immediately and three days after the bite. Human immunoglobulin is not given.

Prevention

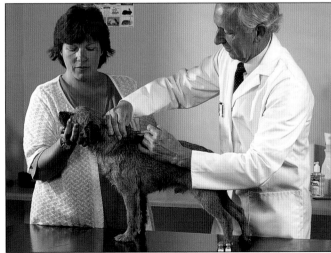

In the past, the main techniques for controlling rabies have involved quarantine and the destruction of stray dogs. Nowadays domestic animals are vaccinated against the disease, whilst efforts are made to control reservoirs of rabies in the wild. Vaccination offers protection for about five years and can be extended by giving boosters. Mass vaccination of human populations in endemic areas is unlikely due to cost.

Mass human vaccination against rabies is prohibitive on grounds of cost. The main preventative measure is widespread animal vaccination.

Prognosis

If treated before symptoms develop, full recovery is possible. Once symptoms are established, treatment using sedatives and analgesics is supportive only and death is almost inevitable.

Depression

Depression is a mental state that involves mood disorder, leaving the person feeling 'low'. There are a variety of symptoms, both physical and mental, which can be mild or severe.

An episode of depression may occur singly or recurrently (with intervening periods of normal mood). In both cases, the condition is referred to as unipolar depression, because there is only one direction of mood change.

Some people, however, develop depression in the context of a manic-depressive illness, called bipolar affective disorder. In this case, there are manic ('high') episodes as well as low mood swings.

Although the vast majority of features of unipolar depression would apply equally to bipolar depression, it is thought that there may be some subtle differences between the two.

CLASSIFYING DEPRESSION

As well as the distinction that is currently made by psychiatrists between unipolar and bipolar disorders, classification is based on its severity, recurrence and the presence or absence of psychotic symptoms.

Only rarely, however, does a depressive illness become so severe that the individual loses touch with reality and becomes psychotic (whereby delusions or hallucinations are experienced).

Depression is primarily a disorder of the mood. This is in contrast to mania, in which there is elation and elevation of mood.

Some people are reluctant to visit their GP to discuss feelings of depression, but this is often the first step towards receiving treatment.

Who is affected?

At any given time, approximately 10–15 per cent of people in this country will be suffering from moderately severe depression and 2–3 per cent from severe depression.

Every year, about 10 per cent of the population develop a depressive illness, although many more cases may remain undetected. Typically, onset is in the late 20s and, overall, women are twice as likely as men to get depressed. Inner-city housing, low social class, unemployment, poor education and being single are other important associations that have been recognized.

New mothers are also at risk of becoming depressed – in the six weeks following childbirth, 10–15 per cent become depressed enough to warrant some kind of help.

Among the many factors that can increase vulnerability to depression are a lack of social support and a difficulty in forming close relationships.

What causes depression?

Attempts have been made to distinguish between depressive episodes, which are understandable in terms of traumatic life events (reactive or neurotic depression), and those that occur spontaneously, depending on factors within the individual (endogenous depression). Although it is tempting to classify further on this basis, the initial observation that 'reactive' depression is less severe, and forms a separate entity, need not necessarily be true. In every case, there must be a mixture of causes that are both internal and external.

Genetic factors appear to be important (more so in bipolar depression), as are hormonal changes, such as increased cortisol levels and abnormal control of thyroid hormones.

Adverse events, especially those associated with losses such as bereavement and physical illness, can trigger depressive episodes. It seems that underlying vulnerability to such events can be increased by circumstances – for example, abuse or parental separation in childhood, unemployment, low social class and poor self-esteem.

CHANGES IN THE BRAIN

There is known to be a change in the function of several neurotransmitters and their receptors in the brain during periods of depression. Most research has concentrated on serotonin and noradrenaline, the hypothesis being that depression is associated with decreased activity of both of these chemicals. It is now accepted that this represents a huge oversimplification and that many other neurotransmitters are likely to be implicated.

The key features of depression are a persistent lowering of mood and loss of enjoyment, interest and motivation. There are also important changes in biological function, thinking and behaviour.

■ **Biological symptoms**
These are most prominent in severe depression and include: sleep disturbance, typically with early morning wakening; decreased appetite; weight loss; reduced sex-drive; fatigue; aches and pains; psychomotor disturbance – slowing of movements, thought and speech or, in rare cases, agitation.

The mood is often worse in the morning and lifts as the day goes on. In very severe, life-threatening cases, an individual will refuse to eat or even drink.

■ **Mental symptoms**
Thought content is extremely negative, with ideas of guilt, worthlessness and hopelessness. People can find it hard to imagine any sort of future, and ideas of self-harm or suicide may be common. Concentration and memory can be severely impaired; in some cases in the

Frontal lobe
The part of the brain concerned with controlling voluntary movement and other functions; it is also the centre for conscious emotion

Area of abnormal activity
It is thought that in depressed people, part of the cortex of the frontal lobe is overactive, leading to an abnormal fixation on emotional state

Research has attempted to identify the specific areas in the brain that are affected when an individual is depressed. This cross-section through the brain shows one such area.

elderly, the degree of impairment can be such that it is difficult to distinguish between depression and dementia.

Other symptoms that occur as part of a depressive illness include anxiety and phobias, obsessions, irritability, agitation and restlessness.

■ **Behavioural symptoms**
The ability to function from day to day, both socially and at work, is decreased – at least to some extent. People may avoid leaving home and isolate or neglect themselves, and facial expressions and body language of the severely depressed may be easily recognizable.

MILD DEPRESSION
Anxiety and obsessive symptoms in particular appear to occur more frequently in mild episodes; indeed, rather than differing merely in terms of severity, mild depression may represent a separate syndrome. Other important differences of mild

A common feature of mild and severe depression is insomnia. A chronic lack of sleep can serve to exacerbate symptoms of fatigue.

depression include a tendency to initial insomnia (difficulty falling asleep with subsequent oversleeping in the morning), an increase in appetite and the presence of few biological symptoms. The pattern of variability throughout the day can vary, with a worsening of mood in the evening.

PSYCHOTIC DEPRESSION
It is important to identify psychotic symptoms, as they represent a severe illness, where the individual has begun to lose touch with reality. Symptoms are usually in keeping with the patient's mood: delusions often concern illness, death, punishment, guilt or persecution; hallucinations (which occur less frequently and are usually auditory) are distressing – for example, a voice that accuses, urges suicide or confirms the patient's low self-esteem.

Depression in older people

Although the prevalence of depression is almost identical in elderly and middle-aged people, the diagnosis of the condition can often be missed in the older group. This is probably because the features of low mood can be less obvious; elderly people may not complain of feeling depressed or suicidal at all, perhaps going to see their doctor with physical problems or simply sleep disturbance, a degree of which is normal in old age.

It is always important for the doctor to bear the condition in mind, however, because of the relatively poor prognosis in

this group. Elderly depressed patients (especially men) are at a high risk of suicide and, for this reason alone, early detection and treatment is of paramount importance. It is also very important in preventing relapse and depressive episodes of long duration, which are more likely in people of this age group than in younger people.

It is easy to overlook depression in older people, but the problem is significant. It is often difficult to diagnose, as it can be hard to distinguish between depression and dementia.

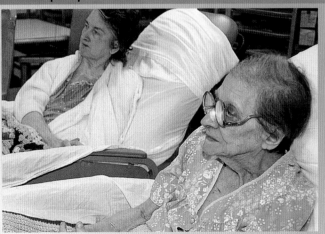

Managing depression

Before taking steps to manage depression, it is important to recognize the type of depressive illness that the patient is suffering from. The most appropriate treatment can then be administered.

The diagnosis of depression would, at face value, appear relatively straightforward but in practice can be rather difficult.

IDENTIFYING DEPRESSION

It is important to distinguish between depression and the normal sadness that would be expected in response to bad news or a significant loss, such as a bereavement or the development of a major physical illness. To justify the diagnosis, there must exist some degree of other characteristic symptoms in addition to low mood; the severity and duration of change is also vitally important.

Depression should also be distinguished from adjustment reactions (representing abnormal psychological responses to such life changes as redundancy, divorce or moving house), which often result in a mixture of anxiety and depression. Neither of these will be sufficiently severe to justify a clear-cut diagnosis of anxiety or depression alone, however, and the biological symptoms of the latter will be absent.

PERSONALITY DISORDER

Borderline personality disorder (one of many recognized personality disorders that represent lifelong maladaptive patterns of behaviour, attitude and experience that cause distress to the individual or society) has, as one of its core features, an instability of emotion; people with borderline personalities typically complain of chronic lack of enjoyment and frequently have a low mood and suicidal ideas.

It is very difficult to distinguish between someone who has a low mood in the context of an abnormal personality alone, and someone with a borderline personality disorder who has developed a superimposed depressive illness.

In fact, even attempting to make such distinction merely serves to grossly oversimplify an extremely complex situation; in practice, if someone who meets the criteria for a borderline personality disorder appears to be markedly depressed they would usually be offered antidepressant medication.

DISTINGUISHING OTHER PROBLEMS

Other important conditions that may be hard to differentiate clinically from depression include generalized anxiety disorder, obsessive-compulsive disorder, chronic schizophrenia (a prominent symptom of which is flattening and blunting of emotions and mood), hormonal disorders (such as Cushing's syndrome and underactivity of the thyroid gland), cancer, malnutrition and post-viral fatigue syndrome.

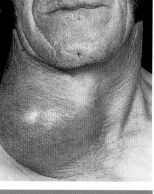

General stress or worry can often leave one feeling low. However, this mood state does not necessarily equate to a depressive illness.

The symptoms of depression need to be distinguished from those that may arise as a result of thyroid dysfunction (the cause of this person's swollen neck).

Evaluating the patient

Initially, the most important step in the management of depression is to make an assessment of severity and risk to the patient in terms of self-neglect and suicidal behaviour.

All cases of psychotic illness and those patients thought to represent a high suicide risk should be admitted to a psychiatric hospital. The vast majority of cases, however, are managed by a general practitioner. Referral as an outpatient to

Most patients with depression are seen and treated by their GP. However, if their illness becomes more severe, specialist attention may be necessary.

a consultant psychiatrist is warranted if there is concern about the severity of the illness, a failure of response to commonly used treatments or recurrent episodes of depression.

It is very important for the doctor to take a history of any abnormal upswings of mood as well as the depressive episodes. Any predisposing factors will also be noted, as will triggers or precipitating events and maintaining factors (which keep the illness going). This helps in the identification of possible targets for change during treatment to prevent deterioration, relapse or recurrent episodes of depression.

Treatment for depression

Most people who suffer from depression will be managed by their GP using antidepressant drugs. In some cases, however, specialist psychiatric care, involving psychotherapy or behavioural therapy, may be required.

Medication

Antidepressant medication is used to treat episodes of all severities. Overall, the response rate to such treatment is good (60–70 per cent) and continuing antidepressants for six months following recovery from a first episode can significantly reduce the risk of relapse.

The classes of drugs most commonly used are the tricyclic antidepressants (TCAs) and the selective serotonin reuptake inhibitors (SSRIs, of which Prozac is an example). Such drugs are thought to exert their influences through effects on neurotransmitters and their receptors, although the exact mode of action remains unclear.

TCAs and SSRIs have different side effects, but neither is without the potential to cause unpleasant or even intolerable symptoms. It is important that patients are warned that although the unpleasant symptoms may appear rapidly, the antidepressant effect will take longer to emerge (2–6 weeks); for this reason, some degree of perseverance is necessary.

COMBINATION THERAPY

Antidepressants can be used alone or in combination, either with other antidepressants or other types of drug. One example is the use of lithium to augment the effects of antidepressants; this approach can be used to treat depression that fails to respond to antidepressants alone.

Patients who suffer from recurrent episodes (especially if they have a strong family history of depression or early age of onset) benefit from long-term

Selective serotonin reuptake inhibitors are widely used in the treatment of depression. One of the best known SSRIs is fluoxetine (trade name: Prozac).

preventative treatment to reduce the risk of recurrence.

Lithium can also be used as a long-term treatment to prevent the recurrence of depression in patients with unipolar depression, and of both depression and mania in those with bipolar affective disorder.

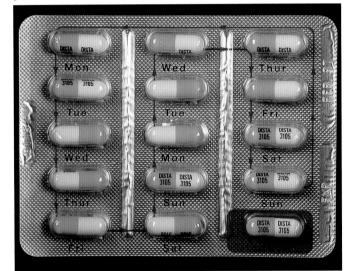

Other therapies

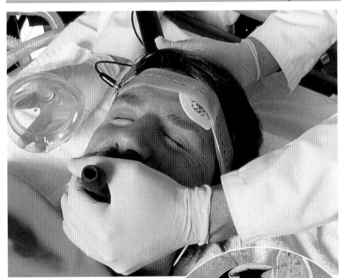

Severe depression that does not respond to drug therapy or is endangering the patient's life may be treated by ECT. This involves administering a mild electric shock to the brain.

Feelings of loneliness, hopelessness and isolation are common when a person is depressed. Counselling may help to overcome these feelings.

Psychotherapeutic techniques can be of great value. The most widely studied is cognitive behavioural therapy (CBT – originally devised to treat depression but since found to have wider applications). In the short term, CBT is just as effective as medication in treating depressive episodes and it may even be more effective at preventing relapses in the future; in practice, medication and CBT are often used in combination.

In some cases, counselling alone may be deemed sufficient for milder forms of depression without the need for psychotherapy or medication.

TREATING SEVERE DEPRESSION

Electroconvulsive therapy (ECT) is reserved for the most severe cases, especially when rapid treatment is required (e.g, if there is refusal to eat or drink) and for situations in which drugs fail to work or cannot be tolerated. In cases of psychotic depression, antipsychotic medication may be added in doses similar to those used for the treatment of other psychotic illnesses such as schizophrenia.

Prognosis

Although a single episode of depression usually lasts between three and eight months, 20 per cent last for more than two years. The severity of the first episode is related to the risk of developing further depressions – a risk of 50 per cent in moderately severe cases, rising to 80 per cent in the more severe.

Psychiatric illness in general (but especially depression) is strongly associated with suicidal behaviour. Among those with severe depression, there is a 15 per cent chance that patients may attempt to kill themselves.

The risk of suicide may be present in depression. It is important that people are aware of support groups, such as the Samaritans.

Post-natal depression

Pregnancy and childbirth are a time of profound
physical and emotional change. However, one in 10 women
develop some form of depression after childbirth.

The immediate post-natal period (the first few days after giving birth) is characterized by a number of physical and emotional changes, and can be a challenging time for mothers.

POST-NATAL CHANGES
As hormone levels fluctuate, many women experience extremes of emotion, and may develop the 'baby blues' – a mild form of depression – for a few days after the birth.

Around 10 per cent of women, however, experience longer-lasting symptoms of depression. Most commonly this condition occurs between four and six weeks after childbirth.

Severe depression with suicidal ideas and psychotic symptoms (puerperal psychosis) is rare after childbirth.

RISK FACTORS
Major risk factors for developing post-natal depression include:
■ History of psychiatric illness, especially depression
■ Mood disorder during the pregnancy
■ Relationship difficulties
■ Lack of support
■ Recent negative life event such as loss of a loved one.
   Minor risk factors include:
■ Low income
■ Complicated delivery
■ Severe 'maternity blues'
■ Physical problems in the baby.

SYMPTOMS
Depressive symptoms include apathy, anxiety, low mood and poor concentration.

Severe depression is often characterized by hostility toward the baby, or even psychosis, and must be actively treated with referral to the specialist mental health team. Mother and baby unit day-care or admission may be required.

Post-natal depression may begin in the first six months after childbirth. Symptoms can affect a mother's ability to look after her baby.

Diagnosing post-natal depression

There is no definitive test to confirm the diagnosis of post-natal depression, which is made by clinical assessment.

HORMONE LEVELS
The period after childbirth is dominated by changes in hormone levels, but there is no evidence that the hormone profiles of post-natally depressed women are any different from those women who do not develop depression. Research has, however, suggested a small increased risk in women who test positive for autoimmune thyroid disorders.

POST-NATAL CHECKS
As well as general monitoring during the post-natal period, the post-natal check at six weeks gives the doctor or health visitor an ideal opportunity to assess the mother's mental state.

The six-week post-natal check may include a questionnaire and a clinical interview. This enables doctors to identify women at risk of severe depression.

Treating depression

In most cases, post-natal depression lasts only a few months. Symptoms are managed by psychological support, with or without drug therapy.

As well as community care support, a variety of psychological interventions prove beneficial to women with post-natal depression. These include:
- Community-based non-directive counselling
- Cognitive behavioural therapy
- Psychotherapy.

DRUG THERAPY

While psychological intervention is effective in the management of mild to moderate post-natal depression, greater benefit can be gained from the simultaneous use of drug therapy.

In those who do not respond to psychological measures and patients with moderate to severe depression, anti-depressants may be prescribed. The few who develop psychotic symptoms will need further treatment with, for example, tranquillizers.

A dilemma arises for many women who may wish to breast-feed their baby while being treated. The advantages of medication for the mother must be balanced against the possible effect on the baby, especially in women on high dose regimens.

HORMONE THERAPY

Following the pattern of hormonal change in the six weeks after childbirth, both progestogens and oestrogen have been suggested for use in post-natal depression.

As yet, there is no evidence to suggest that progestogens are effective. Oestrogen use is unlicensed and is therefore only given as part of clinical trials. It may, however, eventually have a beneficial role for some women.

Antidepressants may relieve symptoms of severe post-natal depression. The drugs take effect within several weeks; full recovery may take up to a year.

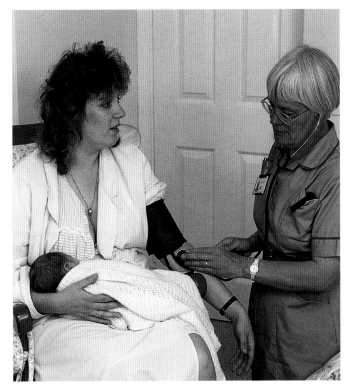

COMMUNITY SUPPORT

While most women will benefit from the community support offered by the community care team, for some a dedicated mother and baby day unit would be preferable. Unfortunately there are very few in the UK and for many, the only alternative is out-patient psychiatric care or even admission.

Involving the community psychiatric nurse at an early stage offers the patient and her family extra support as well as specialist monitoring of her progress.

Regular checks by a health visitor ensures that affected mothers receive extra support. The mother's mental health will be monitored.

RECOVERY

The majority of women, even if left untreated, will recover within three to six months. Ten per cent of women who develop post-natal depression will still be symptomatic a year later, with a smaller percentage continuing with a chronic relapsing mood disorder. Depression can recur in subsequent pregnancies.

Prevention strategies

Awareness of the risks, with prevention plans where possible, can reduce the incidence of depression.

Recognizing the symptoms
Antenatal education, covering the emotional pressures of parenthood, the temporary nature of 'maternity blues' and the risk of post-natal depression, will help women and their partners recognize early symptoms and reduce some of the associated guilt and anxiety.

Antenatal appointments should be used to promote a supportive relationship between the patient and the community care team,

Women who are at risk of post-natal depression can receive extra support during pregnancy. Parenting classes help to prepare for the arrival of a baby.

identifying those women who lack support from their own family and who have few friends.

Depression in pregnancy
If depression develops during pregnancy, it can be managed effectively with general support, psychotherapy and, if indicated, antidepressant therapy.

Although many women want to avoid taking any medication during pregnancy, the use of antidepressants and some newer selective serotonin re-uptake inhibitors (SSRIs) has not been shown to cause any congenital abnormalities in babies. In pregnant mothers with symptoms, the use of drug therapy is essential as the risk of relapse is high.

During the birth and in the immediate weeks following, the mother identified as high risk will benefit from extra support.

Medication in psychiatric illness

Drug therapy for psychiatric disorders has changed the lives of millions of people. Concerns exist, however, that psychiatry may have become too reliant on drugs, overlooking important issues.

Since the 1950s, drug therapy has revolutionized the treatment of psychiatric illness, radically improving the quality of life and outlook for tens of millions of people with mental illness.

TREATMENT CATEGORIES

There are two categories of treatment for psychiatric illness: psychotherapeutic and organic (or somatic).

Drug treatments fall into the latter category, as they involve treating mental health problems by attempting to change or regulate brain chemistry. Ideally, however, drug therapy should be combined with psychotherapy to achieve a holistic treatment programme for mental illness.

DRUG CLASSES

Drugs for psychiatric illnesses fall into four main classes:
■ Antidepressants – used to treat mood disorders such as depression, anxiety disorders, bipolar disorder and bulimia
■ Antipsychotics – used to treat delusional disorders such as schizophrenia
■ Anxiolytics – used to treat anxiety disorders
■ Psychostimulants – used to treat attention deficit hyperactivity disorder (ADHD) and, occasionally, depression.

RAPID RELIEF

Specifically, drug therapies provide rapid relief from some of the worst symptoms of psychiatric illness, saving lives and allowing proper treatment programmes to be implemented.

Medication can restore sleep patterns (typically disrupted by psychiatric disorders), as well as appetite and energy. This allows patients to focus on their problems and avoid institutionalization.

Drug therapies can also help patients for whom other therapies have failed, although today drugs generally provide the first line of treatment for most psychiatric patients.

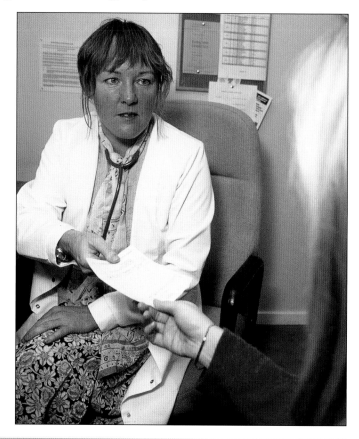

Medication has transformed the lives of people with psychiatric disorders. By altering brain chemistry, drugs relieve the most distressing symptoms.

How mental healthcare has changed

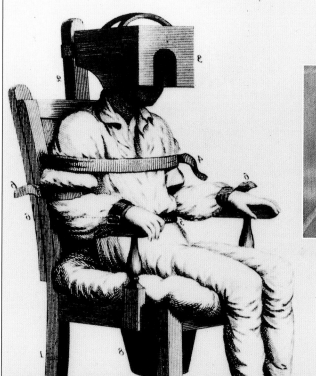

Before the advent of drug medication, physical restraints played a large part in the control of mental illness. Straps and restraining chairs were used.

Many people with psychiatric disorders used to spend their lives in mental hospitals. Effective drug medication means that this is now largely a thing of the past.

Drugs have radically changed the character of psychiatry and mental healthcare. Before the advent of effective drug therapies in the 1950s, severe psychiatric disorders were largely untreatable due to lack of understanding and knowledge, and psychiatric hospitals and asylums had an essentially custodial function.

RESTRAINT

Many patients with mental illness could only be controlled by physical restraints, such as shackles and straitjackets, and lived their entire lives in institutions with no hope of recovery or release. Thanks to drug therapies, most psychiatric patients can now live outside hospitals and many can return to work, family and the community.

Decisions on treatment

Doctors often prescribe drugs to treat mental disorders rather than recommend therapy. However, research shows that both may be equally beneficial.

Drug therapy is aimed at treating the symptoms of mental illness. Psychotherapy helps patients to tackle the underlying causes of their problem.

Some psychologists argue that too many doctors and psychiatrists rely exclusively or excessively on drugs, without exploring alternative treatment options such as psychotherapy.

PSYCHOTHERAPY

Studies show that, in general, drugs and psychotherapies have approximately equivalent rates of success and that for some disorders, such as anxiety and depression, drugs are actually less successful. Drugs can only treat the symptoms of mental

illness, and not the causes, and of course, they carry the risk of varoius side effects.

Psychotherapy provides patients with lasting coping strategies and considers the wider context of a person's life including family, work and friends. It is important to note, however, that often the best treatment plan involves a combination of both medication and therapy. In addition not all patients will respond positively to one or the other.

MEDICATION

There are several possible reasons, however, why drugs are often the preferred course of treatment.

■ Time – doctors are under pressure to see more patients faster, and drugs offer a quick, convenient form of treatment

■ Cost – a course of drugs can be much cheaper than a lengthy

course of therapy

■ Consultations – the patient need only visit the doctor once, rather than the minimum of 10 times for most courses of psychotherapy

■ Stigma – for some patients, psychotherapy carries a stigma: it is easier to view mental illness as an organic problem that can be treated with a pill than as a personality defect.

A major drawback in the effectiveness of drug therapies is the issue of compliance. Psychiatric patients are particularly unlikely to stick to their prescribed course of medication through a combination of dislike of the unpleasant side effects sometimes caused by the drugs and erratic judgement caused by the particular psychiatric condition.

Non-compliance is a particular problem in schizophrenic patients, especially when they have been

Drug therapy can be very effective when used correctly. However, for a variety of reasons not all patients are happy to take drugs long term.

released from hospital back into the community.

LONG-TERM EFFECTS

A succession of new drugs for psychiatric disorders have been hailed as 'miracle cures', only to disappoint in the long term as problems have become apparent. Barbiturates and benzodiazepines – prescribed for the treatment of anxiety disorders – have been shown to be dependency forming, for example.

The long-term effects of relatively new drugs such as Prozac and Ritalin, which may be prescribed for many years, are not currently known. Prescription of these drugs, although very popular now, may carry a heavy price in the future.

Treating mental illness

There are four main classes of drugs used in the treatment of psychiatric illness. Antidepressants, antipsychotics, anxiolytics and psychostimulants are all successful, but work in different ways.

The type of medication used to treat psychiatric disorders depends upon the nature of the disorder.

Antidepressants are used to treat depression that, in its severe form, is a life-threatening illness. Even mild depression has a significant impact on quality of life. Antidepressants help to reduce core symptoms of depression such as suicidal urges and negative thinking, and generally even out the worst troughs of negative mood.

MECHANISM
Antidepressants work by boosting levels of neurotransmitters (chemical substances released by nerve endings) in the brain, primarily serotonin. However, they must be taken for up to two weeks before they start to work, and therefore may not be indicated for suicidal patients.

Antidepressants are not dependency forming, but can have serious side

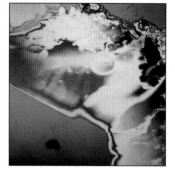

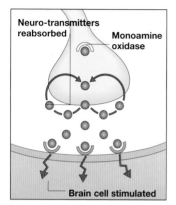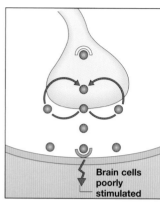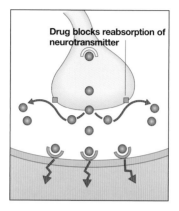

In a normal brain, neurotransmitters are released in sufficient quantities. They are constantly reabsorbed and broken down.

In people suffering from depression, fewer neurotransmitters than normal are released. The result is that brain cells are poorly stimulated.

Tricyclics and SSRIs increase the levels of neurotransmitters in the brain. They do this by blocking their reabsorption after they have been released.

effects, including dry mouth, constipation, blurred vision and delayed ejaculation/orgasm. These are known as anticholinergic effects and are experienced by older patients in particular. The chances that any given antidepressant will work for an individual are 65 per cent. If one drug is not effective, doctors can switch to a different course.

TYPES OF ANTIDEPRESSANT
There are several different types of antidepressant drugs:

GABA (gamma aminobutyric acid) is a neurotransmitter. Levels of GABA and other neurotransmitters are boosted by antidepressants.

■ Monoamine oxidase inhibitors (MAOIs) boost levels of the neurotransmitters serotonin and norepinephrine in the brain by blocking the action of an enzyme, monoamine oxidase (MAO), which breaks them down. Examples include isocarboxazid and phenelzine. They can have severe side effects, and patients should avoid foods containing substances normally metabolized by MAO, such as red wine, broad beans, soy sauce and over-the-counter cough and cold remedies. MAOIs have generally been superseded by newer antidepressants
■ Tricyclics prevent nerve cells from reabsorbing norepinephrine and serotonin after they have

been released, boosting levels of these neurotransmitters in the synaptic gaps. They also, however, produce anticholinergic side effects, including elevated heart rate and decreased blood pressure on standing. Examples include clomipramine and bupropion. Again, newer drugs have mostly superseded tricyclics
■ Selective serotonin reuptake inhibitors (SSRIs) work in the same way as tricyclics, but target serotonin only. Generally, they have fewer side effects than tricyclics and are safer for patients with other, physical, disorders. Examples include fluoxetine (Prozac) and fluvoxamine.

Prozac

Prozac is the trade name for the SSRI fluoxetine. Over 37 million people around the world have taken Prozac, making it the best-selling antidepressant of all time.

In the initial years after its launch, Prozac was hailed as a wonder drug, gaining reams of publicity and support. Inevitably, though, there has been a backlash. In practice, Prozac is not a miracle cure for depression – it is effective at relieving the symptoms of depression in 60–80 per cent of users, a similar success rate to other antidepressants. Also, like other antidepressants, it has side effects, particularly on sexual function.

Recent fears
Disappointment at Prozac's failure to live up to its initial hype has been compounded by growing fears of over-prescription, together with scare stories linking the drug to violent outbursts and suicides.

However, this has not stopped Prozac from increasing its range of uses. It is now prescribed for bulimia, anxiety disorders and some forms of behavioural disorder in children.

When the antidepressant Prozac was launched it gained much publicity. Since this time, over 37 million people have been prescribed the drug.

Other classes of psychiatric drugs

Other drug categories for the treatment of psychiatric disorders include antipsychotics, anxiolytics and psychostimulants.

ANTIPSYCHOTICS
Schizophrenia and delusional disorders are difficult to treat without drugs. Antipsychotic drugs are neuroleptics – they depress the central nervous system, mainly by blocking dopamine receptors, and are sometimes known as the major tranquillizers.

Side effects include sedation, weight gain, muscle stiffness and tremors. In the long term, antipsychotic drugs can cause tardive dyskinesia, an involuntary movement disorder, which can be irreversible.

Examples of antipsychotics are chlorpromazine, haloperidol and the relatively new drug, clozapine, which is highly effective but has severe side effects on the immune system and can only be used with caution.

ANXIOLYTICS
Anxiety disorders such as phobias, panic attacks and obsessive-compulsive disorder (OCD) can be treated with anxiolytic drugs, known as minor tranquillizers. These relax muscles, reduce tension and help restore sleeping patterns, providing temporary stress relief.

HABIT-FORMING DRUGS
However, anxiolytics can be habit-forming, leading to physical dependency, tolerance (need for larger doses) and withdrawal symptoms. In general, antidepressants are

much more effective for treating anxiety disorders, especially OCD and panic attacks. Although antidepressants take longer to have an effect, they are not habit-forming.

Anxioloytics include benzodiazepines, although these sedatives are much less commonly prescribed now than in the past, as awareness of their habit-forming properties has increased. Diazepam

(Valium) is an example of a benzodiazepine.

Before benzodiazepines were discovered, barbiturates were used, but these are even more habit-forming, and carry a greater risk of overdose. Barbiturate abuse was once extremely common in the developed world.

PSYCHOSTIMULANTS
Whereas anxiolytics are 'downers', psychostimulants are 'uppers', increasing the

activity of the central nervous system. Most psychostimulants are amphetamine (a drug that stimulates the sympathetic nervous system) derivatives.

In the 1950s, psychostimulants were sometimes used as 'diet pills' for the treatment of obesity. Today, they may be used to treat depression, particularly in patients who have not responded to antidepressants or elderly patients.

Anxiolytic drugs are used to treat a variety of anxiety disorders. The drugs relax patients and help to restore normal sleeping patterns.

Differences can be seen in the brains of a person with schizophrenia (top) and a normal person (bottom). In schizophrenics the ventricles (white) are enlarged.

ADHD and Ritalin

Today, psychostimulants are primarily used in the treatment of attention deficit hyperactivity disorder (ADHD), a behavioural problem affecting children. Methylphenidate (Ritalin) is the preferred drug, and is believed to help children with ADHD to focus more clearly on their thoughts, thus reducing the mental 'noise' contributing to their symptoms.

Over-prescription
Prescription of Ritalin has increased six-fold since 1990, and up to six per cent of all

Ritalin is a psychostimulant, typically used to treat attention deficit disorder in children. However the long-term effects of this drug are not known.

school-age American boys are now believed to be on Ritalin. Not surprisingly, there has been considerable concern about over-prescription, particularly given the lack of knowledge about the effects of long-term use of Ritalin in either children or adults.

These concerns are exacerbated by debate over the clinical legitimacy of the diagnosis of ADHD.

Side effects
Common side effects of Ritalin include poor appetite, headaches, stomach pain, high blood pressure, nervousness and sleeplessness. Rarer but more severe effects include aggravation of underlying anxiety, depression, psychosis and seizures.

Anorexia nervosa

Anorexia nervosa is an eating disorder associated with mental illness. It is characterized by a person's focus on losing weight, often to an extreme degree.

Anorexia nervosa is the name given to a condition in which people are anxious about becoming overweight and as a result are often very thin. Under-eating, vomiting and excessive exercising are the most common ways used to achieve weight loss. The condition usually affects young girls in their teens. Males who develop anorexia nervosa make up between 5 and 10 per cent of patients referred to specialist clinics; the proportion of boys to girls may be higher in a younger age group.

PROGNOSIS

The weightloss may not be evident at first. However, there are often other associated problems such as depression, anxiety disorders and low self esteem. As time progresses, the focus on weight loss becomes

In people who have had anorexia for longer than five years, X-rays may reveal osteoporosis. Bones become brittle and are liable to fracture easily as a result of a lack of calcium in the diet and low hormone levels.

even more determined and the consequent avoidance of high-calorie (usually high-fat) foods becomes even more obsessive.

People who suffer from long-term anorexia nervosa will go to great lengths to remain in control of their food intake, in order to avoid, as they see it, 'getting fat'. Any weight will make them feel overweight.

The illness can take a prolonged and severe course, resulting in marked emaciation. As well as the harmful physical effects, including fragile

This woman is suffering from advanced anorexia nervosa, and displays the characteristic signs of extreme emaciation. If the condition persists, it is sometimes necessary to admit people to hospital for treatment.

bones (osteoporosis), fractures, heart problems and infertility, anorexia nervosa has profound psychological effects. Personal and emotional relationships deteriorate, leading to social isolation and poor employment and study prospects.

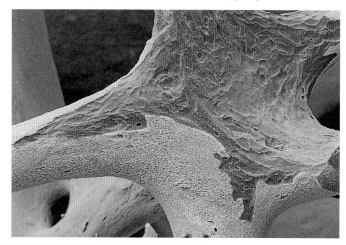

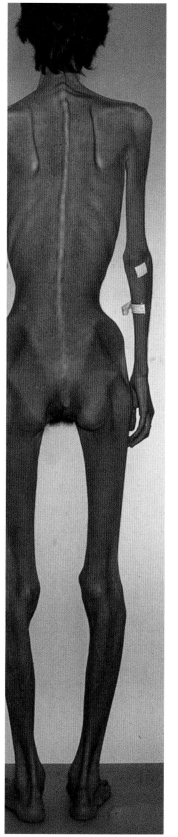

Biological effects of starvation

Anorexia nervosa is a psychological, or mental, illness that stems from an intense fear of gaining weight. The desire to avoid eating overrides any appetite or hunger pains, and gradual starvation can lead to extreme weight loss. In advanced cases, this has serious consequences for the person's

physical condition, including the following:
■ Cessation or lack of menstruation and consequent loss of fertility
■ An irregular heartbeat and low blood pressure
■ Erosion of tooth enamel if a person is vomiting
■ Metabolic and biochemical

abnormalities, for example a low blood sugar
■ Swelling of the hands and feet
■ Anaemia
■ Subnormal body temperature
■ In severe cases, the heart, liver and kidneys can fail

In spite of the physical symptoms, those suffering from anorexia are frequently in denial about their condition, and doctors have to repeatedly explain and draw attention to the problems. In some cases, the patient may 'play along' with the doctor and lie about food intake, or surreptitiously vomit any food that is eaten. In some cases, unfortunately anorexia can be fatal.

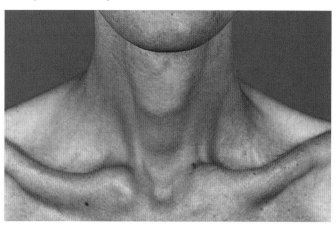

Anorexia is characterized by emaciation, with bones prominent. Up to 25 per cent of total body weight may be lost.

Causes of anorexia nervosa

The causes of anorexia nervosa remain unclear but it is thought to be due to a number of genetic, environmental, hormonal and societal factors. Some experts believe that there may be an inherited aspect to anorexia nervosa, and that those who have a family history of depression, eating disorders or anxiety are able to pass on, in their genes, a tendency to develop anorexia. Certainly, adolescents and young people who develop the disorder show signs of obsessiveness, anxiety and a degree of depression. Our upbringing also influences our behaviours in later life. Family behaviours around eating may play a part in the later development of anorexia. In addition, difficult family relationships are often revealed and frequently family therapy is needed to tease out underlying issues that may be a contributing factor to an eating disorder.

Modern society places great pressures on children as they grow up and messages that over-thin models and physical beauty is the norm has been highlighted as a possible trigger for eating disorders. This coupled with stressful situations, such as bullying at school and puberty, or even abuse, may all contribute to the condition.

Personality aspects, as well as physical characteristics, are passed on from parents to children in their DNA. It is thought that a predisposition to anorexia may be inherited.

From infancy, customs and assumptions concerning food are instilled in the child, often subconsciously. The exact role of family influence in the development of anorexia is unknown, but it may be a factor.

Mental health and anorexia nervosa

In spite of the obvious and visible damage that is done to the bodies and minds of people affected by anorexia nervosa, the condition is often not fully understood by society. The behaviour is seen by some as not as driven by a mental illness but by vanity and the need to resemble the waif-like figures of celebrities or models.

This view trivializes the internal emotional conflict and distress that underlies the condition. Usually, an affected person lacks someone to confide in and seeks alternative ways of coping. Very few people with anorexia will easily admit that they are struggling and will go to great lengths to hide their behaviour, and their weight loss from friends and family. This can often lead to social isolation, which exacerbates the condition even more.

About 50 per cent of people with anorexia are also suffering from depression in varying degrees. Low self-esteem, or a fixed and poor estimate of one's

As with other eating disorders, a characteristic of anorexia is a distorted self-image. This produces an inability to accept that a very low weight is undesirable.

It is oversimplistic to assume that images from fashion and the media force people to become anorexic. However, there is undoubted pressure to conform to a physical 'norm'.

own self-worth, are universal features of all eating disorders, and apply especially in the case of anorexia nervosa. In addition, some may feel a 'compulsion' to behave as they do, and have no control over their actions.

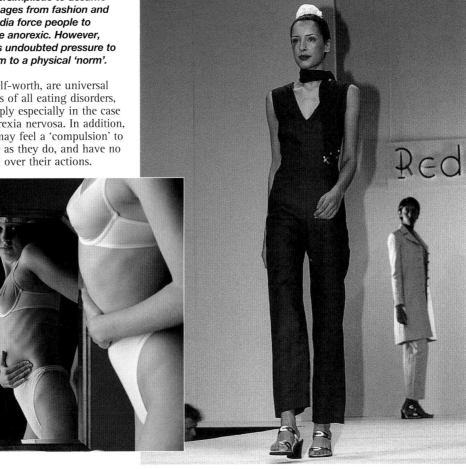

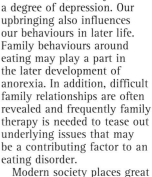

Identifying and treating anorexia nervosa

Identifying anorexia nervosa may be straightforward for a doctor, but convincing a person of their condition can be extremely difficult. Counselling, drug treatment and, sometimes, hospital admission may be required.

DIAGNOSTIC CRITERIA

There is no diagnostic laboratory test to identify anorexia nervosa. However, initial weight loss, not associated with any other medical illness, followed by the subsequent maintenance of a body weight that remains significantly below normal for an individual of the same height, age and sex as the sufferer, is one diagnostic feature of the condition. The peak onset of anorexia nervosa is in the mid–late teens.

HORMONAL DISTURBANCE

Another sign of the condition is a profound hormonal disturbance, which takes different forms in males and females. Young women who have reached puberty and have started to have regular periods find that their menstrual flow lessens and their periods become irregular. In many cases, menstruation ceases completely (known as amenorrhea). The equivalent hormonal disturbance in males reduces the frequency

A common side effect of anorexia is a deficiency of vitamin C (sometimes known as scurvy) mainly found in fruit and vegetables). This can result in bleeding gums and haemorrhaging under the skin.

of ejaculations, and eventually limits the ability to have erections.

Three consecutive months without a menstrual period is taken to be one of the three main diagnostic features of anorexia nervosa in females. The other two are the low weight and the overriding preoccupation with dietary restriction and an absolute avoidance of weight gain. Taken together, these features have been described by one expert as together constituting a 'phobic avoidance of normal weight'.

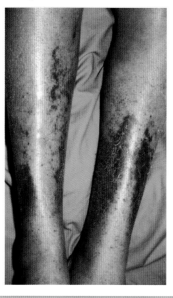

Brain chemistry
A psychogenic (in the mind) aversion to food may affect the chemical balance of the brain, thus affecting mood and mental balance

Fine, downy body hair
Lanugo hair may be present on the patient's body, especially on the back

While there is no single, typical picture of an anorexic's appearance, there are a number of physical and physiological changes that are common to many sufferers of the disorder.

Low pulse and blood pressure
(hypotension)

Amenorrhea
Cessation of menstruation for at least three consecutive months is a diagnostic feature of anorexia; total failure of sexual function is rare

Oedema
Swelling of the lower limbs due to fluid accumulation in the tissues may occur in advanced cases

Anorexia nervosa and brain function

It is known that people can inherit genetically determined constitutional traits or personality characteristics. This may predispose a person to develop anorexia nervosa if the environmental factors are unfavourable. Living with a very low body weight has profound effects on the way the brain works. This is particularly applicable to thought processes and the way in which the brain processes information.

Recent research suggests that differences may be visible on brain scans of teenage girls with

anorexia, compared with girls who do not have it. What is not yet clear is whether the lesions that can be seen to develop as a result of the illness or were there before the girls developed their illness. What happens to the brain after recovery has not yet been established.

Evidence of damage to the hypothalamic region of the brain, which controls hunger, thirst and sexual function, may be revealed by brain scanning. Whether this is a cause or an effect of the disease is not clear.

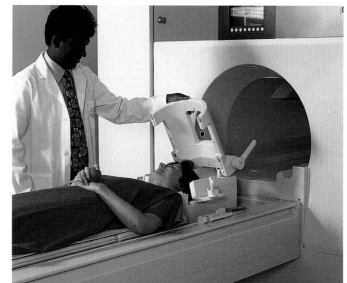

Recovery

Recovery can be a long and difficult process. The patient first needs to regain body weight before embarking on a course of long-term psychotherapy.

Weight gain by itself does not constitute a recovery. However, without restoring weight to at least the lower end of the normal range, recovery cannot take place, as constrained mental functioning means an affected person cannot grasp new ideas or process new information.

Researchers have different views about how attitudes typical of people with anorexia are created and maintained. All agree that restoration of near-normal weight by supervised feeding and counselling or psychotherapy are essential to achieve an increase in self-esteem and establish habits of more flexible thinking. A reward system is sometimes used to encourage weight gain.

Someone who has recovered from anorexia is able to eat enough regular, nutritious meals to maintain a near-normal weight. This enables them to live a normal life, including sustaining personal relationships. Weight gain will also restore any damage to fertility.

Fluoxetine (Prozac) is an antidepressant that is often used to treat sufferers of anorexia nervosa. It controls levels of serotonin, a naturally occurring compound in the body that influences mood.

Severely emaciated patients will require intravenous infusions to stabilize homeostasis and regain body weight. The fatty, vitamin enhanced and mineral-rich solution may contain as many as 3000 calories.

Long-term recovery and support

People with anorexia nervosa require evaluation and treatment focused on biological, psychological and social features of this complex, chronic health condition. Assessment and ongoing management should

After the patient has regained weight, counselling can begin. These intensive therapy sessions may last for months or even years, and are designed to help the sufferer overcome the negative self-image they have of their body.

be interdisciplinary, and is best accomplished by a team consisting of medical, nursing, nutritional and mental health professionals. Treatment should be provided by healthcare professionals with expertise in managing patients with eating disorders, and knowledge about normal adolescent physical and psychological development.

Hospitalization is necessary in the presence of malnutrition, clinical evidence of medical or psychiatric decompensation or failure of out-patient treatment.

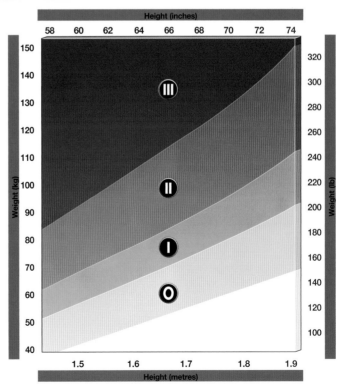

Doctors determine the body mass index (BMI) from an individual's weight and height. The formula is: BMI = (weight in kg)/(height in m)². On the above chart, III, II and I denote grades of obesity and 0 indicates the boundaries of desirable weight. A BMI reading of less than 17.5 indicates possible anorexia.

Body dysmorphic disorder

Body dysmorphic disorder is a mental illness in which people are obsessed with their appearance. The condition causes distress and often disrupts an individual's personal and professional life.

Body dysmorphic disorder (BDD) is a preoccupation with an imagined defect in a person's appearance. If a slight physical anomaly is present, the preoccupation is excessive.

Many people are concerned to a greater or lesser degree with some aspect of their appearance. To be diagnosed with BDD, however, the preoccupation must cause significant distress or impairment in a person's social or occupational functioning.

COMMON CONCERNS

Complaints about shape or symmetry of facial features are the most common, although any part of the body may be the focus of concerns.

People often have multiple preoccupations, which can be specific or very vague, such as feeling that they are ugly.

People with body dysmorphic disorder are excessively concerned with how they look. They may scrutinize themselves in a mirror, looking for defects.

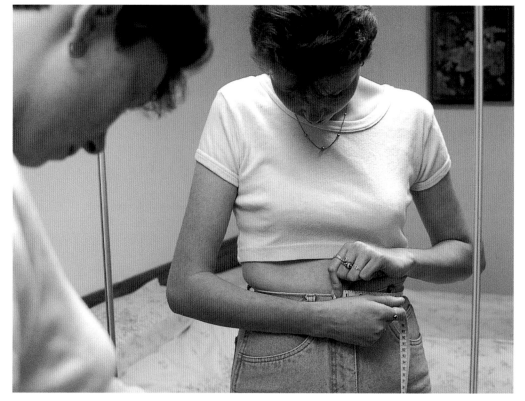

What are the symptoms?

BDD is difficult to control, and sufferers spend several hours a day thinking about their appearance. They often avoid a range of social and public situations to prevent feeling uncomfortable. Alternatively, they may enter such situations but remain very anxious and self-conscious.

Sufferers may try to hide their perceived defect by using heavy make-up, changing their posture or wearing particular clothes. They often feel compelled to repeat certain time-consuming rituals such as:
■ Checking their appearance either directly or in a reflective surface (for example a mirror, CD or shop window)
■ Excessive grooming
■ Picking at their skin to make it smooth
■ Comparing themselves against models in magazines or television
■ Dieting and excessive exercise or weight-lifting.

Such behaviours usually intensify the preoccupation and exacerbate patients' depression and self-disgust.

BDD sufferers may become obsessed with exercise in an attempt to 'improve' their body. They may try weight-lifting to change body shape dramatically.

DEGREE OF IMPAIRMENT

Some sufferers acknowledge that they may exaggerate problems. Others are so convinced about their defect that they are regarded as having a delusion.

Although sufferers often realize that others think their appearance is normal, and have been told so many times, they usually distort these comments to fit in with their views (for example, 'They only say I'm normal to be nice to me'). Alternatively, they may remember one critical comment about their appearance and dismiss a hundred other complimentary remarks.

SEVERITY

Although BDD concerns may sound trivial, a high percentage of sufferers will require hospitalization. Some become house-bound, undertake unnecessary cosmetic surgery or even attempt suicide.

Causes of BDD

Although the condition was first defined over a century ago, there has so far been very limited medical research into body dysmorphic disorder.

In general terms, there are two different levels of explanation: psychological and biological, both of which may be accurate.

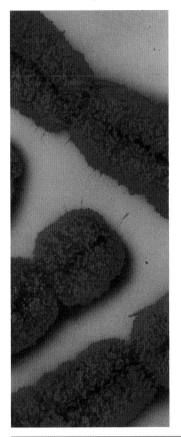

This micrograph shows human chromosomes, which carry our genetic information. A predisposition to conditions such as BDD may be genetic.

PSYCHOLOGICAL CAUSES

A psychological explanation emphasizes that an individual may judge themselves almost exclusively by their appearance, and therefore excessively focus their attention on themselves. Consequently, they may develop a heightened perception of their appearance and become increasingly obsessed about every slight imperfection.

Eventually there is a discrepancy between what they believe they should ideally look like and how they see themselves. Avoiding social situations or using certain behaviours prevents them testing out some of their fears, which in turn maintains their excessive self-focused attention.

BIOLOGICAL CAUSES

A biological explanation emphasizes that an individual has a genetic predisposition to a mental disorder, which may increase their likelihood of developing BDD. Certain stresses or life events, especially during adolescence, may precipitate the onset of the condition.

Once the disorder has developed, there may be a chemical imbalance of serotonin or other chemicals in the brain.

Who is affected?

The incidence of BDD is unknown; studies that have been done have either been too small or unreliable. The best estimate is that one per cent of the population might be affected. BDD may be more common in women than in men in the community, although clinic samples tend to have an equal proportion of men and women.

SEEKING HELP

BDD usually begins in adolescence – a time when people are generally most sensitive about their appearance.

However, due to shame and embarrassment, many sufferers wait for years before seeking help. When they do seek help through mental health professionals, they often have other symptoms such as depression or social phobia and do not reveal their real concerns because they fear that others will think them vain.

The physical changes that occur in puberty can be difficult for many people to deal with. BDD is most likely to arise during the teenage years.

Behaviour therapy and medication

Although BDD can be difficult to treat, certain therapies have led to successful outcomes. To date, however, there have been no controlled trials to compare different types of treatment and determine the most effective.

However, there have been a number of case reports and small-scale trials that have demonstrated the effectiveness of two types of treatment, namely cognitive behaviour therapy (CBT) and anti-obsessional medication.

Cognitive behaviour therapy
CBT is based on a structured programme of self-help so that the individual learns to alter the way that they think about their appearance.

An individual's attitude to their appearance is crucial. This is demonstrated by people who have a physical defect, such as a port-wine stain on the face, and yet are well-adjusted because they believe that their appearance is just one aspect of themselves.

BDD sufferers have to confront their fears without avoidance (a process called 'exposure') and to stop all 'safety behaviours', such as excessive camouflage. This means repeatedly learning to tolerate the resulting discomfort.

Facing up to the fear becomes easier and the anxiety gradually subsides. Sufferers begin by confronting simple situations and

Cognitive behaviour therapy aims to change how patients perceive their appearance. They are encouraged to face their fears to reduce anxiety.

then gradually work up to more difficult ones.

Medication
Anti-obsessional medications such as fluoxetine (Prozac) are thought to be effective. They are called selective serotonin re-uptake inhibitors (SSRIs) and may be used alone or in combination with psychological treatment.

BDD has been linked to another condition, obsessive-compulsive disorder (OCD). SSRIs, which have been effective in the treatment of OCD, appear to reduce the obsessive thoughts, the emotional distress related to the thoughts and also the compulsive behaviour.

Side effects are possible, but the drugs are not addictive and may be stopped without withdrawal symptoms. Medication is especially helpful when a person is depressed, as it may help in improving their motivation.

Bulimia nervosa

Bulimia nervosa is an eating disorder. It is characterized by the affected person bingeing on food and then using various means to prevent themselves gaining weight.

In bulimia nervosa, the affected individual eats large amounts of food over a short period of time and then goes to great lengths to avoid weight gain.

Bulimia nervosa affects both women and men and can occur on its own, or as part of another eating disorder such as anorexia nervosa. Unlike people with anorexia, however, people with bulimia may be of normal weight, or even overweight.

COGNITIVE PROCESSES

People with bulimia have an intense fear of becoming fat and this fear grows to dominate their lives. They feel, to an extreme degree, that their weight reflects their worth as a person and thus determines their self-esteem.

Fears and beliefs about the importance of weight make it almost impossible for bulimic individuals to return to a normal eating pattern. Over-estimation of bodily size and a refusal to accept that they are not fat are adhered to rigidly, despite reassurance from family, friends and therapists.

BEHAVIOURAL PATTERNS

During a binge, the person feels that they are unable to stop eating and that their eating is out of control. However, once the binge is over, these thoughts are replaced by disgust at their

People with bulimia become obsessed with their weight. Affected individuals refuse to accept that they are not over-weight despite reassurances.

Bulimia is more common in women than men and usually develops between the ages of 18 and 30. This disorder is linked with low self-esteem.

behaviour and at the amount of food that has been eaten.

The person then takes steps to prevent weight gain. They may induce vomiting immediately, take laxatives or follow a

vigorous exercise regime.

A diagnosis of bulimia nervosa is usually made if this pattern is repeated at least twice a week for three months or longer.

PREVALENCE

Some studies suggest that one per cent of women and 0.1 per cent of men have symptoms that are severe enough to interfere significantly with their lives.

Physiological complications

Bulimia is associated with binge eating followed by vomiting. This causes physical problems, such as dehydration, which should be explained to patients.

Most people with bulimia nervosa regularly induce vomiting. This can have several immediate consequences; if vomit is accidentally inhaled, damage to the lungs may occur, and forced vomiting can tear or even rupture the walls of the stomach. Frequent vomiting exposes the teeth to stomach acid, which accelerates decay.

Individuals may also lose fluid and potassium through frequent vomiting, and as a result can become dangerously dehydrated. Low potassium levels may lead

to heart arrhythmias and kidney impairment.

LONG-TERM EFFECTS

In the long term, it seems that the metabolic changes induced by alternately gorging and starving the body are associated with the development of Type 2 diabetes and polycystic ovary syndrome. The link in both cases appears to be the development of insulin resistance.

People with bulimia nervosa tend to binge on foods that have a high sugar and high fat content. Rapid rises in blood sugar and consequent insulin secretion followed by fasting may affect the body's ability to metabolize carbohydrates satisfactorily in the longer term.

Genetics and personality

Bulimia seems to be caused by a combination of factors – genetic, personality and environmental.

GENETICS
Eating disorders tend to run in families, and studies on identical twins suggest that genetics may be a major factor. However, it is more likely that certain genes predispose to personality traits that are a factor in bulimia, rather than directly predisposing to the disorder itself. There is also a high incidence of depression and substance addiction among close relatives of bulimics.

PERSONALITY
Individuals with bulimia tend to have certain personality traits – typically, perfectionism, obsessiveness and impulsiveness, coupled with low self-esteem, mood instability and anxiety.

People affected by bulimia tend to have certain personality traits. These may include obsessive behaviour, low self-esteem and anxiety attacks.

They may also have a borderline personality disorder.

Bulimic individuals often have difficulty maturing and dealing satisfactorily with puberty, parental relationships, marriage and sexuality. They also tend to score low on tests of social co-operation. These personality traits are almost always set against a background of a poorly functioning family. The family may be goal-orientated and high-achieving, but may be affected by destructive interpersonal relationships.

ORGANIC CAUSES
Although there are few studies in this area, it is suspected that in some people, a malfunction of the serotonin-mediated satiety signaling system makes it difficult to stop eating. PET scans of people with bulimia have shown abnormalities of the hypothalamus in the brain, but these disappear if normal eating patterns are re-established.

Studies in twins have shown that genetic factors may greatly increase the likelihood of developing an eating disorder.

Environmental factors

It is fashionable to blame the promotion of ever-skinnier models and film stars for the escalating incidence of eating disorders. However, there is little evidence that the media has influenced the behaviour of those people with severe eating disorders, although personal remarks from their peer group may contribute to the condition.

Eating disorders are more prevalent among dancers and athletes, suggesting that the demand for individuals to maintain a low level of body fat in order to optimize performance is a causative factor.

Images of thin models have been blamed for the rise in eating disorders. However, negative personal experiences have a greater influence.

Treatment and prognosis

There is little specific treatment for bulimia, but antidepressants may help in treating any associated depression. Potassium supplements are given to compensate for losses caused by repeated purging. In some cases, high doses of fluoxetine (Prozac) halves the frequency of bingeing and also lowers the frequency of the subsequent weight-reducing activities.

Cognitive-behavioural therapy
Cognitive-behavioural therapy (CBT) may help to address the individual's low self-esteem and their preoccupation with their body, weight and food. CBT also addresses eating habits, dieting

People with bulimia may be referred to a therapist who specializes in eating disorders. The aim of treatment is to establish regular eating habits.

and ritualistic exercise. Patients are asked to monitor their feelings and behaviour. CBT provides cognitive methods to challenge rigid thought patterns. It also suggests techniques to improve self-esteem and to identify and appropriately express feelings.

A combination of CBT and drug treatment is the most effective treatment for bulimia.

Prognosis
Sadly, treatment does not often lead to cure. One study showed that 40 per cent of patients remained bulimic after 18 months; another showed that 50 per cent still had an eating disorder after five years.

Bulimia tends to be a lifelong condition, although it may vary in intensity. There is a small risk of sudden death, but generally the damage to physical and mental health occurs over the long term.

Munchausen's syndrome

Munchausen's syndrome is a psychological disorder that
leads people to seek medical treatment for a non-existent illness.
The condition frequently proves difficult to diagnose and treat.

Munchausen's syndrome is a psychological condition in which an individual endeavours to obtain medical treatment for an illness that is non-existent. The condition is named after Baron von Munchausen, a fictional character renowned for telling extraordinary stories.

HOSPITAL ADMISSIONS

If medical staff are unfamiliar with Munchausen's syndrome, and have not encountered the condition before, they may be misled by the often convincing medical history and symptoms. People with Munchausen's syndrome frequently undergo numerous investigations and procedures – there are cases of individuals with more than 200 hospital admissions.

Every patient with persistent symptoms will be thoroughly examined. In people with Munchausen's, however, tests are continually negative.

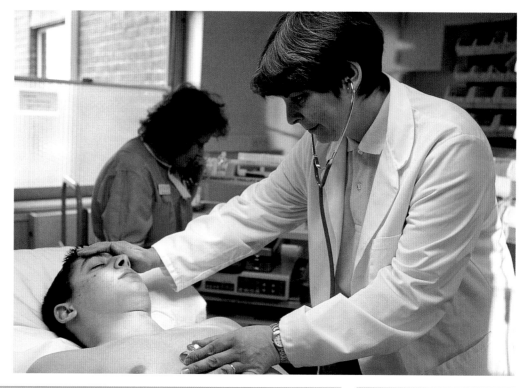

Diagnosis

Munchausen's syndrome is defined by the intentional production of symptoms or illnesses in order to assume a 'sick' role. People with Munchausen's syndrome contrast with those in whom fictitious symptoms may provide financial gain – for example, enable them to claim sick pay. Moreover, although patients may receive drugs as treatment, they are not drug addicts and the procurement of drugs does not appear to motivate them.

DIFFERENTIAL DIAGNOSIS

Doctors may suspect that a difficult patient with unusual or persistent symptoms has Munchausen's syndrome, especially as there are certain symptoms classically associated with the condition. However, other conditions, including real and rare diseases, should always be considered. Munchausen's syndrome can develop from a real illness. For example, a diabetic patient with the disorder may, in order to gain attention, induce episodes of hypoglycaemia (low blood sugar levels) by injecting too much insulin. Such behaviour makes the diabetes extremely difficult to manage.

PSYCHIATRIC DISORDERS

Munchausen's syndrome should be distinguished from other psychiatric disorders, such as somatization. Like those with Munchausen's syndrome, people with somatization have nothing physically wrong with them, but they differ in that they consciously believe that their symptoms are real.

Specific symptoms, such as breathlessness, will always be investigated. 'Real' disorders must be ruled out before a diagnosis is made.

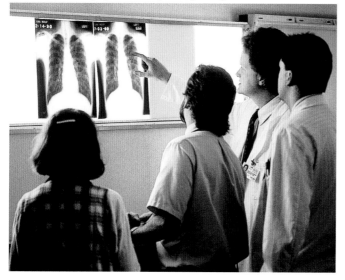

Investigations

Normal tests are usually carried out to investigate any symptoms that a person may present with. In the absence of any positive results, however, suspicions may be raised.

In these cases, medical staff may, if they feel it is appropriate, refer a person for psychiatric assessment. During interviews, the psychiatrist may be able to extract enough information to make a diagnosis.

Some affected people may inject themselves with adrenaline to cause a rise in blood pressure. In this way, they are able to gain medical attention and treatment.

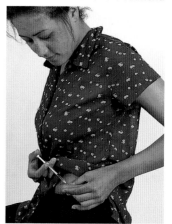

Behaviour

Almost every branch of medicine has experience of individuals who present with Munchausen's syndrome.

SYMPTOMS

Most frequently, those affected by the disorder complain of abdominal, neurological or psychiatric symptoms. They tend to display certain typical patterns of behaviour, and these include:
- Self-admission to hospital Accident and Emergency departments, often relating stories about dramatic events or serious, and frequently fatal, accidents
- A high level of medical knowledge
- A belligerent attitude towards medical staff, especially if challenged about behaviour
- A willingness to undergo any number of investigations or operations. For example, an individual may prefer to have a leg amputated rather than allow self-inflicted injuries to heal and the leg be saved.

Numerous scars indicate that many operations have taken place. This physical evidence may cause doctors to suspect Munchausen's syndrome.

SUSPICIONS

Although Munchausen's patients may be knowledgeable about the medical condition they imitate, there are often certain clues that may alert medical staff.

For example, some individuals have multiple scars as evidence of their previous hospital admissions. Others may complain of a weak leg, for example, but when the 'good' leg is examined, the examining physician may detect that the other leg moves involuntarily.

Some people may imitate unconsciousness, putting up with very painful forms of stimulation without moving or complaining. Yet, if their hand is raised above their head and allowed to fall, it almost never falls onto their face.

It has also been known for people to complain of epileptic

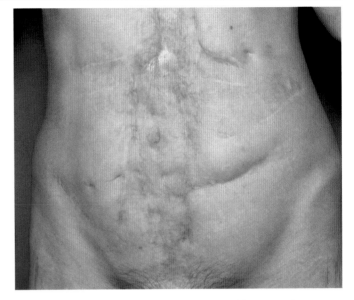

fits, but they have never bitten their tongues and are never witnessed to be incontinent.

PSYCHIATRIC

It is not uncommon for those people affected by Munchausen's syndrome to imitate psychiatric symptoms. For example, they may claim to have had hallucinations and delusions. As a result, medical personnel may mistakenly treat these individuals by prescribing varying amounts of psychotropic (mood-affecting) medication.

Management

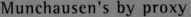

People with Munchausen's syndrome seem unable to control their behaviour and have little awareness of their own motivation.

Referral to a psychiatrist is often helpful in treating people with Munchausen's. However, many people with the syndrome refuse to see a specialist.

CONFRONTATION

Management of the disorder generally involves confronting an individual about their condition. At this stage, most individuals discharge themselves from hospital. Very few will accept a psychiatric referral and, if asked about their condition, they are usually non-committal and unclear. They often leave one hospital to arrive at another with a similar illness.

Rarely, it may be possible to develop a constructive

relationship with the patient, in which their symptoms and underlying fears about illness are discussed. However, people affected by Munchausen's syndrome are often severely disturbed and highly manipulative, and they make little real progress.

Although hospitals frequently exchange information about individuals seeking drugs as well as those feigning illness, issues of patient confidentiality need to be considered.

Munchausen's by proxy

Munchausen's by proxy is a state whereby the patient deliberately harms others (frequently children) to attract medical attention. Most commonly, a mother inflicts harm on her child.

The 'illnesses' may be bizarre in nature, and will never be directly witnessed by healthcare staff. The symptoms rarely follow an accepted medical pattern and typically disappear when the child is admitted to hospital.

Safety of child
These cases must be carefully managed as the safety of the child is paramount, and it is usually very difficult to make

an individual accept their behaviour.

In extreme cases, especially where the illness continues in hospital, covert surveillance can be used to monitor the child. Ultimately, this is the only method of providing definite evidence of such abuse. Accusations made without direct evidence can be extremely damaging and, if unfounded, cause inestimable distress to all concerned.

Injuries inflicted on a child, often by its mother, may be signs of Munchausen's by proxy. In these cases, the child will need to be monitored.

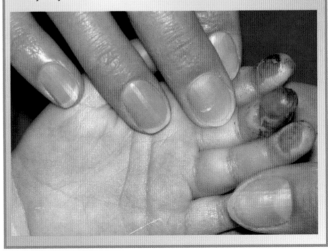

Obsessive-compulsive disorder

Obsessive-compulsive disorder (OCD) is a rare condition, comprising obsessional thoughts, ideas and actions. Patients may be treated by a combination of psychotherapy and medication.

Characteristically, OCD involves a subjective sense of compulsion overriding internal resistance; in other words, the sufferer feels overwhelmingly compelled to perform a particular action, or series of actions, despite struggling against it and knowing that it is an unreasonable series of actions.

The majority of patients have both obsessions and compulsions. Obsessions are characterized by intrusive, distressing ideas or thoughts that do not go away, such as the belief that the front door has

not been shut. Compulsions are actions that result from obsessive thoughts, such as repeatedly checking that the front door is shut. The condition was first described at the beginning of the nineteenth century, and was initially termed a 'monomania' – meaning that once the sufferer had got a fixed idea into his head, he could not get rid of it.

People suffering from OCD exhibit a range of symptoms. The desire to obsessively arrange and rearrange household items is common.

What causes OCD?

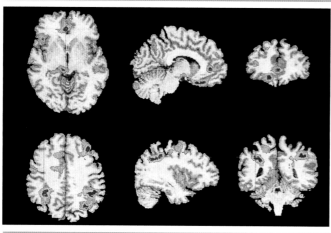

Imaging techniques, such as PET scanning (left), can show which brain regions are active during OCD behaviour.

There are various theories about the causes of OCD, but none of them provides a full, satisfactory explanation for the condition. Current theories include:
■ **Genetic**
Between 5 and 7 per cent of OCD patients have parents with the disorder, suggesting an inherited tendency for the condition. Upbringing, however, seems of little relevance.

■ **Brain disorder**
Advanced imaging techniques to view the brain, such as positron emission tomography (PET), suggest disturbance in brain structures, whilst anomalies of serotonin metabolism indicate a definite brain malfunction.
■ **Psychoanalytical**
Attempts have been made to describe OCD as caused by subconscious aggressive or sexual impulses that trigger internal conflict.
■ **Learning theory**
This suggests the symptoms are ploys to reduce anxiety.

Obsessive-compulsive symptoms

OBSESSIONS
Obsessions are mental fixations that the patient is unable to 'turn off':
■ Obsessional thoughts are recognized by the patient as inappropriate. They may be sexual, obscene, blasphemous, frightening or nonsensical
■ Obsessional fears (also termed phobias) include those of doing something dangerous to oneself or someone else. Common fears are of contamination or unspecified disaster: they may lead to compulsive acts
■ Ruminations comprise the endless reviewing of the simplest actions or brooding over abstract subjects
■ Obsessional doubts are about

tasks one may have omitted to do, such as turning off an oven, or actions that may have harmed other people, such as driving past a cyclist too fast.

COMPULSIONS
Compulsions include repetitive acts, fixed 'rituals' and obsessional slowness:
■ Compulsive acts are those that develop into rituals, such as repeatedly checking that the oven is turned off
■ Fear of contamination leads to washing oneself or other objects or elaborate avoidance of places where there may be dirt
■ Fear of bad luck leads to using the 'magic' of numbers to ward off disaster: doing actions

a certain number of times, or performing everyday activities, such as getting dressed, in a rigid and inflexible order.

Other symptoms vary depending on the patient, but can include:
■ Depersonalization, a strange feeling of unreality whereby a patient feels unreal, or feels that the outside world is unreal
■ Anxiety, often driving the compulsive acts. These acts are intended to reduce anxiety, but sometimes make it worse. A patient who is performing a ritual feels mounting anxiety until they have completed it
■ Depression, common in OCD, is sometimes the primary illness.

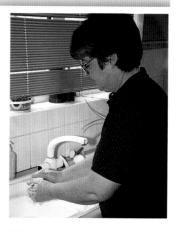

Obsessive cleanliness is a typical feature of OCD. Some patients may feel compelled to wash hundreds of times a day.

Managing OCD

One person in 100 suffers from OCD at any time, but patients can be successfully treated using several methods. Drug therapies, using antidepressant drugs, can be useful and counselling and cognitive behavioural therapy are also very effective.

Psychotherapy

A number of psychotherapeutic approaches are used to treat patients with OCD. In more severe cases, medication will also be used.

The patient may find that the initial assessment with the therapist, involving the unburdening of distressing symptoms, is in itself a relief. The therapist should explain that the symptoms are exaggerations of thoughts and impulses that everyone has sometimes, and do not indicate incipient madness.

Self-help programmes, with encouragement, if possible, from a friend, partner or group can also help. Distractions and physical exercise may be useful. The most effective psychological treatment is

Cognitive behavioural therapy is often very successful in helping patients with OCD. It is necessary for the therapist to be skilled and experienced.

cognitive behavioural therapy, which can reason the patient out of their faulty reactions. Other techniques include:
- Systematic desensitization: a gradual approach. For example, exposure for an hour daily to a situation likely to provoke symptoms, such as doing housework, but without going through the usual rituals
- Response prevention: usually it is sufficient for the therapist to say 'don't'
- Modelling: providing an example for the patient to follow.

Treatment with drugs

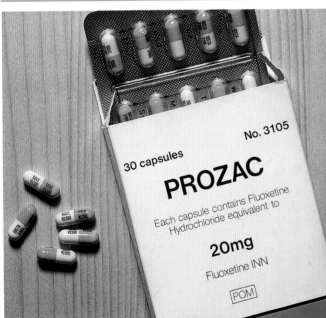

One of the best-known SSRIs is fluoxetine, which is often prescribed for patients with OCD. It is also known by the proprietary name of Prozac.

Recent experience has shown that selective serotonin re-uptake inhibitors (SSRIs), such as sertraline, citalopram and paroxetine, and the tricyclic antidepressant clomipramine can help to improve the symptoms of OCD. Mirtazapine, a serotonergic enhancer that is used in depressive illness, may also be prescribed.

There are possible side effects with all of these drugs, although the more modern SSRIs tend to be safer. Alcohol and benzodiazepines are banned, because of the risk of dependency.

Drug treatment will be considered in many OCD cases, especially if there is a danger that a certain compulsion may lead sufferers to harm themselves or others.

Who is affected?

A little over one in a 100 people will have OCD at any one time, and up to three per cent of the population are at risk of developing it at some time between the ages of six and 70. It is equally prevalent in both sexes.

The condition usually begins in adolescence or early adulthood, with the peak age of onset around the age of 20. Only 15 per cent of sufferers first have symptoms over the

age of 35. Many patients, however, do not seek medical advice about their condition until they reach middle age.

The onset of the condition is usually gradual – although in some cases it can be acute – and the condition tends to run a chronic course, with the severity of the symptoms changing over time. Prognosis is a fluctuating course of symptoms with a 60–80 per cent likelihood of recovery within a year.

Case study

Mrs J had always been meticulous over her appearance, but this had developed into a decontamination ritual: every time she entered her house, she felt compelled to remove all her clothes in the hallway, take a bath and put on clean garments. She was able to conceal her compulsion from everyone except her husband, whom she drew into it. She would not allow him past the door unless he also changed

his clothes. Her feelings were so strong that she could not withstand them.

Her GP thought she was psychotic and prescribed the drug amisulpiride, but she became depressed and her compulsive behaviour was unabated. The GP reviewed the diagnosis and prescribed SSRI antidepressants. After four months, Mrs J's symptoms were greatly improved.

Somatization

Somatization is a disorder in which patients complain of symptoms
in the absence of any physical cause. It is associated with certain
other psychiatric conditions, which become the focus for treatment.

Patients with somatization have symptoms for which no physical cause can be found or where the symptoms are out of proportion to any underlying pathology. Typically, patients with a somatic complaint have multiple symptoms. Somatic complaints may account for as many as a third of all referrals.

When the correct diagnosis has been made, the patient is best treated by their GP.

ACKNOWLEDGEMENT

Even though there may not be an apparent physical cause, somatic symptoms are real and are often disabling. It is important that doctors acknowledge this and explain that no serious medical cause has been found, although this does not mean that there is nothing wrong.

Most patients with somatic symptoms are reassured by discovering that their symptoms do not indicate serious disease, and by normal investigations.

CLINICAL HISTORY

A clinical history will often include pointers to the origin of the symptoms. It is important that a full psycho-social history is included. For example, panic attacks may start after a close relative has a heart attack. It is essential that the doctor asks the patient what he or she feels is the cause of their symptoms, and enquires about their concerns and fears.

In comparison with physical symptoms, somatic symptoms often vary from day to day and tend not to form recognized clinical patterns; moreover, patients often have elaborate beliefs about the cause of their symptoms. In addition, the patient may have high levels of underlying anxiety or depression.

Somatization is characterized by multiple symptoms that have no physical cause. The doctor should examine the patient and then ask for a detailed history.

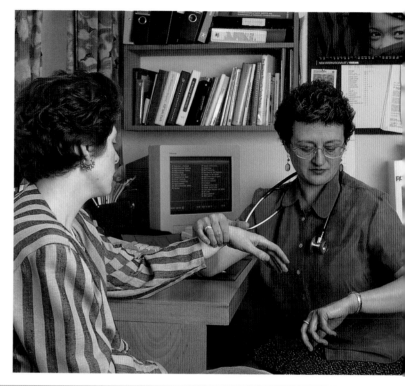

Investigations and diagnosis

Somatization is a clinical diagnosis, made largely from the patient's history. It is almost always necessary to perform one or two investigations to rule out potentially serious medical conditions. Unfortunately, the more investigations that are done the more the patient may become convinced of the physical nature of their condition.

Wherever possible, it helps if the doctor makes a positive diagnosis of somatization within one of the following categories, expecting to revise it if the clinical picture changes:

■ **Somatic syndromes**
With somatic syndromes, a patient complains of a recognizable set of symptoms, thus helping the doctor to make a positive diagnosis. These syndromes include irritable bowel syndrome (IBS), chronic fatigue syndrome (CFS) and globus hystericus (sensing a lump in the throat). Although a high proportion of patients have a psychiatric condition (half of CFS sufferers have depression), the relationship is indirect.

■ **Hypersensitivity states**
Hypersensitivity is an excessive response to the symptoms of a known underlying disorder or even to normal sensations. For example, back pain may become disabling and out of

Hypersensitivity is one form of somatization. Patients believe that a common sensation, such as back pain, is an indication of a serious underlying illness.

proportion to any underlying disorder.

Hypochondriasis is an extreme situation in which the patient is hypersensitive to normal bodily functions such as the heart beating or sweating, fearing each represents a fatal disease. These patients almost always have high levels of underlying anxiety or depression, which heightens their awareness of their symptoms and intensifies any pain they feel.

■ **Psychiatric somatic symptoms**
The physical aspects of a psychiatric condition can become the focus of attention. For example, fatigue, low energy, poor appetite and weight loss are associated with depression; shortness of breath and chest pain are associated with panic attacks; and recurrent minor illnesses with stress.

In the context of the psychiatric diagnosis, the physical symptoms are appropriate. For example, stress reduces immunity, leading to recurrent infections, while fatigue is a well-established symptom of depression.

Treating somatization

Somatization can be difficult to explain to the patient, so plenty of time is needed. During this interview, it is important to try to include the patient's social and psychological background and any other relevant details. At this stage it is helpful for the doctor to explain the cause of symptoms.

ACCEPTING THE DIAGNOSIS
Provided the reality and inconvenience of their symptoms is accepted, almost all patients respond positively. Psychiatric conditions should be treated using antidepressants and cognitive behaviour therapy to help manage underlying depression and anxiety.

It is important that a relationship in which doctor and patient trust each other develops. If the patient refuses to accept the diagnosis or is not reassured, it is better that this is discussed openly, rather than left as an unspoken agenda hanging over future consultations.

TREATMENT OPTIONS
Treatments are available for the following categories:
■ Somatic syndromes – specific remedies may help some symptoms; for example, antispasmodics such as mebeverine are useful for irritable bowel syndrome
■ Hypersensitive states – explanation is one of the most useful approaches while relaxation therapies can help

When treating patients with somatization, the doctor must explain the real causes of the symptoms. This relies on a relationship based on trust.

underlying anxiety. Medication, including analgesics, is best kept to a minimum and is often ineffective
■ Psychiatric somatic symptoms – once the psychiatric condition has been treated, physical symptoms will usually resolve or assume less importance.

Psychiatric techniques

In treating patients with somatization, the psychiatrist must listen to their concerns, discuss their social and psychological background and link symptoms to the following:
■ Anxiety (for example, overbreathing causes dizziness)
■ Depression (lowering of pain threshold and increased attention to physical symptoms)
■ Life events (e.g, stating: 'I see

your chest pain began shortly after your uncle had a heart attack')
■ Another's symptoms (e.g, asking: 'How does your mother respond to stress?')
Explaining the real causes of symptoms also involves demonstrating how symptoms may be generated (e.g muscle spasm from sustained contractions).

Differential diagnosis

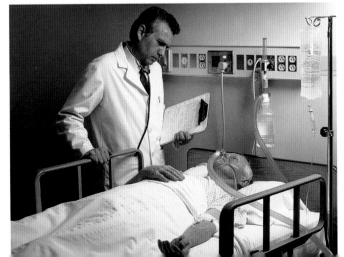

Somatization needs to be distinguished from factitious (invented) disorders and malingering.

FEIGNING ILLNESS
A patient with a factitious disorder concocts symptoms in order to assume a 'sick role'. Munchausen's syndrome is an extreme example of a factitious illness, where individuals give an expert medical history, inventing bizarre symptoms to gain medical attention and undergo investigations.

By comparison, malingering is a conscious manipulation of existing medical symptoms designed to achieve a concrete external purpose, such as avoiding a court appearance.

Patients with somatization may have a detailed knowledge of medical disorders. However, doctors should not confuse this with people who feign illness.

Common pitfalls

When diagnosing somatization, doctor and patient are both concerned that a serious physical condition may be missed.

DELAY IN DIAGNOSIS
Even with modern diagnostic techniques, there is often a delay in the diagnosis of certain conditions, especially when rare. Many neurological conditions, including multiple sclerosis, and rare conditions, such as carcinoid

bowel tumour or insulinoma, are only diagnosed after a considerable delay.

However, without good supporting clinical evidence, it is not ethical to investigate every patient to the extent requested.

Doctors should be aware of physical disorders that are easily missed when considering somatization. Rare conditions are often difficult to diagnose.

Bipolar affective disorder

Bipolar affective disorder is a severe form of mental illness that is characterized by episodes of depression and hypomania. Medication and support are both vital in helping people manage the condition.

Bipolar affective disorder is as common as schizophrenia, yet it is far less researched. It affects 1.2 per cent of the population and is characterized by extreme changes in mood from depression to hypomania (a state of abnormal elation or hyperactivity).

Bipolar affective disorder is named after the periods of severe depression and hypomania that occur: 'bi-' (two) 'polar' (extremes) 'affective' (of emotion) disorder. The condition is also known as manic depression.

CHARACTERISTICS
During periods of illness, the normal variation and regulation of moods is lost. The resulting mood changes may be so extreme that an individual loses contact with reality and develops a psychosis.

People with bipolar affective disorder are more vulnerable to stress, both physically in terms of illness and mentally from lack of sleep and severe anxiety.

POSSIBLE CAUSES
No single cause has been found. The first episode often occurs during severe emotional stress; it may follow childbirth. Rarely, it follows physical illness, head injury or treatment with antidepressants or mefloquine, a drug used to treat malaria. In some cases bipolar affective disorder has a genetic component – a fifth of people with bipolar affective disorder have a parent with the condition.

It is thought that some people are genetically predisposed to bipolar affective disorder. Twenty per cent of patients have a family history of the condition.

Diagnosing types of bipolar affective disorder

The diagnosis of bipolar affective disorder depends upon a person having at least one episode of hypomania. Bipolar affective disorder may be either:
■ Type I – predominantly hypomanic episodes
■ Type II – mostly depressive episodes, with the patient suffering only occasional hypomanic episodes.

'Rapid cycling' describes a pattern of illness with four or more episodes a year. Periods of 'rapid cycling' are interspersed with more stable periods.

Bipolar affective disorder usually develops in the late 20s or 30s, although it is occasionally diagnosed in childhood. People who have depression without episodes of hypomania are described as having unipolar depression.

MOOD STATES
The mood states within bipolar affective disorder include:
■ **Hypomania** – a state of high energy and activity in which the ability to function normally is lost. In the early stages, the individual may appear to work productively and creatively, but this capability diminishes as hypomania continues.

Hypomania is characterized by rapid speech and disconnected thoughts ('flight of ideas'). A person may only sleep for a couple of hours a night. They may become sexually promiscuous, irritable, paranoid, lose their judgement, and spend their money excessively.

Hypomania does not bring happiness, although it may appear to be exciting. Sufferers are not in control, rather they are driven relentlessly by their impulses. They lose insight into their thoughts and behaviour.

■ **Depression** – when life loses its meaning and the future seems hopeless. The patient has neither energy nor motivation. Sleeping is affected; typically a person will wake in the early morning unable to get back to sleep. Thinking is slowed and concentration poor. The person feels distanced from everything and everyone, and suicide is a risk. It is often accompanied by severe guilt and anxiety.

■ **Psychosis** – at the extremes of mood, people sometimes lose contact with reality. Their thoughts may become paranoid and contain many delusions. It is difficult to communicate, and the person has elaborate explanations for their behaviour and experiences.

People with hypomania appear to be full of energy. However, their behaviour is often extreme: for example, they may indulge in compulsive shopping.

Treating bipolar affective disorder

Bipolar affective disorder is a life-long condition that is managed rather than cured. Drug therapy forms the basis of almost all treatment. In addition, psychotherapy and self-management are important for dealing with the disorder.

DRUG THERAPY
There are three main types of drug used in the treatment of bipolar affective disorder. These include mood-stabilizing drugs, antipsychotic drugs used to treat hypomania and antidepressant drugs that treat depression. Other drugs used include sleeping tablets and drugs for anxiety.

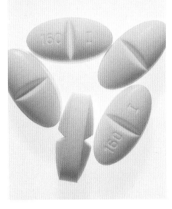

Lithium is a mood-stabilizing drug given to patients with bipolar affective disorder. It is prescribed as a prophylactic, to prevent recurrence.

Treatment for bipolar affective disorder aims to manage rather than cure the illness. Psychotherapy can be used with, or instead of, drug therapy.

■ Mood-stabilizers
The three most commonly prescribed mood-stabilizing drugs are lithium, carbamazepine and sodium valproate. If taken continually by the patient these drugs reduce the number of episodes of illness. Each drug works differently and it may be necessary to try each in turn.
 Newer mood-stabilizing drugs include gabapentin and lamotrigine. On occasion, a low dose of one of the atypical antipsychotic drugs may be used as a mood-stabilizer.

■ Antipsychotic drugs
Antipsychotic drugs are used to treat attacks of hypomania. These drugs sedate the patient and reduce their agitation and hyperactivity.
 Traditional antipsychotics such as haloperidol, chlorpromazine and sulpiride may cause side effects in the extrapyramidal system, the part of the central nervous system concerned with movement, posture and co-ordination of large muscle groups.
 Newer atypical antipsychotic drugs such as olanzapine have fewer side effects and are more acceptable to patients.
■ Antidepressants

These drugs treat depression and may, more rarely, be prescribed long term to prevent depression. They can have side effects but often these effects will reduce significantly after a few weeks. Examples of antidepressants include amitriptyline, dothiepin, fluoxetine and venlafaxine.

During treatment, depression may switch suddenly into hypomania. Newer antidepressants such as fluoxetine are less likely to cause a hypomanic switch.

Stigma

Bipolar affective disorder is a major mental illness and its diagnosis can be devastating for the patient. It affects the core of the person, as well as his or her career and relationships. It can often be difficult to talk about the illness and self-help groups can assist someone come to terms with the diagnosis.

People suffering from bipolar affective disorder can find it difficult to talk about their illness. Mental illness support groups may be able to help.

Non-drug therapy

Therapies that are used in conjunction with or instead of drugs include:
■ **Psychotherapy for depression**
Psychotherapy helps people with depression change 'depressive' ways of thinking. Instead of

negative statements, such as 'the world is against me', they are encouraged to think of specific examples and reinterpret them positively. This is challenging but safer and as effective as drug therapy. Combining

psychotherapy and drugs is most effective in the long term.
■ **Self-management**
Self-management gives a patient with bipolar affective disorder a measure of control over the illness. It involves an individual acknowledging the diagnosis and learning to monitor moods and recognize impending episodes of illness. An individual can then take action to prevent episodes of illness developing further.

BENEFITS FOR PATIENTS
As individuals become more experienced at managing their illness, they can reduce the disruption to their life. This approach depends upon a partnership between the psychiatrist, mental health team and the patient.

Psychotherapy is used to help individuals suffering from depression. Psychotherapists encourage patients to interpret their experiences positively.

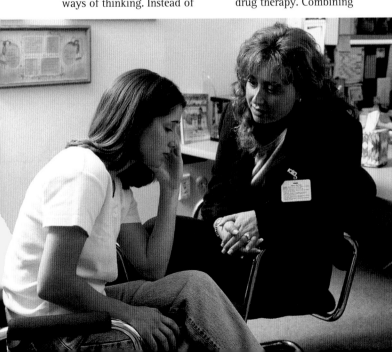

Personality disorder

Personality disorder may occur either in isolation or in addition to other psychiatric problems. It relates to lifelong disturbances of function in a number of aspects of behaviour.

Personality disorder is usually defined by maladaptive, persistent, lifelong and deeply ingrained patterns of individual functioning in several key areas:
- Thinking and perception
- Emotion
- Impulse control
- Behaviour
- Relationships with others.

Such disorders of the person's core character will frequently have devastating consequences and can lead to great distress, both in the individual and society at large.

ONSET

Although the time course is usually described as 'lifelong', it is not unusual for the problem to come to light in adolescence or early adulthood. When personality or behavioural problems arise later in life, there can be several causes, such as:
- Mental illness
- A change in personality due to stressful life events
- Brain disease.

An interesting point is that the severity of the disorder can dwindle with time. This tends to occur more with some types compared with others but, as a general rule, the distress endured by the individual and the conflict with society gradually lessens. By old age, the proportion of patients whose problems can be understood solely in terms of personality disorder is very small.

WHO IS AFFECTED?

Personality disorder is much more common than might be expected; some studies have shown that around 10 per cent of adults suffer with a disorder of mild severity.

The presence of this type of problem tends to bring affected people into contact with health services, especially GPs, emergency services and psychiatric teams. It has been estimated that 40 per cent of psychiatric in-patients can be diagnosed with a specific or mixed personality disorder, either as the sole diagnosis or (more commonly) in addition to another psychiatric disorder.

Surveys have shown that, overall, men are more likely to be affected and that the prevalence is increased in the lower social classes.

RISK FACTOR

Personality disorder is a significant risk factor for deliberate self-harm, suicide, drug and alcohol abuse and, in some cases, progression to specific psychiatric illness such as depression, obsessive-compulsive disorder and schizophrenia. Although symptoms of aggression and impulsiveness tend to lessen with age, the inability to form and maintain close relationships seems to be more enduring.

Personality disorder can cause significant distress, both to the sufferer and to others. Such disorders tend to affect men more frequently than women.

Why does personality disorder develop?

Little is known about the causes of personality disorders. One theory suggests that maladaptive behaviour could be learned within the family.

Since so little is known about the development of personality in general, it is not surprising that the cause of personality disorder remains unclear.

POSSIBLE LINKS

Genetic factors have been proposed, as have events that occur before and during birth which might go on to delay or impair maturation of the brain.

Psychological theories stress the importance of learning in the development of stable but maladaptive patterns of behaviour. Relationships with peers and within the family are significant factors in terms of exposure to abnormal behaviours, but also in terms of subconscious effects on mind and personality development, which are less easily understood.

Personality disorders have been associated with an event during fetal development. Another possible link is a birth problem.

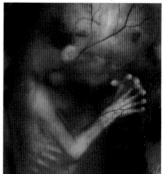

Diagnosing personality disorder

The diagnosis of personality disorder may not be straightforward: the problem
is often long-standing, and there are several different sub-types. Once the specific
disorder has been identified, a suitable treatment programme can be devised.

Personality disorder is difficult to diagnose for two reasons:
■ First, it is necessary to determine that the personality problems have arisen early in development and persisted into adulthood. This can probably only be achieved by taking a comprehensive history from someone who has known the individual well enough to have a good insight into their character and patterns of functioning.
■ The second difficulty is in assessing the nature of the maladaptive personality factors and how far they deviate from normal behaviour patterns. Everyday experience tells us that defining normality is difficult – there is no clear boundary between normal and abnormal.

DYSFUNCTIONAL BEHAVIOUR
Generally, personality disorder would not be diagnosed unless the individual's functioning was at significant odds with the expectations of their culture, sufficient to cause marked distress to themselves or others and difficulties in social and

occupational performance. For these reasons, a diagnosis would not be made on the basis of a single interview alone.

CLASSIFICATIONS
Several classifications of the sub-types of personality disorder have arisen that use slightly different terms and diagnostic criteria. One well-known American system groups the specific disorders into clusters – this can aid understanding of an apparently overwhelming list of terms and symptoms.

This system also highlights the fact that the different sub-types within a cluster have common and overlapping features so that a given person might fulfil criteria for more than one – this is not unusual and mixed personality disorders are common.

CLUSTERS
There are three categories within the American classification system:
■ Cluster A includes odd and eccentric types, characterized by features such as suspicion, oversensitivity, social withdrawal, emotional coldness, odd ideas and perceptions and unusual appearance
■ Cluster B is the flamboyant

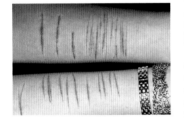

People suffering from cluster B disorders are most likely to carry out self-harming acts. Evidence of self-harming can be seen on this woman's arms.

Personality disorders are hard to diagnose. Many factors need to be considered and patients often show a number of features, such as suspicion.

and dramatic group in which individuals can be much more destructive and violent. Impulse control, mood, self-image, interpersonal relationships and an individual's overall sense of responsibility are all things that can be affected.

This group includes those disorders most likely to result in acts of self-harm (often repeated and sometimes with little or no intention to cause death), angry or aggressive outbursts and acts of violence (which tend

to be carried out impulsively without consideration of the consequences and are sometimes accompanied by a total absence of remorse).
■ Cluster C is made up of disorders characterized by anxiety, obsessional symptoms and undue reliance on others.

Treatment options

The management of personality disorder is complex and varied. Some types will respond poorly to hospital admission, resulting in a worsening of symptoms, distress and maladaptive coping techniques. For others, in-patient care can still have a role to play in some circumstances.

Hospital admission
Periodic crises and dramatic worsening of symptoms can be helped by short-term, well-structured admission to hospital,

Personality disorder takes many different forms, and treatment is likewise varied. Some symptoms respond well to psychotherapy, for example.

with clear goals and boundaries. In some cases, the risks posed to self or to others and the lack of reasonable suitable alternatives to care for the individual in the community necessitate admission to hospital under a section of the Mental Health Act.

In severe cases, detention in a secure hospital with locked wards may be necessary.

Specific treatments
Psychotherapy and psychiatric medication are often used to treat a co-existent psychiatric disorder, such as depression. They can also be helpful in treating symptoms such as aggression and impulsiveness in the absence of any specific illness.

Phobias

Phobias occur when people experience an excessive fear of a certain object or situation. Affected people will avoid contact with the source of the anxiety, but the long-term solution is to confront the phobia.

The term phobia comes from the Greek word 'phobos', meaning terror or panic. A phobia results in extreme anxiety or fear when the affected individual is exposed to a specific situation or object. Often, just thinking about the source of the fear can trigger an attack of anxiety.

AVOIDANCE

A key component of this type of disorder is avoidance. Understandably, people try to resist coming into close contact with what terrifies them. While this behaviour is beneficial in terms of reducing anxiety in the short term, it leads to perpetuation and strengthening of the sufferer's problem in the longer term.

Psychologists explain to their patients that, in order to be cured, they must experience the phobic stimulus often enough to learn and be convinced that it is, in fact, very unlikely to be harmful or dangerous.

DEFINING PHOBIAS

It should be noted that anxiety is an entirely normal emotion that serves many vital functions. It is anxiety that prepares the body for 'fight or flight' when reacting to danger; bodily changes help us to cope with the threat in the most appropriate way.

Certain criteria, therefore, need to be satisfied before a fear can be classified as phobic. Phobic fear represents an excessive response, out of proportion to the risks associated with a situation. No amount of reasoning or debate will help the fear to vanish, as it is not under the individual's control. Rather, the sufferer will try to avoid the source of the fear whenever possible.

Phobias can take many forms; for example, fear of open spaces, known as agoraphobia, can result in people not being able to venture outside.

Classifying phobias

There are three important types of phobia to consider:

■ **Specific phobias** – phobias of this type can be associated with almost anything but are often related to flying, heights, insects or other animals, or blood.

■ **Agoraphobia** – this is characterized by a terror of situations from which easy escape is not possible or for

which help might not be available in the event of an accident, injury or panic attack. Agoraphobia is more complex than the specific phobias in that a whole range of situations is feared and consequently avoided; agoraphobics will often struggle when alone, away from home, as well as in crowded places such as shops.

Agoraphobia is often associated with panic attacks,

which can occur in response to certain triggers or appear without warning.

■ **Social phobia** – this is the fear of humiliating oneself in front of other people. It tends to occur in small group situations with unfamiliar people and so can be distinguished from the anxiety experienced by the agoraphobic in a large crowd.

Typically, the patient describes a sense of being under intense scrutiny, combined with a fear of blushing, shaking, stammering or vomiting.

EFFECTS ON LIFE

The degree to which a phobia affects a patient's life depends on a number of factors, such as the frequency of potential contact with the situation in question. A phobia of flying, for example, is less likely to alter a person's lifestyle significantly than is a social phobia.

Social phobia tends to occur in small-group situations. The disorder leads to marked avoidance of social situations and can cause much distress.

Individual phobias often relate to situations such as flying, or to objects such as animals; fear of spiders (arachnophobia) is included in this category.

Phobic symptoms often occur as part of a psychiatric illness, such as depression, in which case they are not diagnosed separately. A group of primary phobic anxiety disorders is recognized, however, in which the symptoms and syndromes described above occur in the absence of any other illness.

Why do phobias occur?

It has been estimated that the risk of developing a phobic disorder at some point in life is about 10 per cent. In general, phobias are much more common in women than in men – the exception is social phobia, which seems to affect both sexes equally.

PHOBIA DEVELOPMENT
The age of onset and course of these conditions is variable, but they are usually chronic and fluctuating. Specific phobias can develop in childhood or adult life; as a rule, childhood phobias tend to improve, while those that begin later in life are more likely to persist.

Agoraphobia usually begins in early adulthood and runs a prolonged course, whereas social phobia seems to come on after puberty and may gradually improve with time.

ADDICTION
In all cases, the patient should be considered vulnerable to abusing drugs and alcohol, since these substances are initially very effective at 'turning off' unpleasant anxiety symptoms. Repeated use, however, may lead to dependence.

SUGGESTED THEORIES
Theories proposed to explain the development of phobias include:
■ Learned associations between certain stimuli and fear – these associations may lead to avoidance and a subsequent failure to 'unlearn'; that is, realize that there is no danger
■ Hereditary factors – there is reasonably good evidence that predisposition to phobias is in part genetically determined
■ Natural selection – certain objects or situations are more likely to become linked with

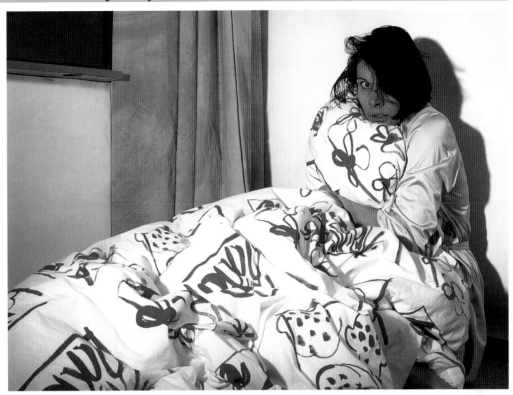

Severe phobias can have a major impact on life. Associated depression and loss of motivation may make even getting out of bed difficult.

fear and anxiety (such as snakes, spiders and heights). This could be explained in terms of natural selection, as individuals who learned to avoid such dangerous stimuli thousands of years ago would have survived longer than others and been more likely to pass their genes on to future generations.

Some animals – such as snakes – are more likely than others to trigger anxiety. Such a fear would have helped to protect our ancestors from danger.

Treating phobias

Drugs (mainly antidepressants) have proved useful in the treatment of phobic conditions, especially agoraphobia and social phobia. However, the mainstay of therapy is psychological.

The key point in all forms of treatment is that the patient is helped to experience anxiety linked with the object or situation in a controlled way, without avoidance, so that they 'unlearn'

Although drugs can be useful, phobias respond best to psychological treatment. Group therapy may be useful in resolving shared problems.

the association. Putting it another way, the patient learns that the stimulus will cause no harm, however anxious and scared it makes them feel.

Some techniques involve 'flooding', whereby the patient takes the plunge and experiences the whole phobic object or event all at once and stays with it until the anxiety begins to fade away.

An alternative approach is 'systematic desensitization', which involves gradual exposure to increasingly anxiety-provoking situations, often accompanied by relaxation, which prevents the anxiety from being maintained.

Post-traumatic stress disorder

Post-traumatic stress disorder occurs in response to a highly stressful experience, such as an accident. Intrusive recollections are common in the condition, which may be long term or may settle with time.

Post-traumatic stress disorder (PTSD) occurs in response to severe stress, either short-lived or continuous.

The condition has been recognized for many years, though under different names. It is now acknowledged that some of the cases of 'war neurosis' or 'shell-shock' seen in First World War servicemen were most likely PTSD, although others were more akin to depressive or anxiety disorders. The actual term 'post-traumatic stress disorder' was probably first used to describe the condition in Vietnam War veterans.

CAUSES OF PTSD
This psychiatric disorder usually occurs in previously healthy people as a direct result of the event in question. The types of situation implicated are extreme and, by definition, would be expected to cause major distress in most individuals.

Personality, genetic make-up and previous experience of mental illness are in themselves not enough to explain the onset of PTSD, although it is thought that such factors can affect vulnerability to this condition and alter its course or severity.

RISK FACTORS
The likelihood of developing PTSD is increased in:
- The presence of certain other personality traits (especially neuroticism) and mental illness
- Women
- Childhood
- Old age
- Poverty

- Social deprivation
- Those of low intelligence
- Those who sustain physical injury at the same time as the psychological trauma.

Certain personality traits (especially those seen in psychopaths, who have a callous unconcern for others' feelings and a limited capacity for feeling guilt and remorse)

The psychological trauma of war can precipitate PTSD. The disorder was experienced by a number of soldiers who fought in the Gulf War.

can, in fact, be protective and reduce the risk of a person developing PTSD.

Triggers of post-traumatic stress disorder

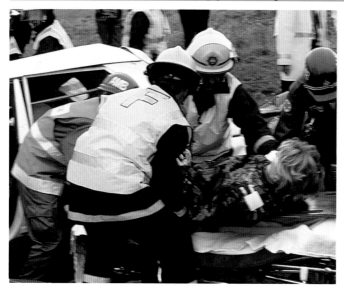

PTSD is triggered by highly stressful events, such as an accident or personal assault. The reaction may be immediate or delayed for several months.

Commonly quoted triggers for PTSD are accidents, war, disasters and assault, although any event can be a precipitant. The risk of developing PTSD seems to be related to the severity of the trigger.

Unlike other, more short-lived, responses to severe stress, there may be a delay before the symptoms of PTSD become evident. This can be up to years in rare cases but is typically weeks to months. Equally, the onset of the disorder can occur very shortly after the trigger.

PREVALENCE
The exact prevalence of PTSD is unknown: studies have shown rates to be around 30 per cent in victims of torture and 45 per cent in women who have been physically abused.

Exceptionally stressful events can lead to disorders other than PTSD; these might occur alone or co-exist with PTSD.

ACUTE STRESS REACTIONS
Acute stress reactions (ASRs) are immediate, but brief, responses to such events and last from hours to days. ASRs are characterized by intense anxiety, agitation and disorientation. They are self-limiting in the majority of cases, but the patient may go on to develop PTSD.

Symptoms of post-traumatic stress disorder

The core symptoms of post-traumatic stress disorder are:
■ Feelings of emotional numbness
■ Unwanted repetitive recollections of an event. Recollections occur either as nightmares or flashbacks (intense memories during the day)
■ Marked social withdrawal and detachment from others, with a loss of normal enjoyment and interest in life
■ Avoidance of factors closely related to the trauma, such as people and places. Exposure can provoke reactions ranging from fear to aggressive outbursts
■ Anxiety – this is common and may be persistent. It is often accompanied by symptoms such as a general state of over-alertness, poor concentration, insomnia and irritability
■ Depressive symptoms – these can be prominent; in some cases a full-blown depressive illness runs alongside the PTSD and is diagnosed as a separate entity
■ Guilt – often present among survivors of disasters.

The picture might be complicated further by harmful use of drugs and alcohol in an attempt to relieve the symptoms. Doctors and therapists must also be aware of the risk of suicide.

UNDERLYING FACTORS
The psychological and biological factors underlying these symptoms remain unclear. The fact that smells and sounds linked to the stressful event can provoke intense and vivid memories has prompted some people to suggest that classical conditioning (a form of learning whereby two objects or events become closely linked and associated) is involved.

Other theories explain intrusive memories in terms of emotionally charged information that overwhelms the normal processing functions of the mind and repeatedly 'spills' out into consciousness. It is thought that the persistently high level of mental arousal seen in PTSD might cause harmless situations to be misinterpreted as threatening.

RECOVERY
Some people who develop PTSD will recover, but it is possible for the condition to persist for years or even for life, with a tendency for the symptoms and their intensity to wax and wane. In some instances, there will be a change in an individual's personality that remains even after resolution of the more active symptoms described above.

Women who are physically abused by their partners are at risk of PTSD. This kind of stress is likely to be long-lasting and requires much support.

Some people with PTSD may withdraw from social interaction and become isolated. This behaviour can complicate the treatment process.

Treating PTSD

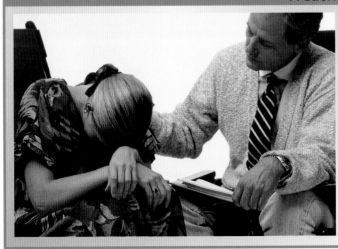

There are two strands to the treatment of PTSD:
■ Psychological therapy
■ Drug treatment.

Therapy
Several different types of therapy are used. The common method is the deliberate reliving of the events in the imagination and reminders of the traumatic events in a supportive setting. Anxiety

Psychotherapy may be used to treat PTSD. People with the condition are encouraged to relive the traumatic event and release their feelings of anxiety.

will be high at first but gradually diminishes in intensity.

Drugs
Antidepressants have been used in PTSD and can have benefits, even in the absence of depression. They have been shown to help relieve intrusive recollections and to assist patients in overcoming avoidance of reminders of trauma.

Such drugs are particularly valuable if low mood or co-existent depression is experienced. Others, including beta-blockers, are used to reduce alertness and mental arousal.

Psychotherapies

Many different schools of psychotherapy exist. All
therapies help the patient to identify, understand, modify or avoid
the psychological problems that may underlie mental illness.

Psychotherapies are therapies based on the theory that mental illness has a psychological cause or component. They are used to help treat a range of psychological disorders, including schizophrenia, depression, phobias and neuroses, sexual dysfunction, eating disorders, addictions and obsessive-compulsive disorders.

INDICATIONS
Psychotherapy can be used to treat almost any form of mental illness, although it is not indicated for acute forms such as severe psychotic episodes or life-endangering depression.

Psychotherapy is usually used in addition, or as a follow-up, to drug treatment, but in many cases it is used instead of drugs. Although drug therapy is now the first line of treatment for most mental illness, drugs are not always suitable. Many people object to drug treatment on principle, and others experience problems with side effects or have an illness that does not respond to drugs. Most importantly, drugs treat only the symptoms of mental illness, not the causes.

PRACTITIONERS
In theory, anyone can establish themselves as a psychotherapist, but in practice most therapists have some degree of training or formal qualifications.

Traditionally, most psychoanalysts are psychiatrists (medical doctors who have specialized in mental health). Most other types of therapist belong to a professional organization, such as the British Association of Counsellors or Relate.

Doctors are unlikely to make referrals to unqualified therapists, but anyone seeking therapeutic help on their own should check that a potential therapist is registered with a reputable organization.

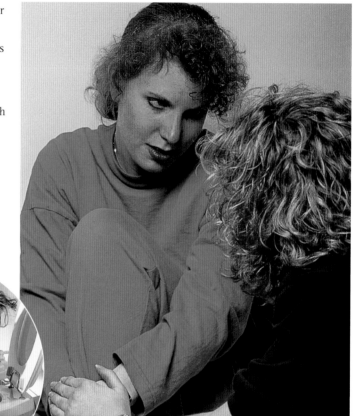

Eating disorders can be effectively treated with therapy. Bulimia is characterized by over-eating, then vomiting.

Psychotherapy aims to help people understand the factors behind their psychological problems. There are a number of schools of psychotherapy.

Principles of psychotherapy

In order for psychotherapy to be effective, a therapist and patient must form an appropriate relationship. The basis of this depends on the type of therapy.

Although different schools of psychotherapy may differ widely in terms of their underlying theoretical models, they tend to share some basic principles in terms of practice. These include:

■ **Establishing a relationship**
The first step in therapy is the establishment of a patient-therapist relationship. The relative status of therapist and patient in the relationship depends on the type of therapy. In some forms of therapy, the relationship is similar to a parent-child interaction;

in others, it is more like a partnership
■ **Gaining insight**
The second step is to allow the patient to gain insight through discussion, as the aim of therapy is for patients to identify and understand their problems by talking them over with the therapist. The degree to which therapists direct patients, as opposed to letting them find their own path, is again determined by the therapy type
■ **Agreeing a plan**
In some schools of therapy, the simple gaining of insight is believed to resolve problems. Others are more practical, and involve patient and therapist working together to formulate a plan to manage and treat illness.

Types of psychotherapy

There are many different schools of therapy, but most fall under one of three broad headings: psychoanalytic, cognitive-behavioural and client-centred.

PSYCHOANALYTIC THERAPY

Psychoanalytic therapy is based on Freud's (1856–1939) theory of the subconscious, and on the subsequent theories of his collaborators.

In psychoanalysis, mental health problems are seen as symptoms of conflicts in the subconscious mind. These result from childhood experiences and

Psychoanalytic therapy is based on the teachings of Sigmund Freud. This therapy focuses on the link between repressed fears and conflicts and mental illness.

the influence of basic drives, such as the sex drive. One example is the Oedipus complex, in which mental illness results from unresolved subconscious childhood conflicts over sexual feelings towards parents.

The patient reveals these conflicts by relating dreams and fantasies, or through word association. The role of the psychoanalyst is to interpret this material and help the patient resolve the conflicts.

COGNITIVE-BEHAVIOURAL THERAPY (CBT)

CBT is based on the theory that mental illness results from dysfunctional or maladaptive thought processes (cognitions). CBT attempts to treat patients by helping them to become aware of these cognitions and to change them and the behaviours that result from them. Unlike psychoanalysis, the mental illness is seen as the problem rather than simply a symptom.

In CBT the patient learns to substitute positive thought patterns for negative ones. Patients practise behaviours such as relaxation and breathing techniques to help overcome anxiety and neuroses.

The role of the therapist is to help the patient to gain insight into maladaptive thought processes, and devise their own coping mechanisms. Results can be produced after a relatively small number of sessions.

CLIENT-CENTRED THERAPY

Client-centred, or Rogerian, therapy helps the patient to

find their own answers through providing unconditional acceptance and encouragement.

The theoretical basis of client-centred therapy varies depending on the therapist, but the most common one is psychodynamic theory, which sees mental illness as the result of dysfunctional social and emotional interactions between people, most significantly between children and their parents.

Cognitive-behavioural therapy teaches relaxation techniques to overcome anxiety. Some types of music have been shown to help a person to relax.

ECLECTIC THERAPY

It is now common for therapists to combine elements of several schools of therapy, using those components that work best for each patient. This approach is known as eclectic therapy.

Family and group therapy

Family therapy involves the whole family of a mentally ill individual who is attending therapeutic sessions. It is based on the theory that individual mental illness is a symptom of problems in the interaction between all the family members (a form of psychodynamic theory).

The therapist's role is to observe the family dynamics and help the family members to understand them and change dysfunctional interactions into positive ones. In practice, however, it can be difficult to arrange for a whole family to attend therapeutic sessions.

Group therapy is a form of psychotherapy involving two or more patients. It is commonly used to treat disorders such as drug addiction.

GROUP THERAPY

Group therapy has become increasingly common in the treatment of a range of disorders including addiction and substance abuse, trauma and mood disorders.

In group therapy, a number of people with similar problems share and discuss their feelings and experiences and provide emotional and psychological support for one another.

A therapist is usually involved to mediate and/ or guide the discussion, and also to introduce a theoretical element, which is usually based on psychodynamic theory.

Group therapy is popular both with patients, as it is self-empowering, and with the authorities, as it is relatively cheap compared with the other forms of psychotherapy.

Treatment of psychological disorders

Different psychological disorders respond to different psychotherapies. Choosing the right type of therapy depends on a number of factors.

Once a patient has been assessed by a doctor, psychiatrist or community mental health team, he or she may be referred to a psychotherapist. The therapist is likely to practise a blend of therapies, although cognitive-behavioural approaches are favoured because they can start to produce practical benefits within a small number of sessions.

CHOICE OF THERAPY

There are many types of psychotherapy, each with their own set of indications, problems and advantages.

Although, in general, different therapies have been found to produce similar rates of successful treatment, equivalence of outcome does not mean that it makes no difference which therapy is used.

A number of factors determine the correct choice of therapy. These include the following:
- Clinical judgement
- Type of mental ill health
- Patient's motivation
- Patient-therapist relationship
- Availability of therapies
- Compatibility of therapy with patient's lifestyle (such as location of therapist).

An initial assessment by a family doctor may result in a referral to a psychotherapist. The choice of therapist depends upon the type of mental health problem.

Factors such as the nature of the problem affect the choice of therapy. This group is receiving counselling for cigarette addiction.

Equivalence of outcome

Studies comparing the outcomes of different types of psychotherapy almost always find that different approaches are equally effective. It has been found that a positive outcome is produced in 70–90 per cent of cases (the rate of spontaneous remission is about 50–70 per cent). In other words, psychotherapies are worthwhile treatments, but they all seem to be equally worthwhile – their outcomes are thus said to be equivalent.

In about 80 per cent of people, psychotherapy has a positive outcome. People with psychological problems often regain a sense of hope.

Common features
Analysis reveals that all forms of psychotherapy share several important factors. These include a theoretical basis that offers patients:
- An authoritative explanation for their illness and the framework for a cure
- A sense of hope
- A feeling that steps are being taken to address the problem
- An influential authority figure (the therapist)
- A logical treatment process for the patient to follow.

Psychotherapies share the above features with other therapeutic models, such as religious counselling and medical treatment.

Therapies and disorders

Although some psychological disorders, such as clinical depression, are now believed to have mainly organic causes (such as imbalances in levels of neurotransmitters), psychological factors play a part in maintaining and worsening their effects. Thus, psychotherapies have an important role to play in the management and treatment of psychological disorders.

MOOD DISORDERS
Client-centred therapies can be particularly effective in helping patients suffering from mild or reactive depression (depression precipitated by events) to identify and come to terms with issues such as bereavement.

Long-term depression may respond well to a long-term treatment, such as psychoanalysis.

Cognitive-behavioural therapy (CBT)

was originally developed to treat depression. It aims to help patients to identify and modify the dysfunctional thought patterns (known as schemas) and behaviours that reinforce feelings of worthlessness and hopelessness, replacing them with positive schemas and behaviours.

For instance, a typical dysfunctional schema in depression is irrational extrapolation: "I burnt the toast, therefore I'm a useless wife and mother". In CBT, the patient learns to reverse this negative schema through positive statements: "In general, I'm a good wife and mother, therefore burning the toast is a trivial mistake."

ANXIETY DISORDERS
It was largely Freud's treatment of anxiety disorders, such as phobias and neuroses, that led him to develop psychoanalytic theory. A psychoanalyst sees anxiety disorders as symptoms of subconscious conflicts, and treats them by attempting to uncover the origin of these conflicts; once the patient gains insight into the source of the problem, it can be resolved. CBT adopts a more practical approach to phobias, based on the theory that a phobia is a conditioned response (the sufferer has become conditioned to associate the phobic stimulus with fear) – curing the phobia requires reconditioning. Techniques used include:

Psychotherapy plays an important role to play in all types of depression. Long-term therapy has been shown to have a very positive outcome.

■ Flooding – exposing the patient to a massive burst of stimuli so that the irrational nature of the phobia is exposed
■ Desensitization – acclimatizing the patient to gradually increasing exposure
■ Relaxation techniques – these are useful in overcoming anxiety and obsessive-compulsive disorder.

SCHIZOPHRENIA
Opinions vary as to the usefulness of psychotherapy in the treatment of schizophrenia. Some theories about schizophrenia argue

Exposing a person to images of a feared object (or the real thing) is known as desensitization. This form of psychotherapy can help to cure a phobia.

that it is a symptom of wider social and emotional difficulties, such as problems between family members. Psychodynamic approaches, such as family therapy, attempt to address these problems.

CBT can help patients to develop coping strategies for use when suffering hallucinations, and also for treating depression.

Sexual dysfunction

Sexual dysfunction, including low libido, impotence and premature ejaculation, may have a psychological cause or component.

Therapies take a number of different viewpoints:
■ Psychoanalysis treats sexual dysfunction by looking for some kind of childhood source of guilt,

Often, difficulties in a sexual relationship are indicative of deeper, emotional problems. Some therapies aim to uncover these deeper issues.

shame or conflict
■ CBT blames distracting, anxiety-producing cognitions that shift the sufferer's attention away from erotic stimuli (such as "What if I can't perform?") and tries to overcome these
■ Client-centred therapy sees sexual dysfunction as a symptom of relationship problems, and treats these, often by counselling both members of a couple.

Sex therapy is a type of client-centred therapy that uses some behavioural techniques, such as sensate focus.

Seasonal affective disorder

For some people, the onset of winter signals the start
of a form of clinical depression. Only long, bright summer days or
light therapy treatment can dispel the symptoms.

Seasonal affective disorder (SAD) is an atypical, recurrent form of depression notable for its seasonal nature. Symptoms always start in early winter and last for five to seven months. There is a full remission in late spring, as the days grow longer and the sunlight becomes stronger.

DISABLING CONDITION
For many people, SAD represents a seriously disabling illness that has a significant effect on life. Self-esteem and mood are very low, motivation for anything seems impossible,

The light on a tropical beach reaches an intensity of around 100,000 lux. At 200 times the strength of light in the home, it acts as an effective treatment.

and comfort is sought in over-eating and over-sleeping.

A remarkable feature of SAD is that its symptoms disappear after a few days of exposure to bright daylight. A mid-winter break to sunny climates can temporarily abolish symptoms, although a return to a winter climate usually sees a recurrence of the condition.

Light therapy is also successful at reducing symptoms of SAD in 60–70 per cent of affected individuals.

POSSIBLE CAUSES
The exact cause of SAD has not been established. It is thought, however, that certain factors may cause some people to suffer a biological imbalance in the hypothalamus (a region of the forebrain) that leads to the onset of SAD. These factors may be related to:
- The number of light photons available (the strength of the light) being inadequate
- The duration of the daily

period of light being too short
- The shift from dark to light and vice versa happening too quickly in winter months.

AFFECTED GROUPS
Seasonal affective disorder affects up to four per cent of the European population, with twice as many women as men reporting the ailment. It

As winter progresses the days get shorter and darker. For some people this reduction in available light triggers a disabling form of clinical depression.

typically affects people aged 20–40, although children and the elderly are sometimes affected.

Symptoms

The form of depression evidenced in SAD is considered to be atypical because some of its symptoms are different from classic forms of depression, such as bipolar (manic) depression.

SAD symptoms
Symptoms include:
- An increase in appetite, leading to weight gain; carbohydrate craving in winter is common. The weight, or part of it, is usually lost again in the summer
- A tendency to sleep

SAD can produce a sense of pointlessness and lack of energy. These may be so extreme that even getting out of bed seems impossible.

excessively but restlessly
- A loss of interest in other people, including a loss of libido
- Extreme lethargy and difficulty in socializing to the extent of being unwilling to leave the home or get out of bed in the morning
- Decreased concentration
- Depression and anxiety. In the most severe cases, this may include suicidal thoughts
- Certain physical ailments such as constipation, diarrhoea or heart palpitations.

Seasonal disappearance
Remarkably, all these symptoms disappear in spring or early summer, although positive feelings may be shortlived due to thoughts of the imminent winter.

Light therapy

The pineal gland

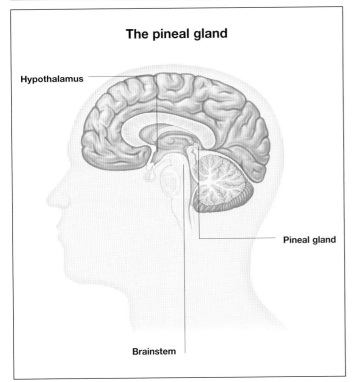

Hypothalamus

Pineal gland

Brainstem

Lack of light on winter days may cause the pineal gland to secrete melatonin by day instead of by night. Melatonin is a sleep-inducing hormone.

Light boxes are the most commonly used device for light therapy. Artificial white light is emitted, which travels through the eye to the pineal gland.

Light therapy remains a controversial treatment, as it is still not known how or why it works.

MELATONIN

It is clear that light therapy works through the eyes, stimulating the retina with bright light to activate brain pathways. This results in measurable changes in the secretion of certain hormones, such as melatonin, which is controlled by the pineal gland.

Melatonin helps to regulate the sleep cycle and is thought to play a role in controlling the circadian rhythm (biological clock). The hormone is normally secreted in the middle of the night (in darkness), a process which is suppressed in the daytime, when it is light.

Shift workers and sufferers of jet-lag are often affected by SAD, and the constant disruption of their biological clocks has led scientists to suspect a causal connection.

ARTIFICIAL SUNLIGHT

Light therapy (also known as phototherapy) consists of exposure to artificial white light provided by special lamps. During the treatment, light travels through the eyes to reach and trigger the pineal gland.

The most important factor in light therapy is the amount of light reaching the patient's eyes, together with its intensity and the duration of exposure.

The intensity of light is measured in units of lux. The standard regimen consists of 30 minutes of daily exposure, usually in the morning, to a light intensity of 10,000 lux, from autumn to spring.

This level of brightness is greater than that in the home (a living room might be 500 lux) but still much less bright than the beach (around 100,000 lux).

TREATMENT

Treatment usually starts two weeks before the typical onset of symptoms or as soon as the symptoms appear.

In order for the light to reach the eyes, patients are usually encouraged to sit around 50–100 cm from the lamp, and occasionally glance at it while performing some other task. The light produced by the light therapy lamps is glare-free. It consists of cool white light, excluding the possibly harmful ultraviolet wavelengths, emitted by flicker-free fluorescent tubes.

The beneficial effects of light therapy are quickly apparent. Within one week, the sombre mood lifts, energy and vitality return and food bingeing decreases. It is important that treatment remains ongoing, however, or the symptoms will return just as quickly.

How safe is light therapy?

Light therapy is a remarkably safe treatment. Any short-term side effects, such as eye strain, headache or sweating, disappear when the light intensity or duration is reduced. The therapy is particularly useful for those unable to take medication, such as pregnant women.

Light therapy can also be used safely in conjunction with conventional drug therapy. Certain SSRI antidepressants, notably citalopram, have been useful in the treatment of SAD.

Concern has been raised about the possibility of retinal damage in the long term. There is a small potential risk of previously unrecognized retinal conditions (such as macular degeneration) being aggravated.

When to seek advice
Certain groups of people should seek ophthalmologic consultation before undergoing light therapy. These include those:
■ Pre-existing retinal or eye disease
■ Any systemic illness affecting the retina (such as diabetes mellitus)
■ Those who have had previous eye surgery
■ People taking medications with photosensitizing effects (such as lithium, certain cancer drugs, melatonin or St John's wort).

An ophthalmologic consultation should precede light therapy treatment. Certain conditions or drug regimes prohibit the use of light therapy.

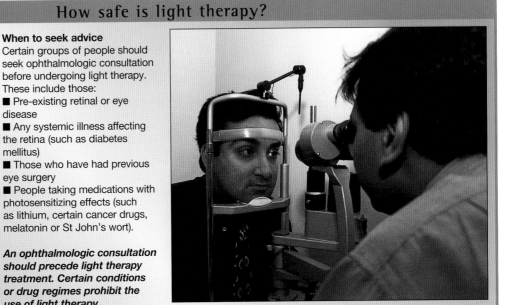

Index

Picture Credits

All images originally published in the partwork *Inside the Human Body* © Bright Star Publishing plc, apart from the following:

Alamy: 29 bottom (BSIP SA), 72 top (RGB Ventures/SuperStock), 81 middle (Mediscan), 97 top right (Phanie), 114 bottom left (Mediscan)

Depositphotos: 6 (Cliparea), 7 top (Serreitor), 7 bottom (Alexei171), 61 bottom (Jazzikov), 78 bottom right (Eleonoras), 87 top right (eddiephotograph), 137 bottom right (Angiolina), 165 top (Ruslan Guzov)

Dreamstime: 70 bottom right (Zuperpups), 111 bottom (Jarenwicklund), 115 bottom (Marilyn Barbone)

Science Photo Library: 146 middle (St. Mary's Hospital Medical School)